School
Can
Wait

School
Can
Wait

Raymond S. Moore
Dorothy N. Moore
with
T. Joseph Willey
Dennis R. Moore
D. Kathleen Kordenbrock

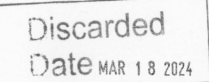
Brigham Young University Press

Library of Congress Cataloging in Publication Data

Moore, Raymond S.
    School can wait.

    Bibliography: p. 235
    1. Education, Preschool—1965-   2. Readiness
for school.   3. Learning, Psychology of.   I. Title.
LB1140.2.M647   372.21   78-19198
ISBN 0-8425-1283-7
ISBN 0-8425-1314-0

International Standard Book Number: 0-8425-1283-7 (cloth)
                                    0-8425-1314-0 (paper)
Brigham Young University Press, Provo, Utah 84602
© 1979 Brigham Young University Press. All rights reserved
Second printing 1979
Printed in the United States of America
79 1Mc, 2.5Mp 40602

To
young children—
our legacy,
society's treasure

Many children
need help in the
first eight years—
some desperately.

Contents

Acknowledgments

Throughout our research for this book over the last ten years, many specialists—such as those in attachment, cognition, learning, neurophysiology, parenting, perception, psychiatry, public policy, reading, vision—from the U.S., Canada, and overseas, have at one time or another lent us firsthand help or a strong word of encouragement. We hold none of them accountable for what we write here, nor do we necessarily imply that they fully concur with our findings.

Among them we list the following: Mary Ainsworth, Yuri Alferov, Sally Allen, Millie Almy, Louise Ames, A. Jean Ayres, and Nancy Bayley; Silvia Bell, Carl Bereiter, Joan Bissell, John Bowlby, and Urie Bronfenbrenner; Leonard Burros, Annie Butler, Bettye Caldwell, Ronald Davie, Paul Dokecki, and Malcolm Douglass; Charles Drain, David Elkind, Martin Engel, Siegried Engelmann, Donald Erickson, and L. R. Fernig; George Fidone, Marianne Frostig, Hans Furth, Ira Gordon, and Alex Grey; Edith Grotberg, Herald Habenicht, Joseph Halliwell, Homer Hendrickson, and Robert Hess; Henry Hilgartner, Marjorie Honzik, Torsten Husén, James Hymes, Jr., and Frances Ilg; Barbel Inhelder, Jerome Kagan, Lillian Katz, Robert Kraskin, and Catherine Landreth; Phyllis Levenstein, Robert Liljefors, William Ludlum, Walter MacGinitie, and Eve Malmquist; George Mayeske, Oralie McAfee, Margaret Mead, Dale Meers, and David Metcalf; George Milkie, Anne Morency, Shigefumi Nagano, Humberto Nagera, and Frank Newton; Glen Nimnicht, Rene Ochs, Earl Ogletree, Anne O'Keefe, and Henry Peters; Jean Piaget, Anneliese Pontius, Henry Ricciuti, William Rohwer, and

Jerome Rosner; Earl Schaefer, Karl Schaefer, Alberta Siegel, Irving Sigel, and Norman Silberberg; A. M. Skeffington, August Steinhilber, Carol Stern, Harold Stevenson, and Robert Strom; Paul Torrance, Helmut and Gisela Von Kugelen, Gilbert Voyat, Otto Weininger, and Joseph Wepman; Burton White, Sheldon White, Paul Yakovlev, Francis Young, and Edward Zigler; the late Milton Akers, Harold Birch, Darrell Harmon, and René Spitz; and the ERIC-ECE staff at Champaign-Urbana, Illinois, the National Institutes of Health, the U.S. Office of Child Development, and the U.S. Office of Education.

Of particular and immediate help in our analyses of more than 7,000 ECE-related studies were our research associates at the Hewitt Research Foundation: Wong Yew Chong, Ingram duPreez, and senior research associate Martha Lorenz. The principal investigators of our basic studies were Pascual Forgione, head of our Stanford public policy team; David Metcalf, who directed our neurophysiological project at the University of Colorado Medical School; and Robert Moon of the Council for Exceptional Children and Andrews University, who directed our analysis of the 1970 National Elementary School Study data on 80,000 children and 3,500 schools.

Raymond S. Moore

Introduction
Interrelated Facets of
Early Childhood Development

Trends in Early Childhood Training

We are losing ground academically and behaviorally in the education of our children. The expenditure of ever larger sums for our schools appears to provide little or no relief. The more time and money we spend, the greater the problem grows. It is possible we do not fully understand the developmental needs of our children and that we place our personal freedoms ahead of theirs. We are captivated or persuaded or pressured by conventional wisdom and practice in a system that places vested interests ahead of helpless youngsters. It is conceivable that we are paying our money for state "services" that endanger our children, then paying it again for state attempts at their remedy— remedy of the very problems that they, with our cooperation, have created.

We look at one facet of a child's life and overlook others, and we think we have done quite well by them in providing fine institutions for their care. A little thought, however, will tell us there are indeed public policies that correlate with losses in learning ability and with negative behavior in our children. Legal and social pressures over the last several generations have taken children ever earlier out of the family and home and have placed them in institutional settings—with attendant transfer of both parental responsibility and authority to the state or other agencies. This basal change deserves our deepest study if we have any concern for the welfare of our children or the survival of our society.

Problems of human ecology tend to be as difficult as they are crucial. Yet if our society does not have the wisdom and self-

1

lessness and courage to undertake their solution, we will awake to find ourselves on our way to totalitarianism or annihilation. A number of child and family specialists believe we are already well along on that road.

We attempt in this book to place the developmental needs of our children in a thoroughly documented context that includes the crucial facets of their growth. The reader may weigh this study against present policy and practice in his town and state and nation.

Concerns about Out-of-Family Care

Powerful and dynamic interactions affect the many facets of a young child's development, learning, and fulfillment as an adult. These factors are often studied individually, but they are infrequently brought together for systematic study. Yet it is of vital importance to educational policy and practice as well as the security of the home that this be done, for these variables are common denominators of later accomplishment and of the child's satisfying personal development.

In spite of current trends toward ever-earlier schooling or out-of-family care, strong, research-based data suggest that *whenever possible* parents should be their children's only regular "teachers" or care givers until the youngsters are at least eight or ten years of age. Unnecessary out-of-home or other alternative care may endanger the child socially, emotionally, behaviorally, and even academically. In such cases the psychological and sociological implications for the family and for society may be disastrous as parents relinquish their responsibility—and authority—during their youngster's crucial developmental years. Indeed we may be paying heavily for early childhood education that ultimately develops problem children, only to pay much more to remediate the problems we have created. We pay not only in dollars but also in anxiety and in loss of human potential.

We assume that much research is still needed to confirm certain hypotheses against unnecessary early out-of-family care. Yet ample cross-disciplinary evidence is in hand to call for policy reform in early childhood education (ECE). Wherever possible this reform must be directed more toward preserving the integrity of the child's home life and less to institutionalizing children at ever earlier ages. Indeed any substantial body of *systematic* evidence supporting care out of the family as normally desirable is

2

hard to find, and some leading psychologists believe it does not exist.

The presentation of the research itself may be better understood if we first lay down the background for these conclusions that so clearly cut across conventional patterns.

Background for Concerns

In the late 1950s, with the gradual refinement of the science of electroencephalography (EEG), several EEG-based studies of the young child's brain, when brought together, led some neurophysiologists to conjecture that a youngster's central nervous system may not be ready until eight or nine years of age or older for the sustained high cortical effort that enables him to learn basic academic skills on a quality level. The possibility existed that until this age a child is dominated by emotions more than reason, causing his or her studies to become often unnecessarily difficult.

Inquiry among students of the brain revealed that, because of the state of the art, some EEG techniques and conclusions from available studies might be presumptuous. Within a few years, however, the influence of psychologist Jean Piaget began to be felt in North America, and his experiments were replicated with consistently similar results. Of particular note were his stages of cognitive development in the child. His "period of concrete operations," for example, suggested that the child's cognitive ability usually flowered into maturity somewhere from age seven or nine to eleven or later. Until this maturity was reached, the child would not be able to bring consistency to abstract reasoning or to the understanding of motivation or the relation of cause and effect. Thus, when asked to assess the relative "naughtiness" of Jimmy, who accidentally broke five saucers, with Johnnie, who deliberately and angrily smashed one, a four- or five-year-old's answer is often, "Jimmy," because "Jimmy broke the most." Many children, even at seven or eight, have little appreciation of motives or reasons. They are not fully reason-able.

It could be logically hypothesized that since both the visual and auditory perception apparatuses—primary tools of learning—are literally extensions of the brain, they may be limited in terms of the time parameters of brain development (see chapters eight and nine). In addition, a sound quality of abstract reason-

3

ing would be necessary if the child were to bring full and satisfying meaning to academic types of learning, such as reading and arithmetic.

Clinical evidence showed that five- and six-year-olds, and even some at seven or eight, had difficulty reading without considerable frustration and with more than rote meaning. This was especially true with boys. Furthermore, clinical observation suggested that visual and intersensory perception were problems for typical five- and six-year-old readers. They would stumble along, uncoordinated, using their fingers to guide their eyes across reading lines. But seldom if ever were eight- or nine-year-olds seen doing this unless they had been habituated to it from their earlier years.

Many normal children, frustrated with their inability to read with understanding, often turned away from reading. Many others, excited at first with the prospect of school, lost their motivation after a struggle with tasks beyond their years; by grade two or three or four they had developed an apathy toward school from which they were seldom aroused. Investigation revealed that this experience was common in elementary schools. In fact, some experienced observers, such as Claremont's Malcolm Douglass (192) suggest that the increase of reading failure among California school children—one of the poorer records in the nation—was due in part to the early schooling practices in that state. Citing the work of Joseph Wepman and other reputable researchers, he reasoned that if California schooling were delayed until age eight, the likelihood existed of greatly reducing reading disability—possibly to as few as 2 percent of the children in some areas.

Research into Early Childhood Development

A combination of reports on neurophysiology, cognition, and clinical experience in developmental psychology and remedial reading led a team at the Hewitt Research Center to explore the possibility of a correlational study in neurophysiology and cognition. A study was tentatively designed in which neurophysiologists on the one hand and learning psychologists on the other would independently study common groups of young children from ages three to nine. Correlation of their findings was to be made by an independent team of biostatisticians.

Specialists at the United States National Institutes of Health (NIH) recommended as chief investigator David Metcalf, University of Colorado Medical School child psychiatrist and EEG specialist. Dr. Metcalf, well known as a creative but conservative researcher, was vitally interested in the project and willing to undertake it even at personal sacrifice.

By the time the services of Dr. Metcalf were secured, a Hewitt-funded literature search necessary for such a study was already well advanced. The search and analysis of studies in cognition and neurophysiology (including vision, hearing, intersensory perception, and other sensory-motor areas) led to an interest in related areas and opened new horizons, including social development and affective areas: parental attachment, parental attitudes, comparative school entrance-age studies, and comparative cost-effectiveness of preschool and day-care intervention as compared with parent education in the home.

In 1970–71 a sense of urgency arose relative to ECE issues because of the proposed federal early childhood legislation. Much of the effort on the part of the legislators was laudable, but some of the preschool and day-care provisions appeared inconsistent with systematic research findings. A number of state efforts were also of concern. Research was ignored or misused at times. The California state school superintendent had gone so far as to declare that the concept of school readiness was now outmoded—a statement that from almost any point of view seemed unwise.

Because of urgent legislative needs and on the advice of several consultants, the Hewitt Research Center published a preliminary report of ECE trends and issues that was conclusive in several respects, although far from exhaustive. With the specific counsel of several distinguished developmental and learning psychologists, the Hewitt Research Center adopted an advocacy position, first published in the *Phi Delta Kappan* (June 1972), then in a popular version through a *Harper's* article (July 1972). According to the *Harper's* staff, this article resulted in more letters to the editors than any other in their history, letters indicating a high degree of concern and agitation about this topic. The *Kappan* version also generated several guest editorials and an ongoing debate in that journal for some months.

In June 1973 the Office of Economic Opportunity, later the Community Services Administration, at the suggestion of both

5

Democrat and Republican members of the Senate and the House, made a grant to the Hewitt Research Center to facilitate a more complete analysis of scientific literature relating to the ECE issues. Along with the literature review funds, the OEO made three joint ECE basic research grants to Hewitt for (1) a correlational pilot study on neurophysiology and cognition at the University of Colorado Medical School, (2) a study of the background of state school entrance-age laws, conducted at Stanford University, and (3) an analytical study of relevant data from the National Elementary School Survey involving some 80,000 children, carried out by the Hewitt Research Foundation.

All four projects were based on the premise that research and practice must work together if they are to be of any real benefit to society. The researchers assumed that a common ground of testing was necessary for communication and for interrelating theory and fact. In an attempt to meet this obligation, they established the following guidelines or cautions for evaluating research, theoretical literature, and clinical findings.

1. Research analysts and consultants may hold divergent views, but, with integrity and competence in the field, they must have prime concern for the welfare of children.

2. A simple, clear interpretation should be sought in analyzing any data. Simplicity in reporting findings is of course not necessarily simplistic. Some of the finest pieces of ECE research have been found hidden in heavy volumes obscured by professional language and statistical anomalies. Every researcher or analyst who produces quality work must feel obligated not only to report data in a technically correct manner but also to translate it into the language of the layman; otherwise little interdisciplinary understanding occurs.

3. Sharing of findings in the various disciplines is a particular need. For example, learning specialists should be aware of a child's affective needs and of the extremely close relationship of neurophysiological development and visual and auditory perception to appropriate school performance. It is such interrelating of research in constituent ECE disciplines that primarily gives substance to this book.

4. There is need among ECE specialists for systems orientation—comprising an overall view, yet with goals clearly in mind. Toy manufacturers may promote their products, private pre-

school operators may lobby for voucher systems, parents may demand their "freedom," and labor organizations may urge more preschools to provide jobs. These represent vested interests. But professionals must not lose sight of the larger goal of optimum development for all children.

5. Another factor that has skewed ECE perspective is the frequent interpretation and overemphasis of the ghetto. The poor must have help, and to date much of the ECE focus has been on them. Yet groups in higher socioeconomic strata (SES) must not be left without benefit of scientific knowledge lest they also succumb to social and personal deterioration and fail to bear their share of society's obligation in developing the child and restoring the home. There is little question that some of the most serious early schooling damage has been inflicted on higher SES children. In contrast, many low SES homes have produced more responsible children.

6. An area related to both items 2 and 4 is that of ECE semantics. When, for example, is a *preschool* different from *nursery school*, different from *day care*, different from *kindergarten?* At almost any ECE meeting two or three of these terms will be used synonymously. Yet some ECE specialists insist on sharply discrete definitions. Such conflict is self-defeating for the ECE movement. Instead, why not remain flexible and, where necessary, work to resolve these differences with common understanding? All these terms apply to the period before regular schooling, and it may be that so-called *preschool* in its best form is closer to a typical definition of quality day care. Any disparity of use should be carefully qualified.

Similarly, what is the difference between *disadvantaged* and *deprived? Handicapped* and *impaired?* We find in one state that children are never retarded, only impaired. This is fine-line talk. On the other hand, we can understand caution about use of such phrases as *lower class* as compared with *middle class.* No one of course should be called low class, for low income or low socioeconomic status is not *ipso facto* low class, with the onerous nuance of those words.

7. The *date* of a study or paper does not necessarily make it good or bad. Despite this fact, many planners are critical of reviews utilizing findings that are not contemporary. Some are even doubtful of studies that date back more than five or ten years. This view is neither scholarly nor farsighted. Studies

should be appraised on the bases of design and validity of stated objectives, integrity of interpretation, and overall value to a field of knowledge. Well-done studies that have withstood the erosion of time are among our scientific monuments. Some of the best experimentation in the area of reading reaches back several decades, and many excellent studies probing school entrance age date back generations.

8. A scientist or scholar may be criticized for becoming an advocate—whether pro or con—on any issue. But if he is convinced of the truth of his position and does not clearly delineate it when faced with contrary practices, then who should do it? It is presumptuous to assume that somebody somehow will come along and happen to do the job. Indeed, what better test can there be of "truths" and scientific techniques than the challenge of advocacy? If, in the opinion of the scientist or scholar, there is sufficient reliable and consistent research evidence to support his position, advocacy should not be equated with prejudice, extremism, or exaggeration.

9. The attitudes of scholars toward other scholars must be open, with a mutual willingness to examine findings. It may be that a scientist is entitled to criticize a colleague, but this criticism is inappropriate when it is done at the expense of children or human welfare. Scholars often demean their colleagues, sometimes in their own institutions, then go on to overstate their own findings. Such attitudes in the educational-political realm of ECE often damage the ECE cause and destroy the benefits sought for children.

10. A careful analysis of data may lead to unexpected but noteworthy findings. Studies are usually designed to yield information about a specific problem, yet the data collected may also provide insights into related problems. For example, from an international study of achievement in arithmetic (358) an alert analyst, William Rohwer, observed that the earlier children went to school, the more negative were their attitudes toward school (574). Both Torsten Husén and his colleague, Robert Liljefors, confirmed this finding from this and later studies involving language and science (359, 433), although their research had been designed for another purpose.

Placing ECE Literature in Perspective

An examination of early childhood education literature must

8

necessarily focus on specific aspects of the subject. Yet findings must be interrelated in broad and systematic context, or erroneous conclusions and policies may be derived from them. The sheer quantity of theories, studies, demonstrations, projects, and programs of all sorts that have appeared in the last decade have left even some serious students of early childhood in confusion. How, then, can parents and teachers or busy administrators be expected to find their way through such a literary morass? And on what basis can concerned citizens and legislators plan for the best possible opportunities for children to develop into happy, responsible, and productive members of society?

Representative reviews have dealt with child development and early learning from a multidisciplinary point of view (340, 342, 319, 318, 138). Our urgent concern here is for an organization and interrelation of literature that might suggest new answers to the perplexing ECE questions relating specifically to the child's readiness for out-of-family study and care. Although we have included only a few references to infancy and toddlerhood to provide a proper perspective, a great deal has been researched for these years. Our emphasis here is on children's learning and education in the home, preschool, and primary grades from about ages three through nine or ten.

In the mass of literature related to early childhood education, it would be impossible to identify all the factors influencing early learning. Each of the specific areas in this volume has been selected because it represents findings indicative of strong influences on early childhood learning. From a careful analysis of the literature, we have identified the following factors as major influences on learning in early childhood:

1. The significant people in a child's life.
2. The nature of the material environment.
3. The interaction of people and the environment to provide opportunities for experience and exploration.
4. Values and self-esteem developed within the family and cultural context.
5. Physical, neurophysiological, and cognitive development and maturation.
6. Human and environmental resources that help develop the potential of the whole child for learning and living.

In 1972 under the auspices of the Hewitt Research Foundation we conducted a broad investigation of approximately 3,000 sources in early childhood education research and other literature. From the wide range of areas examined we found a synthesis of information for further study. Many literature reviews are limited in scope to analyses in a specific area so that indepth treatment is possible. This method makes it possible for teachers and students to analyze the research base for the conclusions. The Hewitt investigation, on the other hand, traces the single idea of school readiness—relating to the home—through many areas. In most instances we report the findings and discuss their significance. Scholars and students who are interested in a more detailed study of the data may refer to the bibliography.

As noted earlier, the relationships observed in the Hewitt method of study made it clear that powerful and dynamic interactions influenced various aspects of early childhood development and learning. And to ignore any of these was to distort the sum of all of them. The Hewitt study related the cognitive development of children to the factors of (1) family, (2) self, (3) culture and home environment, (4) development and maturation, and (5) structured learning programs.

We began the search by examining existing reviews of early childhood literature to locate references to influences on early learning. We then carefully checked the bibliographies of relevant items for further sources, after systematically identifying articles published in professional and research journals since 1960. We discovered unpublished sources by searching annotated ERIC (Educational Resources Information Center) bibliographies at the Champaign-Urbana campus of the University of Illinois. In addition, a large number of interested people provided clues to materials that might otherwise have been overlooked, including many antedating 1960. And finally, nationally known professionals in early childhood education, representing a wide range of views, were selected as consultants to suggest further references and to critique the project.

These various sources yielded more than 7,000 studies and papers that we screened in selecting the literature to be reviewed. About 1,000 items were closely analyzed and categorized, of which 700 or so have been included here. Organized and integrated, they point to solutions for some of the current dilemmas in early childhood education.

Scott (607) cautions wisely that much "research" in education fails to produce new information that can be used beyond the situation in which it is acquired. It is not safe to assume that methods yielding certain results in one place will have the same effect in other circumstances with different teachers and children. Situational variables are responsible for much evidence that suggests trends but does not provide hard data. And in this review some single studies may be inconclusive by themselves. But when the findings of such studies, in concert with the findings of many other studies, all point in the same direction, the implications deserve examination.

In analyzing literature for facts and trends and pointing out relationships between them, a scholar is of course obligated to maintain a regard for truth. To examine information honestly, he must be alert for clues from any source that may lead to further knowledge. While recognizing the value of careful investigation, he also recognizes that much information is available that has not been adequately investigated but that, if validated, could add immeasurably to knowledge and understanding. Although materials of this nature sometimes cannot alone be accepted as fact, they often suggest problems for further study.

It is obviously unscholarly, unethical, and unwise to wave aside a possible truth because it does not agree with presently accepted knowledge or conventional practice. Some of the trends here identified in early childhood literature are provocative in this respect. The human variables are so complex, and the divergent opinions so many—often seeming to depend upon vested interests in a particular profession or a political or social policy—that the real influences on learning in early childhood may be obscured.

Here is a challenge to early childhood scholars to reexamine the early childhood dilemma. Although this book is, by its very nature, designed for the specialist in early childhood development and learning, it does not exclude the college student who has developed a special interest in the education of young children. Synopses, examples, and suggestions have been included in order to make the text as practical as possible.

The materials in this book came to light through a systematic search of diverse studies, reports, theories, and hypotheses, all tied together by a common denominator of influences on learning, socialization, and all-around development of the young child. After they have carefully read all our qualifications, if parents, educators, legislators, vested interest persons, or other ECE individuals or groups have found any systematic or replicated evidence contrary to the research facts and conclusions presented in this book, we will be in their debt if they present it to us.

We have tried meticulously to qualify all statements appropriately and have had the manuscript checked and rechecked by highly qualified and eminent psychologists, psychiatrists, pediatricians, ECE researchers, and other ECE specialists and editors. If the analyses are given as careful and objective a reading as possible, we believe they will form in part a foundation for enlightened ECE legislation, policy, and practice and will produce far more fulfilled and less frustrated children than we often see today.

Thoughtful critics have suggested additional sources that might have been profitably analyzed. And even as this manuscript is being completed, further sources continue to become available. We have identified some trends, and the challenge for an open-minded search for further truth is left with those concerned enough to pursue it, and, whenever possible, to translate it into policy and practice.

1
Dilemmas in Early Childhood Policies and Practice

Synopsis. Changes in the structure of society in the last thirty-five to fifty years have brought about conditions that pose many problems in early childhood, such as reading failure, learning disability, delinquency, and breakdown of family ties. In an attempt to solve these problems, legislators have created programs involving much planning and great cost to the nation. Yet the dilemma persists: What factors, present in early childhood, are the common denominators of later accomplishment and satisfying personal development—leading to a secure, responsible, altruistic adulthood? We believe research will provide some of the answers to these questions.

A brief review of child study in this century shows a progression, beginning with facts only in the early stages, followed by the study of physical and mental growth measures immediately after World War I. During the depression years of the 1930s studies were made on the effects of socioeconomic deprivation on child development. This concern was followed after World War II by emphasis on personal-social development.

In the late fifties, however, the advent of the space age focused attention upon the cognitive functioning and intellectual development of children. The assumption was that accelerated intellectual development during childhood would lead to improved quality of performance throughout life. During the early and middle sixties, social reform produced the early childhood intervention movement for the disadvantaged. Preschools appeared nationwide, and early schooling for all was often urged.

However, the late sixties and early seventies brought doubts as to the effectiveness of these ECE programs. Many scholars questioned the wisdom of preschool education for the masses. Some suggested that the greater emphasis should be on strengthening the family structure and educating parents and future parents in the needs of children and in their adequate care as the means for solving these problems of early childhood.

Fluctuating Programs for Young Children

The current interest in programs for young children is a reflection of major issues in society. Although widespread agreement dictates that something must be done for the nation's children, much confusion reigns as to what the real issues are. Meanwhile, early childhood projects and demonstrations have proliferated across the country—public, private, church-related and commercial. A few of these appear successful in making healthier, happier children. But upon closer look the results of most are puzzling. Gratifying progress has been made, for example, in identifying needs in child health and nutrition. Yet after spending huge sums of money and tapping the resources of interested people and organizations, many ECE programs seem to have contributed little of lasting benefit to children.

Many perplexing early childhood questions remain. Changes in the structure of society have often stranded children on islands of insecurity or have driven small children to seek their peers as models in lieu of disinterested or ill-informed parents who should and could have supplied the attachments so badly needed. The shift of the population toward urban centers, the crowding and poverty of the inner city, a technological society with increased freedom for women, economic circumstances that seem to make it desirable or imperative for mothers to work outside the home, greater social acceptance of the breakup and restructuring of family units—all these conditions pose problems for early childhood and demand adjustments children cannot make by themselves.

Thus, many of our children need help, some of them desperately. In an attempt to remedy the situation, concerned researchers and educators have focused attention on almost every imaginable kind of out-of-family care program for the preschool years. For example, some have urged the need for day care for the child's socialization; others have stressed academic readiness. Some have sought to provide a warm, caring atmosphere; and some have supplied little more than custodial care. Some have

14

hoped to provide freer communication between social classes, while others have been concerned for care within those classes. A few may have succeeded in bringing the child greater freedom; others have appeared to be confused about their goals.

Some early childhood programs have made it possible for business and professional women to leave their children and pursue their work. Welfare mothers have also been freed to work, although their earnings have often failed to equal the cost of their children's care at public expense. This is particularly true when remediation costs are concerned—for those problems that may have been incurred by institutionalizing these children. Such programs for young children are supposed to provide antidotes for the negative effects of poverty, ignorance, neglect, and the general inability or indisposition on the part of adults to meet the needs of children. Unfortunately, scant evidence exists that they have had the expected success.

In view of all this planning and large expenditure of funds, why have so many children in so many early education programs seemed to profit so little? When children in some programs have made noticeable social and intellectual gains, why have these gains so often tended to disappear after a few years? These questions lead to an even more basic question: *What factors present in the early childhood years are the common denominators of later accomplishment and satisfying personal development?* Research is continually in progress, and all the evidence is not yet in, but certain trends 'suggest answers to these questions.

Early Childhood as a Field of Study

Understanding early childhood issues requires knowledge of not only current research, theories, and practice but also of the history of early childhood and the principles of child development. Since basic principles bridge both time and cultures, they can provide a stable perspective for the examination of early childhood findings and theories.

Such principles are provided in part by McLean (458), who reported a brief history of thirty-five years of research in child development, and Anderson (20), who summarized the child development movement. Their historical data trace the major emphases of child development studies from early in this century. Anderson noted that a cataloging of facts is typical of the early stages of any life science. This cataloging of structures, functions, and behaviors of the organism serves to locate problems and develop hypotheses for further study. (See also report of May and Vinovskis [448] in chapter twelve.)

Late in the last century, several psychologists informally observed and cataloged the behavior of their own children, and Edward L. Thorndike, Robert S. Woodworth, and Alfred Binet pursued studies of children's learning early in this century. Yet the main impetus for studying children came after World War I. New measurement techniques had been developed during the war, and hundreds of psychologists eagerly used them. People were concerned about the physical and mental defects that had been found in servicemen during the war. It was a logical time for beginning a systematic and organized investigation of the growth and development of children.

Such studies emerged in a number of universities. In 1916 Lewis M. Terman at Stanford began following the progress of gifted children. Bird T. Baldwin initiated measurement of the physical growth of infants and children at the Iowa Child Welfare Research Station in 1917, and Arnold Gesell continued Baldwin's studies at Yale in the early twenties, as did Walter F. Dearborn at Harvard and Frank N. Freeman at Chicago. Baldwin published a monograph on the mental growth curves of normal and superior children in 1922.

The Laura Spelman Rockefeller Memorial made available funds for research in child development and parent education in 1926. As a result, a number of research centers flowered. These included the Child Welfare Institute at Teachers College, Columbia University (1924), the Yale Psycho-Clinic (1926), the Iowa Child Welfare Research Station (1927), and Institutes of Child Welfare at Minnesota (1925), Toronto (1925), and California (1927). In these institutes nursery schools were established where children—mostly from two to five years of age—might be observed and studied. With the help of other funding sources, still other organizations emerged that were devoted to the study of children, such as the Merrill-Palmer School in Detroit (1920) and the program in Child Development and Family Life at Cornell (1925).

The emphasis in the research was then largely on measurement—of physical and mental growth curves, of intelligence, language, and social behavior. Everything that could be measured at that time was measured, and the results were compiled to

16

give fairly accurate descriptions of children at various stages of development.

The economic depression of the late twenties gave rise to a new focus in child study during the thirties. The effect of socioeconomic status and child care practices on the development of children became of vital interest. Kurt Lewin's field theories of the relation of children to their environment, analyses of the family and of parent behavior, and the effects of deprivation were major trends in ECE studies prior to World War II. Longitudinal studies from the twenties began yielding scientific data, and child development as a scientific area for investigation became more firmly established.

The research was interrupted by war, but, like World War I, World War II brought still newer measurement techniques. Whereas the measurements following World War I had focused on relatively concrete and observable variables, these new measurements spawned by a more technologically complex war turned attention to projective techniques and measurements of the less observable aspects of personality.

Thus, during the early fifties a great deal of attention was given to the study of factors contributing to the development of the self. The self-concept became a basic consideration in human development. And by the sixties the literature was replete with such theories and ideals.

In the late fifties, with the advent of Russia's Sputnik and the space age, diverse individuals and groups abruptly labeled inadequate the education and achievement of American children. Within a few years interest in personal-social development was subordinated to an almost frantic analysis of cognitive functioning and intellectual achievement. Whereas going to school and learning had been considered a right and a privilege for all American children, now, in the minds of many educators and policy makers, it became an obligation.

The study and measurement of children for the purpose of discovering how the human organism grows and develops in its various environments was still of interest to some. But this was overshadowed by the new emphasis on ways and means to induce cognitive and social development at earlier and earlier ages. The thesis suggested among other things that the more rapidly a child developed, the better would be the quality of that child's performance throughout life. Many ECE specialists became less and less concerned about what happens to an individual in the normal process of growth and development and more intent on how a society can *make happen* what it thinks ought to be.

From an extensive analysis of intelligence and experience, Hunt (356) concluded that environmental encounters might be governed "to achieve a substantially faster rate of intellectual development" during the early years of childhood that would eventually lead to "a substantially higher adult level of intellectual capacity." Hunt visualized environments that would promote a "self-directing interest and curiosity and genuine pleasure in intellectual activity" without the grim urgency of "pushing" children. He further noted that as each child's potential was maximized, individual differences in intellectual development would be increased rather than decreased.

Lip service was widely given to the welfare of children, but in the final analysis teachers and child-care workers often submitted to pressure from those in authority to make children produce academically. And why shouldn't children produce? Experimental research was showing that they could learn reading and some mathematical concepts relatively early. At first sight it seemed a great waste of human potential not to capitalize on such ability.

This concern for early learning coincided with social reforms of the sixties that focused on children who were thought to be disadvantaged. Their environments were perceived to limit the development of sensory awareness so that traditional learning was difficult. It seemed to many of these theorists that the obvious answer was to provide enriched environments, with deliberate early sensory stimulation and exposure to basic concepts—for example, in reading and math. Such intervention was expected to help these children keep up with their more advantaged peers. Further benefits were available in child health and nutrition services, and parent involvement increasingly became a key factor in many of the programs.

Head Start and Other Compensatory Programs

Powerful social and political factors combined with research efforts to produce Project Head Start in the summer of 1965. Head Start began as a part of President Johnson's War on Poverty and was administered through the newly created Office of

Economic Opportunity. Its guidelines were developed by experts in pediatrics, public health, nursing, education, child psychiatry, child development, and psychology. Over one-half million children were served in Head Start classes during an eight-week period. It was specified that 90 percent of those enrolled must meet the current federal poverty guideline.

During the summer of 1966 approximately that number of children again attended Head Start programs, and 171,000 enrolled for full-year programs (531). Head Start was described by some enthusiasts as "the country's biggest peacetime mobilization of human resources and effort" (113). But by 1967 investigators of Head Start programs began to question its lasting effects. Time and again Head Start evaluators reported that large gains in achievement were made during the preschool year, but these gains were not maintained when the children entered the public school system. They believed a follow-through program was needed to insure the benefits of Head Start were carried into the primary grades.

In 1969 Head Start was moved from the Office of Economic Opportunity into the Department of Health, Education, and Welfare. The Office of Child Development was created, and Dr. Edward Zigler of the Child Study Center at Yale University became its director. It also included children and family programs. In the spring of 1970 President Nixon declared that most compensatory programs had not helped poor children catch up. He announced the Early Learning Program that was planned as a strong experimental base for building new day-care programs.

The controversy over Head Start culminated in the Westinghouse Report (153, 291), which evaluated 104 Head Start centers across the country and concluded that summer Head Start programs were ineffective. Year-round programs were recommended. For programs to be effective, they should extend downward to infancy and upward into the primary grades. Parents should be taught to teach their own children, and more attention should be given to language development. Some Head Start centers should be purely experimental.

The Westinghouse Report was severely criticized by many social scientists and statistical experts. Nevertheless, the White House approved it, and the news media largely interpreted it as indicating the failure of Head Start. Yet it could also be deduced that Head Start had brought some unexpected blessings.

Among these was the frequently observed effect of making parents more constructively aware of their children and the privileges and rewards of responsible parenthood.

However, unrealistic expectations as to what Head Start could accomplish prevented objective interpretation of its effectiveness and caused disappointment at the "failure" of the project. While Head Start did not appear to produce lasting cognitive and affective gains, observers generally agreed on its health and nutritional benefits. Head Start is still under question by many, but extensions such as Follow Through are rising in public interest. (See more on Head Start in chapter twelve.)

Head Start appeared to be flexible and adaptable to individual situations and communities. Indeed, as many different philosophies existed as communities and programs. Broad differences existed in curricula and techniques; methods of handling children, equipment, materials, supplies; facilities, professional staff training, salaries, age of children, recruitment and screening processes of children, community variables, and racial balance. Some areas of agreement were apparent: "the aim to break the poverty cycle; similarity in class sizes (fifteen to twenty children), and paid personnel (two to four staff members), plus unpaid personnel; and the belief that children under six years of age can be educated. Educators also agreed on the need for speech and language training.

Follow Through was started as a pilot venture in the fall of 1967. It was designed to extend Head Start services from preschool into the primary grades. It was to be a comprehensive program that would provide for the education, emotional, physical, medical, dental, and nutritional needs of primary grade children who had previously received the same services in Head Start. Parent participation was to be an integral part of the program. Follow Through became an experimental program. It undertook a strategy of planned variation to assess the effectiveness of many different ways of working with poor children and their families in many different cultural and environmental situations throughout America.

In conjunction with Follow Through, the Head Start Planned Variation Study was conducted in 1969 (87). Eight preschool models were selected to participate in the study:

1. The pragmatic action-oriented model, sponsored by the Education Development Center in Newton, Massachusetts.

2. The academically oriented preschool model, sponsored by Wesley Becker and Siegfried Engelmann of the University of Oregon.

3. The behavior analysis model, developed and sponsored by Don Bushnell of the University of Kansas.

4. The Bank Street College model, developed and sponsored by the Bank Street College of Education in New York City.

5. The Florida parent-educator model, developed and sponsored by Ira Gordon of the University of Florida.

6. The Tucson early-education model, originally designed by Marie Hughes and sponsored by Joseph Fillerup of the University of Arizona.

7. The responsive model, designed and sponsored by Glen Nimnicht of the Far West Laboratory for Educational Research and Development.

8. The cognitive model, developed and sponsored by David Weikert of the High Scope Educational Research Foundation.

During the 1970–71 school year, the Stanford Research Institute undertook the first national evaluation of Planned Variation in Follow Through (87). Fourteen different approaches were classified into five groups, based on their major emphasis in working with poor children and their families:

1. The structured academic approaches of (a) Don Bushnell, (b) Lauren Resnick and Warren Shepler, (c) Juan Lujan, (d) Charles Smock and (e) Siegfried Engelmann and Wesley Becker.

2. The discovery approaches of (a) the Banks Street College model, (b) the Education Development Center model and (c) the responsive environment model.

3. The cognitive discovery approaches of (a) David Weikert, (b) Ira Gordon, (c) Dan Wolfe, and (d) Joseph Fillerup.

4. The self-sponsored approaches of local school district staff.

5. Parent-implemented approaches in which there were high levels of parent participation.

Researchers planned to include a further six approaches in the continuing study, which would bring the total up to twenty.

Although the results from the Head Start and Follow Through Planned Variation studies were highly tentative, they provided important future directions for research on the relationships between school experiences and the growth of young children (87).

21

In February 1971 five leading pioneers in the development and evaluation of approaches to the education of disadvantaged preschool children presented papers at the first annual Hyman Blumberg Symposium on Research in Early Childhood Education (649). The symposium was held at Johns Hopkins University. The experts were (a) Carl Bereiter—The Academic Preschool, (b) David Weikert—Curriculum, Teaching, and Learning in Preschool Education, (c) Oralie McAfee—An Integrated Approach to Early Childhood Education, (d) Todd Risley—Spontaneous Language and the Preschool Environment, and (e) Marion Blank—The Treatment of Personality Variables in a Preschool Cognitive Environment.

In April 1972 six leading researchers in the development and evaluation of approaches to the education of disadvantaged children presented papers at the second annual Hyman Blumberg Symposium (650). On this occasion the experts were (a) Samuel Ball and Gerry Ann Bogatz—Sesame Street, (b) Irving E. Sigel, Ada Secrist, and George Forman—Psychoeducational Intervention Beginning at Age Two, (c) Joan S. Bissell—Planned Variation in Head Start and Follow Through, (d) Merle B. Karnes—Research with Young Handicapped and Low-Income Children, (e) Virginia C. Shipman—Disadvantaged Children and Their First School Experiences, (f) Scarvin B. Anderson—Educational Compensation and Evaluation: A Critique.

In his critique of the two Hyman Blumberg Symposiums editor Julian C. Stanley (650) offered his personal opinion that

from the careful research of Carl Bereiter (1972), Gray and Klaus (1970, Merle Karnes (this volume), Oralie McAfee (1972), David Weikart (1972), and others [we find] that great expenditures of time and effort have not yet succeeded in permanently elevating IQ's of disadvantaged children much. Large gains the first year are common, but tend not to persist through the primary grades (pp. 7, 8).

Johns Hopkins psychologist Stanley (650) commented further on the symposiums:

Surely one learns from reading this volume and its predecessor that there are severe limits to the effectiveness of current preschool intervention efforts. Also, its cost is probably far higher per child than more effective teaching in the greatly restructured school system should be (pp. 9, 10).

In fact, Glen Nimnicht, at one time a chief psychologist and leading proponent of Head Start, became convinced he should turn in other directions. He suggested that, for a young child, twenty or thirty minutes daily on a mother's lap reading and playing with her was more profitable than several hours of nursery school (515).

In 1972, while still on the staff of the U.S. Department of Health, Education and Welfare, Joan Bissell (87) presented a paper at the Second Hyman Blumberg Symposium. One of her conclusions was that

the Head Start and Follow Through Planned Variation studies provided preliminary information about the variety of educational experiences available to young children. . . . This information was a first step in the development of a 'menu of alternatives' from which communities and parents can choose what best fits the needs of their children (pp. 105, 104).

On the other hand, Bissell admitted that the findings were inconclusive. A few Head Start programs and experimental preschools seemed to be effective in producing relatively large and lasting cognitive gains in low-income children. Nevertheless, the majority of Head Start and other compensatory preschool programs had not produced lasting increases in the intellectual development of little children.

She described the dilemma of early childhood:

The current situation regarding knowledge of the effects of preschool programs is problematic. On the one hand, little conclusive information exists about the total range of the effects of programs or the processes which underlie these effects. On the other, the federal government's involvement in education and child care programs for preschool children continues, as does the interests of state and local governments, industries, and groups of parents (p. 65).

Many pointed to the examples of European countries, such as Britain, Denmark, France, Germany, Sweden, and Switzerland, which had led in the preschool movement. Several states considered legislation for making early schooling available to all children down to age three or four and California went so far as to propose that by the age of eight all children should have mastered the basic tools of learning in reading, oral and written language, and arithmetic (140).

It was not a simple matter to sort out the many facets of the situation. Proponents stamped for the traditional school viewpoint—to build a "solid foundation" and later learning will be more easily acquired. Others were concerned with social action policies and the economics of welfare. Employed and "liberated" women lobbied for child-care programs, and teachers' federations were concerned as teaching jobs dwindled with a declining child population.

Legislative proposals became stop-gap measures. Political considerations became overpowering. The child's overall needs seldom were clearly defined, although general agreement existed that families as well as children needed counsel and other assistance. The major focus generally centered on remedy rather than prevention—what to do with families and children in a damaged society rather than seek the real cause of damage.

Then a series of thought-provoking articles appeared from such scholars and researchers as Urie Bronfenbrenner (118, 119), David Elkind (216, 217), Raymond Moore (495, 496), Meredith Robinson (571), William Rohwer (574, 575), Earl Schaefer (595, 596, 599), Burton White (717, 718), Sheldon White (721, 722, 723), and Ed Zigler (754, 755). The conclusions of these scholars were reached independently, but they expressed a similar concern. They questioned the wisdom of early preschool education for the masses of children, particularly in terms of academic orientation or readiness programs. Some suggested that rather than removing children further from an already weakened family structure, the efforts of society might well focus on strengthening families and educating parents to provide adequate care for their children.

And it has since become clear that many parents concurred— by instinct and in fact but with a variety of outcomes that point up the confusion reigning in policy circles. In California's Napa County, for example, the Larry Williams family kept their seven-year-old home in the face of laws requiring school entrance at age six. The district attorney determined that the state would likely lose the case at the trial level and if it won would probably lose on appeal. He asked the judge to dismiss the case.

In Queen's New York when Barbara Franz, a widow, took her six-year-old Johnny out of school because he was becoming frustrated and nervous, she was hailed into court and convicted.

24

Her crime was her attempt to provide family care for an immature child.

In northern Michigan, in a highly similar case, the district attorney and judge decided that the court was not a "proper forum" to determine if the Larry O'Guins should be held accountable for keeping their six-year-old boy out of school. The case was thrown out of court.

In southwestern Michigan Judy Waddell was warned by her neighbors and the school authorities about keeping her seven-year-old out of school. He was enuretic day and night; he was only five years old physiologically, according to the family pediatrician who advised that he be kept home. Because Mrs. Waddell agreed with her physician and other child specialists and wanted the best for her son, she stayed home with him. For this "crime" she was arrested and reluctantly jailed by the county sheriffs on the demand of the local public schools. As this book goes to press, she has been on trial for nearly three years as a patient judge tries to unravel the developmental needs of a child from the vested interests and politics of rigid laws requiring the ever-earlier institutionalizing of little children.

In Fallbrook, California, Dick and Marjorie Schaeffer were disturbed at the attitudes and habits their young children were developing in a nearby parochial school. They explained their concern to the local public school principal, who understood their dilemma and arranged for them to care for their children at home under the general guidance of a credentialed teacher with whom Mrs. Schaeffer conferred every two or three weeks.

They were at war with the law—with the legislators, who were influenced by, among others, educators, labor unions, and the women's liberation movement. These parents were charged as lawbreakers for doing what they thought was best for their children. Everyone offered either religious or scientific reasons, or both, in addition to their affection and concern for their children. Some school authorities were understanding, some vindictive.

Parents and their little children are in trouble. The inconsistency both within and among the states leaves parents confused. Sometimes the family is pushed aside through the demands of the law. Sometimes it is sustained. And ironically, a recent

25

Stanford study of school entrance laws shows that no state with laws requiring five- or six-year-old school entrance has based early entrance requirements on facts derived from systematic research (238). The essential pressures come primarily from vested interests and conventional practices.

2
The Role of Parents
in Early Learning

✳

Synopsis. *A child relates to people and to the world primarily through interaction with parents or parent surrogates. This effective tie or attachment makes it possible for the child to define himself* as a person, separate yet related to those around him. Premature interference with this tie often threatens the child's stability and the satisfactory performance of his role as a social creature.*

Attachments and quality of care influence learning from birth through early childhood and into the school years, and the strength and quality of attachment is principally determined by the amount and kind of care given by the mother or mother figure. This affectional bond gives stability to the child's uncertain world and contributes to a healthy independence.

The home appears still to be the best place for acquiring a healthy attachment. At present no substitute is known for the family in this respect. Frequent interaction with both parents enables the child to accept separation with the least problem. Nevertheless, most children cannot tolerate separation from their mothers before the age of five; and for the insecure, this intolerance may continue until age eight and for some as late as age ten.

Even the best day care cannot completely neutralize the negative social, emotional, and cognitive effects of mother-child discontinuity. Yet for some years a clear trend in U.S. child-rearing practices has been for parents to arrange for out-of-family care. Furthermore, legislators who induce or mandate very young children out of home and into school through school

---

*We recognize that the term *child* may mean either a female or a male, but until we have in our language one pronoun denominating both, we will use the masculine.—The editors.

27

entrance age laws are contributing to this pattern, albeit without any systematic research basis.

 Because the child's development and learning are influenced more by the attitudes and child-rearing practices of the parents than by social status or economic factors or by teachers, parent education becomes a primary concern for any society that would provide models to which the children safely attach themselves.

How a Child Sees Himself

A current trend is for young children to learn more and more about the world in which they live from people outside their own family in environments theoretically prepared for teaching and learning. Preschools of various kinds have burgeoned—nursery schools, kindergartens, and a variety of day-care programs. Or children may learn from people who are not physically present but who appear in two-dimensional substance on a television screen. According to Yarrow (748), "Today's children are reared by more influences and by fewer significant persons." This trend must be examined in relation to the role of parents in early learning.

Life in a technological culture is often extremely complex, and a child's family may not be able to teach him all he will eventually need in order to cope with it. It is true, however, that acquiring the skills to live with technology will have little meaning if one has not first learned to live as a secure and happy human being. Historically, this has been a major role of parents—to teach children in their early years that they have a place, a responsibility, and a worthy future as individual persons in a society of human beings.

The importance of the function of parents and families for the strength of a society is apparent in both history and anthropology. An individual's heredity may be either highly desirable or extremely doubtful. His environment may be good, bad, or indifferent. But more basic than either of these is *the method of dealing* with hereditary influences and environmental factors (19). This historically has been the domain of parents through the years of infancy and early childhood.

How a child relates to people and to his world is still largely the result of interaction with parents or parent surrogates. As we

28

have said, it is this affective tie developed in close and stable association with a small primary group that makes it possible for a child to define himself as a person. Premature interference with this tie often threatens the child's stability and the satisfactory performance of his role in society.

While the importance of this primary attachment is generally conceded, some disagreement exists as to when the attachment process is completed. Whether or not the development of attachment extends beyond infancy is an important question to answer correctly if we are to arrive at sound early childhood policy decisions.

Attachment and Dependency

Some relatively recent reviews (9, 747) and a comprehensive discussion by theorist-researchers (267) provide an extensive background for examining attachment and dependency in human development. The growth of significant interpersonal relationships during the first year of life is generally considered of primary importance for all later development.

Although the *attachment* and *dependency* constructs are not synonymous, they are both centered around what Yarrow (742, 744, 745) calls an "object relationship" or a "focused relationship." Yarrow and Pedersen (737) define this as a relationship characterized by strong interdependence and intense affect. Bowlby (104, 106) and Ainsworth (6, 7) simply label a child's affectional tie to an adult, particularly to his mother, as "attachment." Other researchers (266, 279, 265) have referred to a child's smiling, vocalizing, watching, and crying in response to his caretaking environment as "key social behaviors" without limiting their meaning to a concept such as attachment or dependency.

In discussing similar phenomena among animals Harlow and Zimmerman (317) speak of an "affectional system" or "affectional attachment," while Scott (605, 606) uses the terms "primary social relationship," "primary bond," and "social attachment."

These labels all apply to behaviors sharing some of the same origins that may nevertheless be quite different in purpose and function. To understand the real impact of infant-adult interaction and its potential for positive effects in later development, one must make a distinction between attachment and dependency.

29

Attachment has also been defined as an enduring affectional tie that an individual forms with another specific individual (8, 9). An attachment may change over time; but it is not transient, nor does it imply emotional immaturity—characteristics found by definition in dependency. Attachment may be a characteristic of all ages—infancy through adulthood—and it is essential for healthy development and emotional maturity. It implies a discriminating social responsiveness in seeking proximity to one particular person. It is the result of learning by experience from a significant relationship and of being cognitively aware that a particular person exists even though not actually present (8). It in fact carries no connotations of immaturity at any age (62).

Strong early attachments aid in the development of perceptual discrimination (746) and sensorimotor intelligence (61). In Geber's study (258) of Uganda infants, tribal children were strongly attached to their mothers and experienced almost constant interaction with them for the first two or three years of life. According to Geber, they were a part of all the mothers' activities, and their early motor and intellectual development progressed rapidly. The African children showed a lively interest in test materials and maintained excellent personal-social relations with the tester, smiling and trying to communicate with her. According to Gesell measures, by seven months African children were two or three months in advance of European children in adaptivity, response to language, personal-social relations, and motor development—especially posture. However, Uganda infants brought up in the European way provided a distinctly different picture. Left much of the time in cribs and cared for according to a schedule, often by nannies, they tended to develop according to norms established for Western children, and in some respects were lower than Western children.

While these evidences of early mental development do not necessarily correlate with later intelligence or achievement, they do point up the influence of attachments on learning. Attachments, warmth, and loving care continue to affect learning all through early childhood and into the school years (432, 590).

Gewirtz (268, 269) further refers to attachment as a directional force within an organism that controls behavior by the unique influences of *one* person. The strength and quality of this attachment is determined by the amount and kind of care given

30

by the mother or caregiver (9, 746), and it is generally formed only with a single, consistent caregiver (746).

Furthermore, an attachment is an affectional bond that gives stability in a world full of uncertainties. The mother or mother figure to which the child has become attached affords a safe base from which to explore the unknown, a place to which one can return when things "out there" become too threatening. Beyond the first year of life a well-established attachment contributes to a healthy independence (746). An emotional stability then evolves that builds a desirable independence and makes it possible for a child to persevere in spite of frustrations (268)—to stay with a task or problem until a goal is reached.

Dependency, as noted, is not synonymous with attachment. In fact, these constructs are related only in that the parent or caregiver is usually the central figure in both systems (610). Dependency is transient and implies an emotional immaturity as the individual grows older (8). It may be defined as the response to stimuli from any one of a *class* of persons (8, 268), or it may derive from a lack in parental responsiveness during a child's infancy (456). Dependency originates in the infant's reliance on its mother and other adult caregivers and may be defined as a set of behaviors that denote helplessness. This is natural in infancy. It is age-appropriate behavior. However, it should decrease with time in the course of normal development (62, 62).

Gewirtz refers to dependency as a *class* of learned behaviors that come under the control of stimuli from a *class* of persons. So there will be different sets of responses from interaction with different kinds of people. In dependency nothing is sure. The child must then sort out what is acceptable behavior and what can be expected from interpersonal relationships that are frequently changing. The people on whom one is dependent all have different expectations, so problems are met with routine, adaptive responses of low or moderate intensity (268). Relationships are diffused (269), and a child seeks reassurance by seeking help, attention, admiration, and approval from any person available (8, 269, 270, 610). Bowlby (104) calls it a "cheerful undiscriminating friendliness" with a "shallow attachment to any adult within the child's orbit." According to Bowlby, such children are extremely insecure and tend to go to pieces when they must function outside a structured environment.

Janet Kastel (390), head of teacher seminars that service a number of Israeli kibbutzim, points out a young child's need for solitude to work out his own fantasies. This in fact is an essential to positive sociality—first to be sure of himself without interference. She notes how in certain of the kibbutzim, which are not family oriented, children do not even have time or place to cry alone without the other children looking on and possibly making fun. So, she says, they accommodate. And they grow up more and more dependent upon their peers in all social and emotional respects. Initiative and creativity are stifled. They do not learn the vital art of making independent decisions. By the time they reach adolescence and come face to face with the need to do their own thing—without group approval—they often appear virtually helpless, are caught in a traumatic confrontation, and many times cannot make such decisions at all. Indeed, Miss Kastel says, they make very good soldiers.

Gewirtz (268, 270) suggests that attachment may be a form of dependency that comes under the control of stimuli from one person, or very few other persons. Help-seeking or attention-seeking that results from a diffusion of caregivers, however, is termed socio-emotional dependency and should not be confused with a normal dependence on others for assistance that is *really required* in normal daily living. This latter type of dependency is purely instrumental and is used constructively in a great many social interactions.

The determination of attachment and dependency behaviors is rooted in qualitative differences first in the mother-child relationship. During the first year of life, these differences not only affect the development of attachment but also influence the development of the cognitive capacity to grasp the concept of person-permanence and to realize that persons still exist as separate entities even when the child cannot see or hear them. Infants with a secure attachment to the mother have been observed to be more advanced in this concept than infants with a disharmonious mother attachment (61, 258). At first, the biological status of mother and child determines the nature and type of interaction between them. Recurring interaction sequences in feeding, holding, and transporting lead to mutual response patterns. Thus the basis for an attachment is formed (136).

The best place for acquiring a healthy attachment appears to be a healthy family environment. A child will learn to respond to some extent to all the people who appear consistently within the family, but his primary attachment will be to the one or two who give him the most care. Even when that care is lacking in some things that are usually considered essential, there is at present no known substitute for the family for developing an equivalent healthy attachment in children (9).

An attachment that assures stability for the child also makes it possible for him eventually to be separated from the attachment figure without trauma or protest, especially as he acquires experience and becomes cognitively able to handle the fact of separation. Spelke and colleagues (643) found that the intensity of an attachment was *not* reflected in a child's crying when separated from his parent. A child was more likely to protest separation when interaction with a parent, in this case with fathers, had been limited. Children who had experienced frequent interactions with *both* parents were able to accept the separation with the least upset. Research suggested that children who interacted frequently with both parents had a greater variety of experience in a stable environment and were, therefore, cognitively precocious. This enabled them to accept the fact of separation with more assurance. On the other hand, children with minimal interaction with parents cried the most when separated from them.

In Boston, researchers established an experimental day care program, using a cross section of working and middle-class families, carefully selecting as caretakers mothers with warm nurturing personalities (385). They established 1-to-3 adult-child ratios up to age thirteen months and 1-to-5 for those who were older, up to twenty-nine months. The psychologists set up a control group of mothers who cared for their own children at home. The children in the two groups were "carefully matched."

The researchers studied intellectual growth, social development, and the child's ability to achieve a close relationship with the mother. The day-care children were in custody seven hours daily, five days a week. They found few if any dissimilarities between the home-reared and the day-care children in the three study areas.

However, the researchers had some reservations, for the fathers were not studied. Nor was there indication that the mothers of home-reared children were as carefully selected as the caretakers of the day-care youngsters. The psychologists also suggested that (1) the sensitivity of their methods may not have been adequate; (2) the factors measured may not have included or accommodated the key variables; and (3) the study may not have been extended long enough to have captured emerging differences in the future. The careful selection of caretakers in combination with the small adult-child ratios seems to preclude the study from generalizing communities at large—both in terms of finding so high a quality of caretaker and of prohibitive fiscal costs for low adult-child ratios.

Children two or three years of age who can accept separation with equanimity, however, may show distress when they discover they are alone in a strange situation (260). They still need the assurance that they can return to a stable attachment figure whenever necessary.

Although cognitive awareness enables a child to handle the fact of separation, it does not follow that there will be no emotional effect on an older child. When children thirteen to fifteen months and two to three years of age were observed in strange situations—both in the presence and in the absence of their mothers, the constant presence of the mother appeared more necessary for normal behavior with the younger ones. The older children also reacted to the mother's absence by a decrease in activity and by crying, but they recovered completely in a shorter time than the younger children when the mother returned (168).

In the Cox and Campbell study the mother was absent for only a few minutes. Other studies show the negative effects of total separation on children in institutions (103, 104, 105, 106, 107, 631, 671). In an intermediate area, Blehar (92) studied the effects of long, daily separations in a day-care situation. She found there were possible disturbances in attachment and separation distress, and these were a function of the age of the child at the time day care began. Children who began day care at twenty-five months tended to exhibit a massive detachment. Those who started day care later, at thirty-five months, maintained their attachment, but it was an anxious attachment. They were still in need of reassurance from an attachment figure.

Bowlby (104) has concluded that most children are not really able to tolerate separation from their mothers before the age of five. Normally after that a child who is happy and secure in his

34

mother's love will not be unbearably anxious if the separation is not prolonged. But, Bowlby observes, children aged five to eight who are insecure, doubtful of their mother's feelings toward them, and "liable to emotional troubles can easily be made far worse by a separation experience." They often believe they have been sent away for naughtiness. This in turn leads to anxiety and hatred, which results in a vicious cycle in parent-child relationships. Bowlby (106) states further that "throughout the latency of an ordinary child, attachment behavior continues as a dominant strand in his life." It is only as adolescence approaches that this attachment to parents begins to weaken.

The stress of separation from an attachment figure is frequently intensified by an accompanying change in the environment (743). For a very young child this strangeness and unpredictability in his surroundings may be as traumatic as the separation itself. Even for older children such novelty and unpredictability heightens the sense of loss of the attachment figure (744).

Just how an early attachment affects behavior at later ages is not yet conclusive, but according to Ainsworth (8), clinical evidence suggests that significant relationships exist. And Bowlby asserts that the foregoing dangers from broken attachments may continue until some children are eight to ten years old. The deprivation resulting from a lack of attachment may occur at any social level (9), in affluent as well as disadvantaged homes. Ainsworth also says that even the best of day care cannot completely neutralize the effects of mother-child disharmony. The responsibility rests ultimately with the parents, the ones with whom children form their primary attachments.

The anxiety, fear, and stress generated by separation from parents may move beyond the creation of emotional problems or neuroses to develop serious learning and behavior problems. It is true that mild anxiety may heighten activity and facilitate learning. But when anxiety becomes acute or chronic, it "produces disorganization of cognitive responses" and may result in low performance, erratic conduct, and personality disorders (589).

When parents actively dislike or are indifferent to their children, perhaps there might be an advantage in placing these children with surrogate parents. Lewis (430) noted that some children gained rather than lost from such separations. Yarrow

(744) also believes that a child might well be removed from "grossly inadequate parents in a depriving and hostile environment." But Yarrow states further that everything possible should first be done to improve the family situation, or the children should temporarily be given alternative care in their own homes.

This suggests a difference between out-of-family and out-of-home care. When "out of family," a child may derive a certain amount of security from the "home nest" even though the family is not present. This is typical of "nanny" care. Out-of-home care may provide alternatives to the home but will sacrifice the quality of security. Bowlby (102) concurs generally with Yarrow on the basis of clinical experience and studies by Simonsen (629) and Theis (671). He suggests that the home must be very bad before it is bettered by a good institution.

Parental Attitudes

The same environmental circumstances that contribute to either permanence or instability in a child's life also have some influence on parents' attitudes toward children. For the most part, however, parental attitudes are more deeply rooted in events, customs, and personal experiences.

An example of an attitude that seems to be associated with early parent-child interaction appeared in a study of the effect of hospital practices on later maternal behavior. Mothers in hospitals who were permitted sixteen hours of additional contact with their infants beyond what was normally experienced showed an attitude of greater interest and concern for their children than mothers in a control group who had had normal hospital experience. The assessment was made a month after the mothers returned home (401).

Another group of mothers—whose children were left in an intensive care nursery for longer than two weeks because of low birth weight—gave evidence of having personality problems unrelated to the circumstances of birth and early interaction. Records of these mothers' visiting patterns during the infants' hospital stays showed that disorders in mothering behavior occurred exclusively among mothers with attitudes of little interest toward their infants. These mothers visited their infants infrequently—fewer than three times during a two-week period. Mothers who visited their infants more than three times in a two-week period gave no evidence of such disorders in spite of the lack of parent-child contact (225).

Most parents' attitudes have resulted from the environments in which they have lived and from association with a great many people and influences. Thus the family, education, religious institutions, the public media, the economy, and prevailing status symbols all have their effects on how parents perceive their children and what they expect those children to be. These attitudes, in turn, influence the quality of the motivation of children, especially as attachments are formed. Programs of parent education that do not account for these factors are incomplete (451).

Out of the milieu of social and economic forces parents have distilled their own beliefs that shape the future of their children. On the basis of comprehensive data from public schools in the United States, Mayeske (449) concluded that children's motivation for learning is primarily social in nature and origin, and the beliefs and aspirations of parents are a greater influence on school achievement than social status or economic well-being. Durkin's study (199) of over 5,000 California school children confirms this conclusion in revealing that those youngsters whose parents provided many books and similar learning materials generally excelled in reading.

Differences exist in the learning and achievement of children with different socioeconomic backgrounds, but these appear to be more a result of the attitudes of parents and of aspects of the lifestyle that are not entirely dependent on economic factors. For instance, the results of an investigation (125) of the way in which mothers attached meaning to their own and their children's behavior in a mother-teaching task implied that the greatest differences among socioeconomic groups in stimulating children to learn were in the areas of guidance and enrichment.

A Brandis and Bernstein (111) analysis concludes that parents of middle and lower socioeconomic status differ significantly in their attitudes concerning the adjustment of their children to school, and they differ in the preparation of their children for school. They also differ in their attitudes toward work and play and toward the use of toys by their children. Major differences exist among social classes regarding the value of books and reading, and these differences are apparently related to learning abilities. In all of these respects, a child from a low socioeco-

37

nomic level is usually at a decided disadvantage in comparison with middle-class children.

McCandless (451) notes that an *effective* environment for a child is one to which the child has sufficient maturity to bring meaning. Even though a child may be surrounded by stimulating toys and materials, he may lack the motivation to learn because these things are beyond his ability to experience. A simple but organized environment to which a child can actively relate probably provides the greatest stimulation for learning. For this reason, poverty-level homes may provide as much stimulation for children as those that are more affluent, especially when activities are experienced in a satisfying relationship with a parent or other adult. The family and home influence is more likely to be a better predictor of educational functioning than socioeconomic status (413).

Furthermore, many low-income parents have educational and occupational aspirations for their children equal to those in higher income groups, and they strongly believe they have a responsibility for their children's learning (426). But they, as well as parents of other socioeconomic levels, need help to know *how* to proceed. As suggested by McCandless (451), parents should develop attitudes about their children's value and the use of materials available to them. And above all, they must develop positive attitudes about their own worth as parents and the effect of their interaction with their children if they are to provide optimum care.

Mothers in low socioeconomic status groups sometimes feel they have little influence on the development of their children. They may see themselves as powerless and unable to change things (481, 392). The attitude of parents toward such a simple thing as talking to a child may set the stage for positive or negative development in the future. Weikart and Lambie (703) found that some low-income mothers considered talking to a baby silly and unimportant. Failure to understand that infants can communicate with people and can express emotions can result in a lack of maternal stimulation that may, in turn, hinder cognitive development (679).

Early mother-child interaction is an essential factor in a young child's language development, and the quality and consistency of this interaction profoundly affects his communication competence. A child responds to communication before he understands words. Hostility or warmth are readily transmitted by voice tone and body language—eyes, facial expressions, and other forms of communication. His mother shapes his information-processing strategies and influences his future mental growth and personality development through her linguistic and regulatory behavior. If this mother-child relationship is inadequate or incomplete, the child's language development may be retarded (707).

The influence of sociolinguistics on the learning of a young child is emphasized by Brandis and Bernstein (111). They found that the measure of communication and control by the mother *before* the child goes to school is related to the verbal behavior of the child at the end of his second school year.

When parents are themselves frustrated or apathetic, when life is unrewarding and apparently futile, there is a tendency to be satisfied with a low level of child care. In a study of Appalachian mountain mothers (545), such feelings resulted in social withdrawal, lethargy, and declining intelligence in children. In addition, impulsiveness in some of these mothers was linked with a way of life that made children hostile and defiant by the time they were five. The work of Skeels (632) tends to confirm this conclusion. Indifferent care by orphanage staff brought withdrawal and deteriorating intelligence, while warm, responsive "mothering"—although given by retarded teenagers—assured increments in intelligence and sociability.

It must be emphasized, however, that children of low socioeconomic status are not the only ones who may suffer from parental attitudes toward their learning. Children from high and middle levels of society often are hurt by parents who go to the opposite extreme. These children are sometimes under such tremendous pressure from their parents to achieve that they succeed academically at the expense of mental health. Some retain lifelong feelings of neurotic strain, while others succumb to psychoses or severe neuroses (428).

That children perceive the attitudes of their parents and behave accordingly is illustrated in the findings of Darvin Miller (473). In this instance children's perceptions of their parents were significantly related to their social behavior in a nursery school. Parents who were perceived as accepting their children fully and who were also firmly in control exerted a positive influence on their children, who exhibited self-assured social behaviors and a certain independence associated with the security that comes from positive parental attitudes. Conversely, children who perceived their parents as punitive or overindulgent tended to be dependent, with negative social behavior.

In relation to learning, children's awareness of their parents' attitudes is closely linked to their intellectual development. The education and IQ of the mother seem to be less significant in this respect than the mother's attitude toward herself (328) and her expression of maternal warmth (425, 556). Radin, in fact, found that a child's ability to respond even to a compensatory program was greatly affected by maternal warmth. Schulz (603) suggests that our inferring children may do poorly in school if they do not go to school early builds a fear of failure into both parents and students.

Early learning in preschool boys who were observed with their fathers correlated definitely with father behaviors, particularly in relation to both acceptance and restrictiveness. Boys gained significantly in IQ when fathers used reinforcement and consultation and also demonstrated sensitivity over a period of time. But boys whose desire to explore was apparently blocked by their fathers showed only limited cognitive growth (557).

Yet restrictiveness that limits exploration must be differentiated from the necessary limits imposed upon a child for his own safety and for protecting property and the rights of others. The security of knowing limits and the freedom to explore within them help a child to achieve. Radin and Kamii (558) discovered this attitude in middle-class mothers led to a high probability of their children's success in school. But the attitudes of low-income mothers often tended to be self-defeating. They were inclined to be protective and intrusive and to control their children with little respect for them as individuals (480, 522).

A thoughtful, informed firmness indeed appears to produce good results. Drews and Teahen (202) found that mothers of high academic achievers were more authoritarian than mothers of low achievers. Mothers of high achievers appeared to know what was best, and their standards were accepted by their children.

Such successful authoritarian practices are generally complemented by rational responses—a willingness to answer to the principle or basic why involved in the parental action. This is in contrast with dominating, intrusive, and coercive parental at-

40

titudes that have a negative effect on children's apparent intelligence (38, 357, 95, 72).

Child-rearing Practices

Whether a child-rearing practice can be termed "good" or "bad" depends upon the criteria used. Key among such evaluation standards are the physical well-being and psychological health of children as they grow up in their own particular cultures. Basic early physical and psychological needs are much the same in every society but are met with varying degrees of success, depending upon the prevalent customs of child rearing (659).

The most basic of these needs include (1) opportunity for physical development and health—with strong concern for sound nutrition and constructive exercise; (2) learning to communicate through language; (3) acquiring concepts basic to the organization of the culture—relating to time and space, using tools, expressing emotion, and learning accepted behaviors; (4) identifying one's self as an individual, first in the family and later in the larger society; and (5) relating to reality, existence, and the supernatural through religion or some metaphysical orientation. This latter aspect of child rearing is concerned with the inculcation of values, morals, ethics, and attitudes regarding life and death, including sexual conduct and the ultimate purpose of human existence.

In meeting needs that involve a heavy emotional impact, such as personal identification, values, and the basic issues of life, a parent or other principal caregiver exerts a strong influence. Spitz (646) found that this child-adult interchange is the central psychosocial factor in an infant's life. This raises important questions concerning the widely held thesis that young children make their most rapid gains out of home in a group of their peers.[1] In areas of intense feeling the confidence and affection of involved adults are more important than actual child-rearing techniques. Maturity of the parents and their own psychosocial responses are the most influential factors in child-rearing success.[2]

[1] See "Issues and Likely Solutions," chapter 13, on "Home or School Socialization of the Child."

[2] The psychosocial maturity in parents urgently calls in turn for a high degree and quality of *parenthood education.*

41

Baumrind (49) found that firm, loving adults—demanding but understanding—generally help children become self-reliant, self-controlled, competent, mature, and buoyant. And the spontaneity of such children is not affected even by adversely high parental control. Baumrind noted, however, that parents who were firm but punitive and unaffectionate could affect their children adversely. Such children tended to be anxious, restless, and alienated from their parents. Children of moderately loving parents who lacked consistency and control were dependent and immature. Such uncertainty in parental control was apparently reflected in unsureness of child behavior.

Spitz (646) referred to a similar effect. Mothers with an infantile personality, shifting between hostility and over-protectiveness, had children who were slow to respond socially and were also slow in acquiring manipulative ability. The solution advocated by Spitz was education for parenthood, especially for mothers. He suggested that legislation be arranged so that mothers could stay with their children. Yet in 1968, nearly twenty years later, the Low and Spindler study of child-care arrangements in the United States (436) showed a trend in the opposite direction. And a study of school entrance-age laws (240) strongly suggests that legislators who induce or mandate little children out of home and into school do so without any sound or systematic research basis. They appear to be almost capricious in their use of early childhood data.

The number of mothers who have felt it necessary to arrange for the care of their children while they work has steadily increased. At the time of the Low and Spindler survey 25 percent of all U.S. mothers living with their husbands and having pre-school-age children were in the labor force. Twenty percent of mothers living with their husbands and having children under three were working. In addition, a great many widowed, divorced, or separated mothers of young children were also working. This survey showed a clear trend in U.S. child-rearing practices to arrange for out-of-home child care.

But employment of mothers is not the only reason for out-of-home care. Those who are concerned about children's learning give a more pragmatic reason, especially for children from disadvantaged homes. Declining IQ scores among the disadvantaged seem to be related to the emotional effects of child-rearing conditions. Wiener, Rider, and Oppel (727) concluded that "something happened to lower-class children after the age of three that was both emotionally disturbing *and* intellectually impairing." Their data suggested that child-rearing conditions were the cause, but the specific variables were not determined.

Umberto Nagera (504), director of the Child Psycho-Analytic Study Program of the Children's Psychiatric Hospital, University of Michigan Medical School, made a direct connection between early childhood emotional disturbances and certain child-rearing practices. He used the term *developmental interference* to refer to "whatever disturbs the typical unfolding of development." Unjustified demands made of a child in early and rigid toilet training, inflexible feeding routines and premature mother-child separation with lack of maternal stimulation were identified as having a potential negative emotional impact.

Aspects of child rearing that are usually normal at a developmental level can become serious interferences if demands are made that a child cannot handle. Nagera noted that culturally determined interferences—such as behavior expected of children at a particular age—may be actively imposed upon a child without regard for individual rates of development and needs. Because of differences in individual rates of development, a demand made of one five-year-old, for example, may be beyond the ability of another five-year-old and may be totally inappropriate for a three-year-old. These inappropriate demands disturb the normal course of development and eventually hinder rather than speed up the developmental process.

In the early 1970s Martin Engel (221), then director of America's National Day Care Demonstration Center in Washington, D.C., discussed a related problem:

The motive to rid ourselves of our children, even if it is partial, is transmitted more vividly to the child than all our rationalizations about how good it is for that child to have good interpersonal peer group activities, a good learning experience, a good foundation for school, life, etc., etc. And even the best, most humane and personalized day-care environment cannot compensate for the feeling of rejection which the young child unconsciously senses.

Variables in Parent-Child Relationships

The overriding importance of positive, consistent parent-child interaction is far more evident in literature related to early childhood learning than is commonly understood. Important among these influences are (1) the degree and quality of the involvement of child and adult, (2) the desirable freedom or autonomy on the one hand as opposed to the restrictiveness engendered by the interaction on the other, and (3) stability and firmness as opposed to inconsistency and indulgence on the part of the adult.

Children from stable homes with a considerable degree of contact with their mothers may be expected to form strong attachments. Little, Kenny, and Middleton (435) found a significant trend in relating child-adult interaction to the development of intelligence: A strong interaction with parents in stable homes was positively related to an increase in IQ over a period of time. On the other hand, children from less stable homes appeared, for some reason, to have higher IQs at age four, but by the age of seven the situation was reversed. Generally children from stable homes with many opportunities for positive interaction with their parents showed a significant rise in IQ, and those from unstable homes with less opportunity for positive interaction had a significant decrease in IQ. As the children grew older, stability of the home and contact with parents became increasingly important in producing cognitive gains.

Although a considerable amount of parent-child interaction appears to be preferable, smaller doses are far better than none. Saltz and Johnson (590) found that an experimental group of children one to six years of age living in an institution definitely benefited from part-time mothering by foster "grandparents" over a period of several years, without any special environmental stimulation. Their control group of institutionally reared children did not have this mothering but was given much general environmental stimulation. While this stimulation was somewhat effective, these children gained less in IQ than those who had grandparents and no special stimulation. These findings appear consistent with those of Skeels et al. (632) whose orphans, mothered by retarded teen-agers, developed rapidly in intelligence.

On the other hand, many adults exercise authority over children without sufficient interaction to develop a real attachment. This may be true when older siblings and other adults (besides the parents or caretakers) are present in the household, and an undesirable spirit of rivalry is generated in the home. Under these circumstances Abramson (2) observed children expressing violence in fantasy. According to Tulkin and Kagan (679), children interacting with a number of adults other than their own mothers may be less likely to be involved in activities of the home—less disposed to explore and manipulate their home environment.

According to Sylvia Bell (62) the quality of exploratory behavior, which begins in infancy, is influenced by the quality of the mother-child interaction. This affects both the child's attachment to its mother and its early cognitive development. Mary Ainsworth shares with Dr. Bell the research-based conviction that cognitive and social development are intimately interrelated, and that mother-infant interaction influences both (10). Geber's (258) work in Uganda would certainly seem to support their conclusions.

During a child's first eight months the maternal qualities of sensitivity and appropriate maternal responses to infant signals were found by Bell (62) to affect significantly all aspects of cognitive development. In the last quarter of the first year, and possibly thereafter, cognitive development is fostered by a constant maternal role coupled with conditions permitting a child to explore his surroundings, to initiate action on the environment, and to receive feedback on his actions. And the quality of this exploratory behavior stems primarily from the mother-child relationship.

Factors in the quality of parent-child relationships that have been shown to have a positive effect on children include such variables as *acceptance* (473), *warmth* (425, 556), *happiness* (479), *expression of affection* (479, 49), and *firmness of control* (49, 50, 194, 473). All these appear to be integral parts of stabilizing, self-worth inducing experiences. And, according to Milner (479), the awareness of such happy experiences in parent-child interactions is a characteristic of children with high mental maturity scores.

On the other hand an investigation by Roff (573) of specific factors in parent-child relationships that were predictive of adult neuroses pointed heavily to kinds of parent-child interaction that were quite the opposite of these stabilizing qualities. The families of neurotics were differentiated from other families primarily in terms of the subtleties of parent-child interaction. Neurotic adults generally reported they had experienced in their childhood parental neglect or repudiation and lack of affection.

45

Some reported their parents wanted to be rid of them, and some parents exhibited vigorous physical violence.

So the evidence suggests that adults largely determine child behavior by the quality of the interaction they build. In his discussion of the social ecology of human development, Bronfenbrenner (119) concurs.

Parents' Responsibility

In order to assure positive conditions and motivation for their children's learning, the first responsibility of parents is to understand their own relationship to their children and their children's developmental needs. Robert Hess (327) sought to identify the things mothers could do that would develop cognitive ability and educability in their children, even in poor environments. He concluded that the mother's own behavior and cultural background was the influential factor. Although mothers' backgrounds cannot be basically changed, mothers can form attitudes that have a strong, positive influence on their children's emotional and physical environment, even in extremely limited circumstances.

Regardless of social class, parents can be helped to use their own abilities as parents and as their children's earliest teachers. Miller (478) found differences related to social class in the teaching *effectiveness* of mothers largely because of differences in their teaching styles. In all social classes he found that mothers used varying degrees of specificity in communicating with their children, but mothers in the lower socioeconomic levels tended to be less specific and precise, conveying a more passive attitude. This passivity tended to have a negative effect on their children's cognitive development.

• From work with disadvantaged children, both black and white, Liddle and Rockwell (432) assert that the most important learnings in life begin in the family. When children lack loving care, they are unprepared to succeed in a traditional school situation. According to Liddle and Rockwell, such children may have no idea what education is all about or why they are in school, and it is difficult to achieve when expectations are not clear.

Schaefer (597) observed that children model after parents in attitudes, moral knowledge, vocational interests, and personality. This suggests that the influence of parents on children is greater than that of teachers. A logical conclusion would be that teachers should work to effect desired changes by teaching the parents and trusting them to develop in their children the attitudes and motivations necessary for learning.

On the basis of literature reviewed, Schaefer reached the conclusion that parents must be taught skills for educating their own children in their early years. Gordon (284) recognized that the "overwhelming influence of deleterious life circumstances" can be a real obstacle for parents who are willing to assume the responsibility for their children's early learning. These parents need help in mobilizing their own potential and that of their environment to meet the developmental needs of their children.

Schoolroom assistance by parents is not the same as their direct interaction and teaching of their children themselves (329). Nor are ignorance and poor attitudes effectively remedied simply by involving parents in school-home programs for their children. This was strongly suggested by a follow-up study of mothers involved in Head Start programs (154). Parents need more than participation in their children's educational activities. They need education themselves, education showing them how they can be effective influences in their children's development.

The preponderance of evidence indicates that the key role of a parent throughout the years of childhood is simply to be the kind of warm, responsive, and relatively consistent person to whom a child can safely become attached. Early development and learning are actively dependent on this relationship. Parents are chiefly responsible for a child's early learning by their attitudes and responses to the child in frequent interactions. There is little if any evidence showing that this role can be successfully assumed by anyone else except by parent surrogates or attachment figures who become very much involved in positive ways with a child on a relatively permanent, continuous, and consistent basis.

The extent to which the child's attachment is diluted by care out of the home or is broken by indifferent, unresponsive, or overbearing parents will dictate his relative stability and sense of self-worth. To the extent that he is unstable or is reliant on his peers for his value system and his decisions-at-large he will be ill-prepared both socially and cognitively for his tasks as a child and as an adult.

3
A Child's Values and Self-Concept

Synopsis. A child's system of values and his self-concept are inextricably bound together and are concurrent in their influence on learning. Thus, a major task of early learning is an individual's identification of values—of defining his sense of self-worth.

The role of parents is crucial in establishing a sound sense of worth in a child and building his value structure. This is first and best accomplished by the example of the parents themselves. During his first six or seven years a child absorbs the values of his family, although the full understanding of these values may not be grasped until adolescence or later. The influence of the family, especially the mother, is of prime importance in establishing and maintaining values and the associated self-concept.

In order for children to function effectively in a peer group, they should be able to comprehend reasonably their social identity within the primary family group. Age seems to be a significant factor in their relative understanding of the structure of the family and their place in it. In less than a generation the shift from parents to peers as the primary models appears to have moved substantially down from about grade seven to early grades, and it is believed that social contagion—imitating attitudes and activities of peers—is now already well developed at the preschool level. Such peer orientation seems to have negative effects upon the attitudes and behavior of young children. This is consistent with findings that children who start school later—and wait therefore to come under the influence of their school peers—tend to be superior in achievement, behavior, sociability, and leadership.

When a child has achieved a positive sense of self-worth, he will adapt more constructively to the world outside his home. He will be less

49

threatened by authority figures who control his environment; and if he has strong, internalized values and standards, he will be less vulnerable to peer pressures.

An abiding need exists for developing in the young necessary values and self-worth for social competence. Yet early socialization in the family context is being undermined by younger and ever younger out-of-home care, with the result that children are left socially and morally to rear each other and to randomly gain their values and a sense of worth from their ever younger and more insecure peer group.

Awareness of Self and Early Learning

Self-awareness originates early in life (720, 227, 166). And the success or failure of academic learning appears to be influenced to a great extent by a child's concept of himself (123, 124, 141, 122, 272). So the self-concept must be considered an important and integral part of early learning.

ECE researchers and scholars have proposed a variety of hypotheses on the development of a high quality of self-worth in a child. Weininger, for example (708) believes that the concept and awareness of oneself is related to body image, and body image seems to be a function of certain kinds of early experiences. These experiences include exploration of the body, masturbation, and wounds.

But the child does not come by these concepts alone. He is no island. The views of those about him are often key influences. The reaction of parents,* particularly the mother, toward these experiences, is a prime factor in the child's growing awareness of self (112).

Elementary children as a group have difficulty maintaining positive self-concepts for the first few grades after they are enrolled in school (652). Felker (230) reports a study of suburban middle-class children in a relatively new school and with an excellent faculty: From the time of the children's early entrance to school at kindergarten or first grade, they showed a steady

---

*While our references to parents primarily concern mothers and/or fathers, care should be taken to evaluate the suggestions from cited studies also in terms of parent surrogates.

downward trend of self-concept as they met the pressures of the early school years—until about grade five, when their self-concept began to improve.

The self-concept is also closely associated with value orientations (739). In fact, a child's self-concept and value system are likely to have the same origins (341). Wylie notes that terms applied to self-esteem, such as self-respect and self-acceptance, also carry value connotations and are sometimes used interchangeably.

Not only do values and the self appear inextricably tied together, they are also mutual or concurrent in their influence on learning. As long ago as 1890, James (366) recognized that personal values largely determine the worth attached to one's self—the measurement used in self-judgment and in evaluating personal achievement. More than seventy-five years later Coopersmith (166) provided essentially the same joint appraisal of values and self. He concluded that experiences are interpreted and modified according to the values and aspirations of the individual. If the individual lives up to his ideals, he generally maintains a high degree of self-esteem.

The values that interact with this achievement of self-esteem, however, do not represent objective, established data but are the personal convictions acquired by an individual through his unique life experiences. Thus, a major task of early learning is helping a child consciously and subconsciously determine his self-worth and to identify values that become the foundation for later learning.

Acquiring Positive Self-Concepts

The earliest, distinct awakenings of the self originate from the quality of care and the trustworthiness of the caregiver (223, 664). From this basic sense of identity a child can move on to acquire a sense of being "all right"—of being what other people expect him to be.

As experience accumulates and attachment to significant adults develops, the infant's awareness of himself as a person with an individual existence becomes more firmly established. Purkey (550) observes that during a baby's first year he finds boundaries between his body and the outside world. He gradually learns to discriminate "me" from the "not me" and to attribute intention to the acts of others.

51

Even during the first few weeks of life a baby begins to sense his own worth in the awareness of others' appraisals. Approval, warmth, and consistency carry the message that he is wanted, loved, and valued as an individual. On the other hand, pity, concern, hostility, indifference, or disapproval give rise to feelings of negative worth, of being unwanted and of little value. The role of parents is crucial in establishing a sound sense of worth in a child (441, 177, 615, 468, 166).

Now enters a factor calling for far more wise and objective attention and effort than has heretofore been demonstrated by educators and early childhood specialists. A parent whose own sense of worth is well established will, of course, find it easier to transmit a positive self-concept to his child. The parents' acceptance of each other as worthwhile persons will also influence the acceptance they provide for their children (227). Because a child must perceive himself as fully accepted and because parental approval is primary in this perception, the climate parents create must be a positive one.

Tocco and Bridges (672) have also demonstrated that a child's self-concept bears some relation to the parents' self-esteem and related attitudes. For example, mothers from a deprived level of society representing black, white, and Indian ethnic groups have a definite influence on their children according to their level of self-esteem and their view of teachers and schools. Mothers with high self-esteem have a more positive view of their children, of teachers, and of schools. Their children also have high self-esteem and a positive attitude toward school. Studies by both Daugherty (176) and Mildred Smith (636) suggest that parental self-concept and attitude toward schools can, with care, be remarkably improved.

The findings of Bledsoe (91) indicate that boys generally have a more difficult time establishing self-esteem than do girls. Bledsoe found elementary school boys to be significantly lower than girls in self-concept scores, and these scores correlated with both IQ and achievement for the boys but not for the girls. It may be that girls desire more social approval than boys and respond to measuring instruments in a way that produces error variance rather than genuine measures of self-concept. Chapter ten provides further insights into sex differences that may relate to relative maturity levels of boys and girls and their possible influence on self-worth, particularly in western societies.

A study reported by Girona (274) provides further support for the idea that personality variables related to self-esteem may be influenced by emotional involvement with significant adults. For ten weekends college students carried out special activities on a one-to-one basis with six- to nine-year-old children from the Miami Children's Center (for parentless children). In that brief period, the children showed a significant progressive increase in a sense of self-worth and a willingness to assume responsibilities. The interest and attention of the college students also brought positive changes in the children's intelligence scores and lessened their dependence on nurturance.

Becoming Aware of Values

So children embrace values as they become aware of themselves by interacting with significant people in their lives. This is consistent with and supportive of the well-established fact that children learn best by example. Parents and other adults with a firmly based system of values can provide a strong foundation upon which children can build their own value structures.

Parents with a sound sense of values do not find it necessary to immortalize themselves in their children (12). And children who receive positive acceptance and respectful treatment from their elders are far more likely to accept the values of their parents and worthy elders (341). This is essentially a restatement of the fact that the same conditions that produce high self-esteem, acceptance, and regard for others as persons of worth also produce stable and realistic values (166).

The values of adults become apparent in the quality of their treatment of children—the degree of their consistency, warmth, and responsiveness and the kind of behavior they foster or permit. This, in turn, gives rise to rudimentary values in a child, to an awareness that certain rewarding experiences facilitate the *good-me* while anxiety-producing or forbidden behavior more often relates to the *bad-me*. There are also experiences one hardly dares admit to his conscious mind, experiences of intense anxiety associated with "such awe, horror, loathing or dread" that they are relegated to a personification of *not-me*. These experiences are not clearly connected on a cause-and-effect basis and remain well in the background as guides for organizing future behavior (664).

The *good-me* and the *bad-me* are common, however, and can be well understood. From these concepts of himself a child begins to distinguish between right and wrong, to identify the values approved by the significant people in his life. In discussing a child's growth toward maturity, Neubauer (510) says that a child absorbs the values of his family between the ages of four and six. It is at this time that he begins to ask, "Who am I?" And he finds his first social identity within the family group.

Interrelating Values, Self, and the Primary Group

Within the family group a child first learns that people need each other. This happens even in relatively bad homes (102). He receives care, but he also learns that he can contribute to the care of others as he becomes capable of doing so and can cooperate in family endeavors (368). Interaction within a primary group of closely knit persons without deliberate or regular interference from other individuals or institutions gives the self an opportunity to develop and establishes more firmly within a child the values governing the group.

Although family values are absorbed during the preschool years, real understanding of these values increases with age (208). Indeed, a full understanding of the moral issues involved may not be attained until adolescence or later. Edwards found that, in general, children probably do not have a clear grasp of certain moral concepts before the age of fifteen.

Edwards also confirms that the influence of the family, especially the mother, is of prime importance in establishing and maintaining values and the associated self. In his study, which included 700 children from seven to fifteen, he found that the influence of the mother on her child's acquiring moral knowledge increased as the child grew older. This primary group influence was not generally supplanted by the peer group, even into the teen years, as had been expected.

Parental understanding, consistency, and reliability as models in developing a child's sound and steady value system are crucial in clarifying family ideals. It is important that parents know where they are going ideologically. Although family values are dominant in a child's pattern of beliefs and values, these values may be so hazy in both articulation and practice that the child never knows for sure what they are; therefore he may absorb conflicting values from other significant people in his early years. And there will usually be difficulty reconciling values as understanding increases. This finding is supported by Van der Veen et al. (688) in a study of the congruence of value orientations held by parents and the self-images of family members.

Attachment to Peer Influence

Finding one's place in a peer group is a highly essential part of growing up in all cultures. This process of social identification outside the primary group, however, as Coopersmith (166) observes, will often threaten self-esteem when there is conflict between personal values and group values. In general, people tend to judge their personal worth by values espoused by the group. Thus the social norms of the group often become internalized as self-values.

In 1959 Charles E. Bowerman and John W. Kinch (101) worked with a sample of several hundred students from the fourth to the tenth grades in the Seattle public schools. They studied age trends and the tendency of students to turn to their parents on one hand or to their peers on the other for opinion, advice, or association in their activities. In general, they found a turning point at about grade seven. Before that, most of the students looked primarily to their parents as their companions and their models for behavior, but after that the peers seemed to have as much or more influence.

About ten years later Condrey, Siman, and Bronfenbrenner (164) made a similar study on parents and peers as influences on children. They found a larger percentage of peer independence at each age and grade level than had Bowerman and Kinch. Bronfenbrenner (118) and others have concluded that the shift from parent to peer influence is not only much more pronounced, but it has moved down to earlier grade levels. Bandura (42, 43, 44) and others at Stanford University have conducted experiments that suggest children's imitating attitudes and activities of peers is already well developed at the preschool level. Bronfenbrenner refers to this as "social contagion." He also found that peer-oriented youngsters described their parents as "less affectionate and less firm in discipline."

This attachment to peers seems to be influenced by weakness at home—a lack of attention and concern there—rather than by the strength of attraction by the peer group. In fact, children

55

who have such peer orientation tend to have a negative view of their friends and of themselves, to be pessimistic about the future, to be less likely to accept responsibility and leadership, and to have a greater tendency toward errant behavior. This is consistent with Forester's (239) findings that children who started later in school (and therefore came under the influence of their school peers later) tended to come out better not only in achievement and behavior but also in sociability and leadership.

Beginnings of Social Relationships

Unfortunately, children are often expected to function effectively outside the family in a peer group before they have reasonably comprehended their social identity within the primary family group. Sweet and Thornburg (667) found that age was a significant factor in preschoolers' understanding the structure of the family and their own place in it. The older the children were, the better they could identify and understand familial labels—good, bad or indifferent—and their own relation to them. White children did better than black children, but the reasons are not yet clear. Whether this was indicative of family structure or of communication ability or of other variables was not determined.

The influence of the family, and of mothers in particular, as we have mentioned, appears to be related to those self-perceptions and aspirations associated with academic achievement. Webster (698) drew such conclusions in a study of adolescents, and the family behaviors that led to these findings were identified as attention and support shown by mothers when the children were six to ten years old. The greater the amount and the higher the quality of this early attention, the more favorable were the youngsters' later self-perceptions.

Yet other developments spotlight the primary or family group as the provider of stability and acceptance that a child can take for granted. For example, neurological data indicates that small children often have difficulty in reprogramming for new situations. For example, a parent may shout "Stop!" when his child is about to throw a rock at a passing car. But the child throws it anyway. Even though a child may *know* what he is supposed to do, he may be unable to master his actions because of genuine neurological inability to alter his reponse patterns to verbal commands that are yet complicated to him (547).

56

Pontius suggests that this neurological inability to accommodate quickly, if at all, to unaccustomed circumstances normally exists up to four years of age, and for some children even longer. It could be much easier for the child in a preschool situation, for instance, if a familiar person were available to interpret the situation for him. Pontius finds here a basis for later behavior, that is, some juvenile delinquents who, under certain stressful conditions, cannot act according to what they know they should do.

As long ago as 1931 Alexander and Staub (11) were concerned with the early identification of behavior that might result in later delinquency. They referred to all children as potential delinquents if appropriate later socialization did not take place. Sometime between the ages of four and six, they pointed out, normal children begin to repress their nonsocial tendencies, and they transform them into socially acceptable behavior by the time they reach puberty.

Many years later, from 1950 through 1974, Glueck and Glueck (275, 276, 277) reported a study of five hundred delinquents who, in retrospect, were found to be slightly over eight years of age on the average when maladaptive behavior first became apparent. Some had shown signs of delinquency even earlier in the first and second grades. The Gluecks (275) speak of "the child's first attempts to adjust to the codes and authority imposed by adults outside the home" as "the acid test of his social adaptability." If a child faces this test with amorphous values or before he is developmentally able to handle the testing of the self, the consequences can be disastrous.

No doubt delinquency implies complex behavior, and there is no easy way to completely account for or predict it. It seems clear that children who fail to absorb and eventually internalize meaningful values and self-worth during their early childhood years are candidates for delinquency.

Values, Self, and Society

For most western children the time inevitably comes when they *must* learn to adapt to the world outside the familiar boundaries of home and its immediate neighborhood. This may be an experience either of eager exploration or of threatening anxiety, depending on the child's ability to meet the situation.

If he is ready for it, his positive sense of self-worth will expand as he accepts other people and embarks on a creative social adventure that will be surprisingly stable in the years to come. If he is not ready, he enters the larger social group with a personal identity handicap likely to remain with him throughout his future struggles to find and maintain his place in society. The strength and maturity of the self-concept in essence predicts the quality of socialization available to a child.

Northway (517) discovered that the sociometric status of children in nursery school and kindergarten corresponded significantly to their sociometric status several years later in grade five. Some growth occurred with increase in age, but the relative level of social status among peers was largely unchanged from nursery school through elementary school. Felker's studies (230), as noted early in the previous chapter, largely confirm Northway's findings.

Since values and a positive self-concept are originally acquired in relation to significant, positive adults, it is natural that in new and changing environments a child will find initial security by relating to available adults—authority figures who control his environment—for example, parents, foster parents, teachers, bus drivers, and recreational personnel. A child who has matured enough to learn that he is a competent, worthwhile person is not threatened by out-of-home adults. He does not essentially depend on their approval nor the approval of his peers. His experience is merely extended and his understanding enlarged by learning to know new people and places and methods. He is better able to put new authority figures in perspective, and he can meet the test of adaptability.

The child, then, who can have the security of a reasonably sound family life until his value system is stabilized—until he is able to reason consistently from cause to effect—will be "his own man." Such a child will more likely enjoy an independence—intellectual and emotional—that will insure a high and positive sociality.

But for some children, adults in authority pose a threat. Formaneck and Woog (241) examined the perceptions of authority figures (father, policeman, teacher) held by preschool and elementary school children. They found that the younger children—preschoolers—are considerably more threatened by authority than the elementary school children. Authority figures tend

58

also to be a greater threat to children of lower socioeconomic status. Teachers in particular are a greater threat to boys than to girls.

Punitive teachers exert a negative influence in general on first graders not yet sure of themselves and their values (408). First-grade children who have punitive teachers tend to be unsettled in conduct, less trustful of school, and less concerned with school-unique values.

Even as late as the sixth grade, children's self-esteem is affected by a teacher's appraisal of them, as revealed in teacher-assigned grades (245). This effect may extend into adolescence or later if a positive self-concept had not been already established and if grades are considered to be an evidence of the teacher's evaluation of one's worth rather than an index of individual achievement. However, the child who has a high sense of self-worth is more likely to feel free to function independently of teachers' assessments.

Eventually, of course, a child's self-concept with its component values will be tested within his peer group. Where learning in the early childhood home environment has provided adequate ego-strength, the peer-group experience will, as noted, usually be positive, moving toward the development of a strong, autonomous moral character. However, the likelihood is that children without the benefits of an optimum early home background, and therefore without strongly internalized values and standards, will be vulnerable to peer pressures (185).

Association with the peer group by its very nature gives children the opportunity to see themselves in relation to others of their age. If self-esteem is high, they can examine differences between themselves and others objectively and independently. They can afford to be different because they sense their own worth. But when an adequate sense of self-worth has not been developed, early association with a peer group seems to demand that individual characteristics be submerged in order to earn peer approval, which, in turn, is required to maintain self-esteem. And a desirable independence is sacrificed, possibly for life, and with it a high and positive sociality.

On the basis of conclusions by Ausubel and Ausubel (35), Crovetto, Fischer and Boudreaux (173), and Hawk (323) some people have assumed that disadvantaged children are likely to have a low self-esteem. But in a study of public school children in a New England city, Soares and Soares (639) found higher self-perception scores among the disadvantaged. A similar study with a larger sample over a wider age-range (640) returned the same results. Again, the emotional climate of the family may be more important than economic or social influences. If the climate is unloving, unresponsive, or inconsistent, low self-esteem can exist in either advantaged or disadvantaged families.

Trowbridge (675, 676, 677), like the Soares, examined children of about nine to fourteen years of age and found much the same evidence: children from low socioeconomic groups showed higher self-concepts than more advantaged children. He also observed that rural and small-town children scored higher than urban children (677).

Yet studies by Lamb et al. (418), and Crovetto, Fischer, and Boudreaux (173) found lower self-concepts for lower socioeconomic children, except for those who were able to raise their self-concept as they learned to perceive themselves similar to others. But there was one clear distinction: the Soares and Trowbridge studies examined children of about nine to fourteen years, while the Lamb and Crovetto studies centered on preschoolers.

Radke, Trager, and Davis (559) noted a sensitiveness in preschool and young school children toward membership in particular social groups. The awareness that they were not like everybody else also affected their self-concepts. What appeared to be a low self-concept among these children seemed to be associated with their inability to cope with an environment different from that to which they were accustomed.

Age or maturity, satisfying experiences, and desirable cultural variables all nurture the development of the positive self-concept a child needs as he prepares to function constructively in the larger society. Analyses of early childhood literature point squarely to the need for developing, while the child is young, the *values* and *self-worth* necessary for social competence. Yet strangely the traditional "system" for this job—early socialization in the family context—is being widely questioned. Children are being rushed ever earlier out of home into institutional settings, and one of the principal rationales is their socialization (490).

In a sense children are socializing each other—gaining their values and sense of worth randomly from ever younger and more insecure peer groups. Theirs in a sense is a negative sociality, ego-centered, seeking approval, rather than developing a positive sociality which is altruistic and independent in thought. Spitalny (645) speaks of children as mirrors for each other. This interaction could provide a positive experience in personal growth if a child's sense of self were securely rooted in a stable family group. But very young children whose value systems have not yet become grounded and stabilized have little basis for assessing the behavior of their peers, many of whom they choose as their examples. This is illustrated by a study of preschool children's leniency toward cheating, in which rule breakers became more lenient toward misdemeanors, while conforming children became more severe (584).

Considering the likelihood that young children are unable to reason consistently until they are at least seven to eleven or older (538, 537), it should not be surprising that risk is involved in turning them out of the singular security of the home before those ages.* For example, place a four- or five-year-old, his values yet unstabilized, in a preschool. He soon finds that the behavior of his peers differs from that which he has been taught at home. Having not yet developed a desirable independence, he readily adapts to his peers, and soon his parents are shocked with his aberrational behavior—his "bad" language, dietary preferences, or willingness to cheat or steal. But their well-reasoned remonstrances are not necessarily accepted by the child, for he is not yet cognitively mature or consistently reason-able. He is guided more by emotional influences than high cognitive perception. This also gives substance to Bronfenbrenner's (118) conclusion that little children are not carriers of sound social and moral values.

Some Practical Suggestions for Parents, Parent Surrogates, or Other Care Givers

(How to build a strong and stable value system, a sense of self-worth, and a positive sociality in children)

---

*From overwhelming evidence from systematic and reliable research, this book strongly advocates home-based education until age seven or eight or later. The reaction of many parents is: "Show us how to be educators in the home." Suggestions to parents have been included as a feature at the end of chapters three, four, five, and six in order to meet this need and to make this book more practical and understandable.

For Children from Birth to Eighteen Months

1. Consistent care by warm, responsive parents is fundamental to the child's emotional security.

2. Firm, loving discipline from his earliest weeks gives the child stability. Such discipline is accomplished by establishing a schedule that is reasonable for him as well as compatible with the family program. Regularity not only enhances physical health by maintaining sound body rhythms of digestion and sleep but also affects mental health. Knowing what to expect gives the child security and confidence.

3. Make your home environment as safe and free of breakables as practicable and allow your child freedom to explore within reasonable limits. When a child is too young to reason with, he must still be taught to obey. Harshness or slapping is never appropriate, but he notes your approval or disapproval by the tone of your voice. Before he is a year old, he can understand what you simply and plainly tell him. Gently divert or distract him the best you can. Moving him bodily from the forbidden item or to the requested place—even a snap on the little offending hand—may be necessary to enforce your request, but generally guidance should emphasize the positive rather than the negative.

4. Refrain from hovering over your child and directing everything he does. To develop self-confidence, he needs to learn to be happy by himself and to do things independently as he grows older. While he does not enjoy isolation, he does need and appreciate solitude to work out his own fantasies.

For Children from One to Three Years

1. The two- and three-year-old loves to be his mother's helper. Make him feel he is needed to help you in your daily household duties. Give him simple one-step requests and always thank him for his help.

2. The toddler's desire to do things for himself should be encouraged.

3. Conversation and incidental learning should be a part of the daily activities for your child, but if at all possible, each child should have a special time when the parent's attention is all his own, such as when the parent reads to him or inspects a plant, bug, or other natural wonder with him. This cements the

parent-child relationship and builds a strong sense of self-worth in the child.

4. Family values need to be clear-cut as demonstrated by your example.

5. Do not discuss the child's strengths or weaknesses with another adult in his presence. Relating his cleverness or amusing escapades gives him a false sense of importance, and negative reports embarrass and humiliate him. The Golden Rule applies here.

For Children Thirty Months to Five Years

1. Close conversations are now needed more and more to thresh out problems and soothe frustrations.

2. Rules should be few and well enforced. As your child begins to understand, give him simple reasons for your requirements. But remember he is not truly reason-able, so do not go into long explanations. He wants your approval and will strive to deserve it if you encourage him by your smiles and words. He will learn self-respect as he learns to respect you.

3. Respect your child's legitimate emotions of fear, frustration, or other unhappiness and help him handle them properly. First show understanding by accepting his honest feelings, but as soon as possible divert him to other activities or happy thoughts. However, don't blame or allow him to blame his problems on others or on things. Help him to face them, solve them—if they can be solved—or forget them if they cannot be changed.

4. Growing up is very important to a child. Yet it is not too easy for him to understand. Find a place behind a closet door or other inconspicuous place where you can measure and mark his growth periodically. Also help him see how plants and animals grow as opportunities become available, such as with plants you grow or pets you own. Snapshots can help record this growth for him to observe and compare.

5. At this age your child never seems to get enough stories, and many have to be repeated again and again. Choose true stories that teach honesty, dependability, industry, and concern for others. Remember, he has enough fantasies of his own. Don't clutter his world with unnecessary fantasies—e.g., television, fairy stories. Screen out violence. Nature stories are among the best for him now.

For Children from Four to Seven Years

1. Any physical skills or abilities add to a child's feeling of competence and independence. This development could be in the area of cooking or gardening as well as in swimming or bicycling. A child should be encouraged and helped to perform many duties around the house for himself and for others as his age and capacity allow.

2. If he has not already had the opportunity to help others outside the family, he should be given the chance to do kind things for others, especially for those who are old, sick, poor, or otherwise disadvantaged.

3. As your child works or plays, he will sing or hum many kinds of songs he has learned. His musical standard will reflect precisely what you have taught him.

For Children from Six to Eight or Nine Years

1. As fast as practicable, the child should be trained to make his own decisions on the basis of family values—working toward self-discipline under parental guidance. Help him to recognize the value of consulting experienced judgment in choosing his activities and friends.

2. He will become aware of auto-driving principles at this time. Your example will be very effective in establishing his future behavior behind the wheel.

3. Pride in and loyalty to his country are easily developed in a child of this age. Teach him to respect his country and its flag. Acquaint him with simple stories about the beginnings of his country. Teach him what liberty means in terms of rules and rights. Celebrate patriotic occasions by letting him display the flag, learn patriotic music, and see a parade.

4. This is an excellent age to teach the child how to prevent illness. He should know the value of good health habits.

4

The Learning Environment

Synopsis. *The early learning of a normal child depends largely on the people and things in his immediate environment, as well as the opportunities he has to respond to them. Among the factors contributing to an effective learning experience are the following: personal approval and acceptance of his behavior by adults; active, self-initiated—though leisurely—exploration and discovery of a healthy, predictable environment adapted to the child's culture; active manipulation of the materials in his immediate world; active interest in a learning task; and less constant exposure to external stimulation rather than more.*

These factors inhibit early learning: disapproval, fear, and uncertainty; confusion in the surroundings or in relation to authority figures such as parents, other adults in the home, older siblings, and teachers; passive absorption of continual sensory stimulation such as television; and structured learning, with its tedious repetition and boredom, particularly before the child is ready cognitively, neurophysiologically, and sensorily. Verbal stimulation does not appear to be as necessary for the development of early learning as supposed.

The quality—warmth, responsiveness, consistency—of the home and family, rather than a particular culture or socioeconomic level or materially enriched environment, is the most significant factor in cognitive and perceptual development. It is not so much the school environment that enables a child to learn in his early years as what he brings to the school. For children who are insecure, socioemotionally dependent, or disadvantaged in other ways, a structured situation will sometimes foster learning. Yet the internal security of a stable home and family, which permits learning without deliberate structure, generally fosters greater progress.

Cultural and social-class differences in experience and modes of think-ing lead to differences in learning processes and rates, making some chil-dren appear disadvantaged whether they are or not. Measuring learning progress by imposed standards, rather than the children's actual ability to achieve, may mean automatic disadvantage for ethnic and minority groups. All children deserve the privilege of developing and learning in an opti-mum environment, but not necessarily a contrived learning situation. Vir-tually all cultures and societies possess the crucial characteristics of a pos-itive atmosphere for early learning. Usually these characteristics are best provided by the parents and home.

Learning and Environment

The extent and meaning of learning in early childhood are largely dependent on the people and things in a child's immedi-ate environment. Much of the recent agitation about early learning is concerned with environmental deficits, especially among the poor and minority groups (160). As vital as are the needs of these disadvantaged children, they have received a dis-proportionately heavy emphasis both in research and in policy making. Thus, certain therapies for the deprived have often been generalized to apply to all children, much as if aspirin had been prescribed for all because a few have headaches.

Learning competence assessed primarily from the observed performance of individuals within any group is, as Cole and Bruner also state, "both situation-blind and culture-blind." Therefore, in order to derive objective judgments, we have sys-tematically studied all groups, regardless of advantage or dis-advantage or of socioeconomic level.

Effective learning, of course, can proceed under a variety of circumstances, depending on the specific categorization of expe-riences within a culture (682). So any attempt to describe an ideal learning environment must be made within an appropriate cultural framework. In the United States, deficient environments are often assumed to be a factor, even the principal factor, when groups of young children do not measure up to the learn-ing standards of middle-class children (345, 273, 39, 381, 658). But Cole and Bruner (160) suggest that this may be a highly suspect criterion. They also suggest that the organizational adequacy of any environment depends on whose point of view is used in categorizing familiar areas of experience.

On the other hand, studies of both animals (181, 705, 581) and human infants (349, 324) indicate that some environmental factors do have a significant influence on basic learning achievement. These factors must be identified and, insofar as possible, be incorporated into a child's environment if learning competence is expected. Nor is this necessarily inconsistent with the Cole and Bruner thesis.

An Atmosphere for Learning

A number of assumptions can be made regarding basic learning: It involves a child's experience with his immediate surroundings (137). It includes information about the people and things that affect him and to which he has opportunity to respond. This acquiring and ordering of information encompasses the affective, social, and cognitive aspects of a child's development (614). It is an integral part of personal and interpersonal growth in self-esteem, sense of identity, and orientation to other people.

How the interplay of personal approval and self-worth contributes to effective learning experiences is illustrated by the responses of five- and six-year-old disadvantaged children to rewards for learning. In Farber's study (226) some children were rewarded for correct responses with candy and others with a verbal "Good; that's right." Those who received personal recognition instead of candy not only showed superior learning but also learned with fewer trials.

Unfortunately, however, adults do not always appreciate the value of approval expressed in such a personal way. So they often ignore it. Teachers frequently imply disapproval of a valuable cultural heritage by expecting or even requiring children to perform according to standards that are inconsistent with this heritage, such as a Mexican in Chicago, a Chinese in San Francisco, an Indian in Seattle, a Puerto Rican in New York. These differences then become deprivations (160) when they might well have been learning assets.

When researchers compared elementary school teachers' attitudes toward child behavior with those of clinical psychologists (673), they found that psychologists are more accepting and tolerant than teachers. Generally the more experienced teachers, however, lean more toward the views of the psychologists in their assessments. A variety of child behaviors considered normal by psychologists are often termed pathological by inexperienced teachers, who generally tend to regard almost all differentiating behavior as abnormal.

It should not be surprising that learning becomes inhibited in an atmosphere of disapproval. A study of teachers' belief systems (320) showed that teachers who were most willing to accept differences in a positive manner and who could interpret situations from a broad point of view were clearly superior in producing desirable atmospheres for learning. However, teachers who frequently expressed platitudes and normative beliefs, who could see things only in *their* way, and who were otherwise inflexible were much less successful in creating favorable learning environments.

To become a competent individual, a child must learn to deal effectively with his surroundings (614). But this is difficult if not impossible when he must cope with fear, uncertainty, and confusion (592). A child from an unstable home or from unstable segments of society is particularly susceptible. For example, Klaus and Gray (402) identified a confused noise background as a hindrance to learning among some disadvantaged children. Such children have more difficulty concentrating and are more easily distracted in a learning situation (165). Conners and his colleagues noted that this distractibility appeared more likely among five- and six-year-olds than among those from nine to twelve.

Confusion may also exist concerning authority figures, whether those figures be parents, other adults in the household, older siblings, or teachers. When there is competition for a child's attention (2) or excessive child interaction with a number of adults (679), a child can become confused if authority is not clearly designated. Abramson observed negative aggression affects in children, and Tulkin and Kagan found a limitation of opportunities for children to explore and to manipulate the environment.

"Paradoxically," says Bronfenbrenner of the preschool child, "the more people there are around, the fewer the opportunities for meaningful contact" (118). This has important implications for any kind of institutional experience for very young children, but particularly for those kindergartens or care centers where continuity of care is not assured and where adult-child ratios range higher than about one to five (487).

When confusion of adult authority and values is minimized or eliminated, adults can more readily provide assurance that makes it possible for a child to explore and organize his own environment. Collard (162) found that lower- and middle-SES children explored about equally, although middle-class children seemed to have more opportunities for experiences around which to organize their discoveries. Collard also observed babies reared in an institution with one adult caregiver for every five babies. These babies gave evidence of insufficient adult attention and had less inclination to explore and fewer ways of playing with a toy than the home-reared babies.

In a study of children one to four years of age, Honig, Caldwell, and Tannenbaum (347) observed that even when these children were surrounded by other children they sought out adults when they needed information. However, adult-child dialogues decreased with advancing age, and the shift was prominent by three years of age. From this study, the researchers concluded that adults in a young child's environment are of "overwhelming importance" for cognitive input, especially during the first four years of life. This provides strong support for high teacher-child ratios in early-environment enrichment programs. It also suggests that any group care without understanding and responsive adults to answer children's questions will be a deficient environment for the child.

Acceptance, approval, and assurance born of a highly predictable environment all contribute to a positive atmosphere for learning. To these must be added as much freedom as is safely possible for a child to explore the environment with whatever interest and challenge it offers. Animal studies by Rosenzweig, Bennett, and Diamond (581) even suggest greater enrichment in brain development when there is larger freedom to explore, particularly in a natural setting.

The freedom to manipulate actively the materials in a child's immediate world helps him to develop a specific, concrete base for learning. Here appears to be a key influence in determining whether or not he will become deprived. Here also lies a significant poverty not often understood among low-SES families—the poverty of freedom to manipulate and to explore. In comparing economically advantaged and economically disadvantaged five-year-olds, Kunz and Moyer (414) found no relationship between the respective environments and children's physical skills, their attempts at problem solving, or the length of sentences spoken. But the disadvantaged children showed a lack of experience with manipulative materials along with a difference in vocabulary and motor skills.

Wolff, Levin, and Llongobardi (737) also observed a relationship between manipulation of materials and learning. They compared kindergartners (1) who produced interactions ("Make the toys do something") between pairs of toys with kindergartners who only observed such interactions. Thirty common children's toys were paired. Two paired-associate lists of fifteen pairs were formed by randomly dividing the toys into stimuli and responses. Two random pairings of the stimulus and response items were then generated. The children had to remember which toys went together, and later they had to re-pair them. Twenty-four hours later the children who had actively manipulated the toys again paired significantly more items than those who had only observed.

This freedom to explore, to move, and to manipulate helps children to learn not only about material things but also about themselves. Carpenter and Shipley (143) describe it as an intellectual and emotional as well as a physical experience. Freedom to explore encourages curiosity that leads to new encounters with both people and things, affording an ever widening challenge for learning.

The extent to which a child is interested in a learning task may have much to do with his performance as a learner. Marshall (444) found that when children who had a poor educational environment, as determined by their area of residence and the education of their parents, were assigned a high-interest, gamelike task they learned as quickly as children from better educational environments. Marshall also observed that children from high-rated environments performed better without the gamelike qualities that added the interest to the task. He concluded that these game-indulged children could complete a dull task simply to get it over with. For them task interest needed to be inherent in the task itself.

The quality of motivation appears to be a transcending factor here. Many "fun and games" conjured up to make learning appealing are apparently highly extrinsic—pseudo-components of the atmosphere of learning, gimmicks that stimulate at the outset but soon pall. These bored, over-stimulated youngsters, their intrinsic motivation cooled, eventually often become passive acquirers of information.

Furthermore, any passive learning should be carefully appraised before using it to strengthen a child's motivation or build his creativity toward positive, constructive ends. For example, by using videotapes that depicted and promoted social integration of black and white children, Colton (163) found that kindergarten children from both integrated and all-white schools gained a significant number of concepts from viewing the tapes. But the passive viewing resulted in almost no active changes in social preferences for those of an opposite color.

This broad principle has serious implications for learning in general, and particularly for young children yet in their formative years. And we shall shortly see that the formative years extend well beyond conventional estimates—in fact up to at least age 8, and for many to 9 or 10 or later. There is evidence that passive absorption of continual sensory stimulation actually reduces the arousal level and dulls responses (367). Brackbill (108) found this to be true whether the stimulant was audio, visual, tactile, or temperature. But perhaps more startling, she determined that this reduced arousal remains relatively unchanged over time, not for just a few hours but for years. This dulling effect, however, was not apparent with intermittent stimulation.

In a technological culture children are often surrounded by mechanical noise and clamor. Motion pictures and television intrude their visual stimulation of light and movement, as well as sound. The findings of both Colton and Brackbill suggest that the real need for an optimal learning environment of many children is for *less* constant exposure to external stimulation rather than more. In the early development of intelligence, the quality of overstimulation in the environment may be more detrimental than understimulation (693).

The alternative to contrived stimulation would appear to be active, self-initiated exploration and discovery of a reasonably predictable environment (143, 581). Gesell and Ilg (264) in fact suggest that nature herself offers children the greatest teaching, especially when allowed to do so without adult interference.

Thoughtful critics of early schooling (216, 571, 574, 575, 576)

71

suggest that a child's opportunity to explore his environment at leisure is being jeopardized by measures that were meant to counteract environmental deficits—to provide for the disadvantaged. Paradoxically, it appears that the very laborious methods employed to stimulate children into learning often lead instead to passivity and wearied boredom—as already inferred by Marshall (444), Colton (163), and Brackbill (108).

The very redundancy in structured learning, the tedious repetition year after year of the same or similar school materials appears to inhibit a child's intellectual freedom to move and explore. And according to Carpenter and Shipley (143) this repetition can actually retard learning. This is especially unfortunate for those children who have reasonably warm and consistent homes, and who, if they could wait until they are a year or two older and more nearly ready academically, could quickly learn the same skills without boredom and unnecessary repetition. *(This assumes that upon school entrance they are placed with their age-mates' social group instead of being locked in to lower grade levels, beginning with the first grade.)*

Indications are that much current preschool or kindergarten stimulation in early childhood is, to use a metaphor from Ames and Chase (18), a two-dimensional effort to force what should happen spontaneously in the natural three-dimensional world of the home.

Even verbal stimulation, so often considered fundamental to early learning, may not be as necessary as has been supposed for the development of basic learning ability. Cole and Bruner (160) define verbal skills as "cultural amplifiers," useful for adapting to a culture. But there is apparently no systematic support for the assumed role of a specific language in the development of cognition. In other words, a child's intellectual ability may in no way be impaired merely because he does not communicate in the commonly used language or according to a prescribed cultural pattern (182, 322, 691, 350, 577).

The Material Environment

Although a learning environment may be materially limited, highly intelligent children may come from low-SES families. It is not their being materially poor that limits learning but rather the apathy, the lack of initiative that sometimes accompanies poverty. As we have already implied, initiative and achievement

72

are not the prerogative or private domain of wealth nor of a particular culture. Families can provide a challenge for learning in quite diverse environments. Vernon (691) concluded from a study of Jamaican, Eskimo, and Indian boys that, in spite of linguistic handicaps, some of these children actually scored very well on tests of verbal intelligence and achievement. Vernon's results indicated that the most significant single influence in these various cultures was the quality of the home and family.

While active exploration and manipulation of materials is essential for optimal early learning, enriched environments alone do not necessarily improve cognition and perceptual development (133). When six experimental preschool classrooms were provided with special equipment to facilitate learning, the enrichment did significantly alter the classroom environment; yet there were no differences in verbal ability or auditory perception between these children and six groups of children from ordinary classrooms. In fact, the control children showed greater gains in visual perception and ability to perform intellectually. While enriched children came out ahead in visual sequential memory, they were surpassed by the control groups in all other areas.

Busse and his colleagues concluded that (1) a "properly" equipped preschool was not a panacea for the problems of disadvantaged children, and (2) there can be too much of a good thing. The greatest gains made by preschool children in general occurred without special equipment. This discovery suggests a simple, natural environment as a criterion for optimum learning during the early years.

The same principles that govern learning (in relation to structure and stimulation) in the environment are also apparent in the effects of urban and rural settings. Children seven to nine years old from a farm community in Norway were found by Hollos and Cowan (344) to do as well or better than children from villages and towns on tests of logical operations, and their performance became markedly better with age. The seven-year-olds in this study were still preschoolers because of later school entrance age laws in Norway, yet late school entrance did not hinder their performance.

Although these Norwegian farm children were considered socially isolated and were limited in role-taking abilities, their general intellectual development had not been hindered. Differences in ethics and values between the farm children and the other groups of child.en may have influenced their performance. Whatever the reason, language stimulation and schooling did not seem to play a major role in developing logical-operations ability in the children.

This clearly raises a question about providing sound learning experiences. Is a school or other institution with a more socially structured environment and material advantages a viable alternative for the ethics and values of a reasonably good home? Relatively little empirical research has been done on the incorporation of family value systems into children's thinking. Yet the evidence of Hollos and Cowan suggests that children tend to make greater progress in learning if they come from homes with clearly delineated value systems. This is a promising area for the objective student.

Studies dealing more specifically with the effects of schooling or lack of schooling on children's ability to learn usually produce similar results. They generally conclude that it is not so much the school environment that enables a child to learn in his early years as *what he brings to the school*. And if there is no school, he can still develop the ability to learn (623, 691, 282, 464, 280). The evidence from these studies suggests that emphasis on attempts to structure an environment for learning is of lesser value than the internal motivation that originates with the child's earliest consciousness of his family, his home, and the immediate cultural milieu.

Furthermore, in planning for the time when the child is ready and should go to school, the meaning of culture for productive school learning appears to be generally underestimated. Weininger (708) urges that educators develop learning environments for children based on various cultures. In the classroom, he feels, there must be a transitional period, a bridge, fashioned for the child in which he makes use of his home experiences—his culture—so that he does not enter school feeling alienated and valueless. Educators need to study and understand the environments from which children come. They should then adapt familiar learning environments so that children can build on whatever knowledge and backgrounds they have acquired from their homes and the cultural assets they offer. This adaptation has special meaning, as noted earlier, in avoiding deprivation among minority groups.

The Home Environment

As a place for early childhood learning, particularly for developing language and social skills, the home and neighborhood have been found to be as effective as carefully planned preschool experiences. Vance (684) reported such results from a comparison of two groups of preschool children. Children in a preschool program designed to improve the language and social skills of disadvantaged three- and four-year-olds gained no more at the end of a seven-month period than children in a matched group of preschoolers who had remained at home. In another program, low-income black mothers participated in activities at home with their own preschoolers (296). The results of this program indicated that more teaching and learning can occur in the home than had previously been assumed.

According to the findings of a longitudinal study on the effects of the environment on mental growth (349), early auditory, tactual, and visual stimulation is best provided by the home and family. This agrees with the conclusion of Collard (162) that home-reared infants receive the greatest variety of stimulation from their environment through social responses within the family.

Holmes and Holmes (345) also reached the conclusion that the home environment could have a significant influence on the learning of preschoolers. In a Head Start-related study, children who consistently gave the highest evidence of learning were generally those who had favorable home environments, including parents who were interested in their development.

The highest scores were made by middle-SES children who were not even participants in the school program. Head Start children with concerned parents scored next highest. Children who were sought out by Head Start personnel but whose parents were not especially interested made the lowest scores, regardless of the extent of participation in the program. Holmes and Holmes suggested that family environments constituted the differentiating factor among these children. Parental concern was a greater influence than the specific provisions of the material environment.

Similar results have been reported in work with elementary school children. Wolf (735) examined relationships between the home environment and the general intelligence test scores of ur-

75

ban, suburban, and rural children who averaged about eleven years old. As with the younger children, the home environment proved to be positively and significantly related to intelligence scores. The better the home, the more stability and interest it provides, the easier it is for children to learn, while disorganized and threatening homes tend to inhibit intellectual development.

When children from kindergarten through grade six, mostly black and from low-income families, received learning support at home, they were able to achieve at a higher level in school (636). This home support included creating a climate conducive to study. Parents read aloud to their children to stimulate interest in reading. And having books and newspapers around and available was found to be supportive. Smith suggested that educators should be helping parents assume these responsibilities for their children's education so that parents will not expect the school to take over their roles. She concluded that the school could not make up for what the home did not provide.

This is also consistent with Durkin's (199) findings in her study of over five-thousand school children. The best readers came from homes in which reading was encouraged and ample reading material was available.

While children seem to learn best when they can relate to a warm, responsive adult, Blank and Solomon (88) found that mere personal involvement on the part of a nursery school teacher was not sufficient to produce significant cognitive change in the disadvantaged child. Even when a teacher worked with a child on a one-to-one basis, learning from a cognitive point of view was not successful, particularly for the low-SES child, without a structured teaching situation along with the teacher's involvement.

This at first seems to contradict studies showing the advantages of relatively unstructured environments, but in reality it is consistent. The security of a healthy early attachment to a reasonably consistent adult contributes to later emotional independence (746). For children who are insecure and socioemotionally dependent (268), the structured situation described by Blank and Solomon provides an external security that fosters learning. But greater progress is fostered by that internal security of home and family that permits learning without deliberate structure (345).

Blank and Solomon also note that in middle-class homes, op-

76

portunities for adult-child verbal interchange come about normally and are not generally limited to short, set times. In lower-income homes, these opportunities are less common, even rare in some homes, and the relatively brief time spent with a teacher is not a satisfactory alternative. This lack of parental responsiveness in the home is identified as a primary cause of children's difficulties in verbal skills and attention span, and maximum use of the time a child has with his teacher is deemed essential.

Indeed, disadvantaged children must not be sold short. They do have the potential to learn (350, 577), and fostering this potential can be done by concentrating either (1) on a structured teaching environment for a certain time each day (88), or (2) on a supportive home environment (345), or a combination of these efforts. For early childhood learning the structured teaching environment has limitations (133, 143). Yet it must often be used, for many homes are so lacking in supportive qualities that they depress the children's morale and hinder learning achievements (611).

Litman (434) discovered limited resources in both low- and middle-SES families. And she found that educationally well-developed children could come from either crowded or spacious homes. It was the *quality* of the home that mattered most. Home environments that provide such opportunities as conversation among family members and reading by adults to children (380) or simple materials and toys to manipulate (427, 296) appear to provide more effective learning opportunities than do the schools.

Influences of Culture and Society

Secord (611) concluded that the types of experience available to a child are determined by the culture in which he lives, and he develops his attitudes and ambitions accordingly. Horowitz and Resenfeld (352) found that persistent behavioral deficiencies were often reversible in children whose experiences had been primarily limited by social conditions.

Culturally determined differences in experience and modes of thinking lead to differences in learning processes that make some children appear at a disadvantage whether they are or not. As noted earlier, teachers sometimes appraise and condemn as a "handicap" a cultural peculiarity that they should have turned into a distinct asset. Stevenson, Williams, and Coleman (658) raise questions about such comparisons based on average levels of performance among populations. They suggest that a more revealing approach would be comparing patterns of correlations among different learning tasks.

The ability to profit from previous experience and to recall previous learning was found by Rohwer (577) to be about equal for two remarkably different groups—white children from a high socioeconomic level and black children from a low socioeconomic level. Variance in learning success for both groups was attributed to the manner in which learning materials were presented. When materials are relevant and meaningful and when they are presented in a way that can be understood (658), learning can occur at all social levels (544).

A positive attitude toward school has also been demonstrated to be an asset for learning. Neale and Proshek (507) found this was not necessarily a problem limited primarily to culturally deprived children, as some have assumed. Fourth to sixth graders from a culturally disadvantaged area placed a high value on school although they considered it something difficult to attain. Socioeconomic standing is of less consequence than is usually assumed in determining attitudes toward school, at least in the United States (79).

The cumulative results of these studies indicate that attitudes, maturity, purpose, and appropriate process are the key contributors to learning success. When due consideration is given to these factors, children from supposedly deprived conditions seem to show an ability to learn that is in no way inferior to that of normal American children (182, 322, 692, 350, 697).

Cultural Imposition

The foregoing studies relating to the learning environment bring into perspective two distinct aspects of the problem: first, the basic conditions that permit or encourage learning and, second, the social and ethnic group differences that assist in organizing experience and mind-hand relationships.

Cole and Bruner (160) suggest that research involving cultural differences is of little practical benefit as long as one cultural system is assumed superior over another. When children of one social group seem to learn less readily than others, the source of the learning difficulty needs to be identified. It may be in the

78

home environment (345, 402, 679). It may also arise from unrealistic expectations of teachers, as suggested earlier, who assess performance from a cultural point of view foreign to that of the child (320, 673).

It has been observed that social class differences in children's intellectual performance appear sometime around the age of three (278, 381, 570). Golden and colleagues suggest abstract knowledge with verbal interaction as factors significantly differentiating social classes during the third year of life. Robinson and Robinson identified the development of verbal abilities between the ages of two and four. These studies point to the possible conclusion that it is not the child's ability to learn that is impaired—that is, to assimilate knowledge—so much as his ability to organize and communicate patterns of thought and behavior.

Radin (555) concludes that skills and attitudes incompatible with middle-class values demanded intervention in early childhood so that disadvantaged children can measure up to generally acceptable academic achievement. But Rist (569) reports that public education practices are not accomplishing this objective. Instead, a child's kindergarten performance usually determines his future position in the class. Measuring learning progress in terms of imposed middle-class standards rather than the children's actual ability to achieve may mean an automatic disadvantage from an early age for ethnic and minority groups who are generally found among the low classes.

Where the immediate school environment is lacking in those essentials that create an atmosphere conducive to learning, every effort should, of course, be made to correct the deficits.* Often learnings and skills may be transferred from a minority group culture to a dominant culture with profit to both (160). Baratz and Baratz (45) suggest that culture-related forms of behavior should be optimally recognized and utilized in educating minority and ethnic groups. They suggest that research efforts should seek to discover the *different* or distinctive cultural assets rather than the negative forms of minority group behavior. When differences are not recognized, individuals of minority cultures may be pressured to conform to the dominant culture. And pressures

*See chapter thirteen for one suggested list of qualities and characteristics of optimal preschool or care centers (487).

toward conformity will leave some individuals deprived in areas of creativity and self-expression (565).

All children deserve the privilege of developing and learning in an environment that promotes optimal physical, mental, and emotional health. But this need not demand nor usually suggest a contrived learning situation. *Acceptance, approval, assurance,* and *freedom to explore an environment that presents an appropriate challenge*— these appear to be the crucial characteristics of a positive atmosphere for learning. These have been found in all cultures—rich or poor, complex or primitive, educated or largely illiterate. And usually they are best provided by parents and home.

Some Practical Suggestions for Parents or Parent Surrogates or Other Care Givers

(How to increase their effectiveness as home-based educators or to do an optimum job in the preschool, kindergarten, or other out-of-family care)

For Children from Birth to Eighteen Months

1. Most teaching should take place incidentally while you go about your household duties and share them with your child in a warm, responsive manner.

2. Be aware of the learning possibilities of your child; then make use of daily activities to help him develop the senses by which he learns. Let him listen to music and help him identify and mimic the sounds of animals and birds. Provide opportunities for him to see flowers, fish, birds, and animals. Show him how you smell. Let him feel the sand, wet and dry. Let him fondle a green leaf, crumple a dry one. Let him play in the water. Smooth, floating blocks of wood are as exciting as expensive toys.

3. Your baby should have a special activity time with you for at least twenty or thirty minutes once or twice daily.

4. Use the playpen for short intervals two or three times a day, but take some time when you can watch him closely to give your child the freedom of the house or the outdoors.

5. Sing to your child, or play recordings of lullabies, or play a music box. Cuddling time, story time, bath time, or bed time are good times for quiet music. Livelier songs and other musical activities can be used when you are caring for him in other ways.

80

6. When your baby is three months old, you can start taking him on a daily tour around his room or the house. Introduce him to objects of various sizes, shapes, colors, and textures.

7. Teach him which items he can safely touch and which ones he may not play with.

8. Weather permitting, the baby tour can move outdoors where he can be introduced to the wonders of nature and other outdoor objects.

9. By six months he can be taught to identify various parts of his body. Later he can learn the functions of his body and how to care for himself.

10. Quietness, calmness, and freedom from artificial excitement build strength in the immature child. Be sure that your child has regular naps and plenty of rest.

11. It is important that the baby explore his immediate environment first, that is, his own yard, or if he has none, the park nearby. Special trips, such as going to the zoo, at this stage are overstimulating to the small child and should not be indulged in.

For Children from One to Three Years

1. In your child's world there is no difference between play and work; therefore allow him to "work" with you whenever he is willing.

2. If your child works with you, you may have to take more time and patience than if you do it yourself, but it is the best preschool education he can have.

3. Toddlers especially enjoy helping Daddy with the outside chores. They also enjoy playing outdoor games, such as hide-and-seek, with him.

4. Give him finger foods to eat. Teach him to chew thoroughly. As he becomes able, show him how to use his spoon for appropriate foods.

5. Encourage independence. He should help dress, undress, and bathe himself. This is a good time for him to begin learning the names and functions of his body.

6. He should learn how to care for his clothes and keep his dresser drawers neat.

7. Shortly after age two, he can wash his own hands and brush his teeth. He can put away his toys.

8. The child who lives in the country or on a farm learns eas-

ily about nature. For other children, parents can create substitute experiences such as window-box gardens, neighborhood parks, pet stores, books, and TV programs about nature.

9. Learning possibilities through music are almost limitless for the young child. There are numerous ways he can be introduced to rhythm and melody such as using bells, clapping hands, and moving arms.

10. Continue his regular naps, with twelve to fourteen hours of sleep daily.

For Children from Thirty Months to Five Years

1. If you find learning to be exciting and worthwhile, your child is likely to feel the same way.

2. When your child is about four years old, encourage him to work with you and assume responsibility for many age-appropriate jobs around the house. Show him how work can be fun. Always work *with* him.

3. The kitchen is a particularly good place to learn. He can even help you prepare the meals and set the table. Train him to be careful, neat, thorough—and to clean up afterward. Allow for some spillage and breakage and take precautions against injury.

4. As early as possible, involve your child in growing things in an outdoor garden or in pots or a window box. Use different kinds of seeds, for example, radishes, beans, and onion sets. Gardening teaches your child many concepts of science and economics, besides being exciting and rewarding. It also helps him develop patience.

5. When your child is mature enough to help in the care of pets, he is old enough to have one or more of his own. It helps him develop responsibility and dependability.

6. Learn a variety of appropriate songs to teach him.

7. If you have a musical instrument or record player, help him make instruments of his own to go with it, for example, blocks to clap together or a drum to beat or beans in a container to shake.

8. He will also enjoy motion songs and marching to music, but avoid music that is loud or has a heavy, complex beat.

9. Your child is old enough now to enjoy family outings. They are all pleasant learning experiences. You can strengthen the impact of these experiences by talking about them after you arrive home.

10. Prepare your child for such special events as having company, going to the doctor, or embarking on a trip. Let him know what is likely to happen and what you expect him to do. Anticipation is often a greater treat than the actual happening.

11. He still needs his regular nap time and plenty of rest to build up his reserves for energy and growth.

For Children from Four to Seven Years

1. Work and play are important to your child at this stage. Take time to play daily with your child. Involve him in everything you normally do in the way of work at home, including gardening, sewing, and woodwork.

2. He is old enough to learn how to be a good host—welcoming, introducing, and making visitors feel comfortable.

3. You can play many games as you go about your daily activities that will teach your child to listen.

4. Give your child a chance to hear and appreciate rhyme and rhythm. You can also teach manners and other bits of wisdom with rhymes, which you invent or find in children's books.

5. By this time your child has a reasonable understanding of the interdependence of the family. Now he needs to learn about various people in the community and to appreciate the services they provide. Short trips, conversations with workers, and discussions at home afterwards are ways of teaching about the community.

6. Art can become a means of self-expression and of experimenting and creating for your child. All you really need to provide is a positive atmosphere, some inexpensive materials such as sand or flour or paper, a place to use or display his creations, and a few ideas gleaned from children's books or magazines. Making useful things, such as gifts or holiday decorations or items for the home, brings a child special satisfaction.

7. Keep your child constructively busy at work or play but do not be a hovering parent. He needs a lot of time alone; but be aware of his needs and share in their fulfillment without worrying about them.

8. Regular nap time is still desirable, at least through his seventh year.

For Children from Six to Eight or Nine Years

1. Almost all the activities suggested for younger children can

be expanded for the child in the beginning of this age group. As noted before, he learns best by discovery and by doing.

2. Work, handled wisely, is still the best experience a young child can have. He can share in almost everything that needs to be done around the home. You should not do jobs that your child can do for himself or for the family as long as he is not actually overworked. Most jobs are far more enjoyable to a child if he does them with you rather than alone.

3. Boys and girls of this age can learn how to use tools effectively in the home so that they can make simple repairs when necessary.

4. As a child enlarges his activities, he will need to learn the rules for whatever tool or machine he uses.

5. These are the years when children really begin to enjoy camping. Planning for the camp, sharing in camp chores, and engaging in activities in nature are all exciting learning experiences.

6. This is an excellent time for teaching conservation of wildlife, streams, and forests.

7. Since children like to cook, watch for simple recipes your child can make, either alone or with a minimum of supervision. The family should let him know they enjoy his cooking.

8. Give a child practice waiting on the family at meal time. With a little briefing, he can make an excellent assistant at the table when you have company for dinner.

9. His horizons have gradually broadened so that now he is interested in people farther away from home and even in other parts of the world. You might invite a family from another country to your home to learn something of their culture. Your guests may even return the invitation.

10. A child can be a great help to his mother in caring for a sick person in the family. Teach him how to apply simple home treatments to prevent or to cure common illnesses. One of the best sources of information for basic health care is the Red Cross book on home nursing.

11. This is an excellent age to teach the child how to prevent illness. He should know the value of good health habits.

12. Insure that he gets plenty of rest—at least ten to twelve hours daily if possible.

5
Readiness for School

Synopsis. School entrance ages, whether by legal or social mandate, generally tend to be arbitrary. In some of the United States, children must enter school as early as age five. In some states they may enter as early as three or as late as nine or older. European societies show the logical result of freeing parents at the expense of children. Holland, for example, requires school entry at age four. In France, for 99 percent of the children, the general entry age ranges between two and three (487).

Although public policy and conventional practices often ignore research, it has found optimum readiness levels for school entrance. In addition to attachment, already considered, readiness for formal school learning depends upon age-linked experience and knowledge contributing to certain cognitive-structural changes that facilitate conceptual learning. Attempts to speed up conceptual learning through specific training have been found ineffective; yet a wide range of ordinary life experiences appears fundamental for optimal cognitive readiness. Corresponding physical and motor readiness must also exist. Children seldom have fully developed perceptual processing ability before age nine, but unfortunately neurophysiological readiness is a variable frequently overlooked in evaluating school readiness.

Readiness for school generally may be acquired at any socioeconomic level. Although social class may influence how a child functions and how his experience-related intellectual abilities develop, some SES differences tend to narrow as age increases and may disappear after age seven or eight.

Acceleration of bright children alone may sometimes be sound practice. However, research shows that delayed schooling with acceleration at a later age is more effective and potentially less damaging—mentally, socially, and emotionally—than early school entrance. In fact, many studies

85

show that, except for certain severely deprived or handicapped children, children who are older at school entrance generally do better in all aspects of learning and adjustment than younger children.

Since children develop at different rates, including sex-related differences, researchers cannot pinpoint a specific age at which they are ready to begin formal schooling. Yet overwhelming evidence on readiness for normal children—including the gifted—points to later rather than earlier school entrance: seldom, if ever, before eight and often ten or older. Delaying school entrance until a child is developmentally ready would require more flexibility in school age regulations in most states, leading to policy reform at local, state, and national levels. This does not suggest that an eight- or nine-year-old should enroll in the first grade, but rather with his social peers. Experience has proven that he usually will catch up with, and often pass, those who have entered earlier.

Arbitrary School Entrance Age Laws

In recent·years many researchers have examined the overall development appropriate for children's academic education. The time to begin formal structured learning should be a milestone in the child's intellectual and social development. Many diagnostic tests have resulted from the search for optimum readiness levels for school entrance (15, 17, 4, 394). Although complex variables are sometimes confusing (452, 115), a systematic review of the literature leads to deep questions and convictions about public policy and conventional practice (198).

School entrance age laws, for example, appear to be generally arbitrary (240). Yet there has been a wide variation in school entrance policies in the U.S. Data compiled in 1966 showed that in some states children could enter elementary school as early as age four, or they could be exempted as late as age nine (654).

Among the United States there are no systematic, research-oriented guidelines to provide reasonably uniform entrance age laws. So parents in Arizona or Pennsylvania are normally free to keep their children at home until eight years or later, whereas such practices in California (139) or Michigan (469, 470) may bring social and legal harassment, arrest, or even jail (491).

86

The United States, of course, is not alone in perpetuating earlier and earlier school entrance. The British primary schools have many children in school at four. In central Europe formal schooling is mandated at that age. Holland, for example, has recently laid down age four as the year to institutionalize their children. France's Ecole Maternalle program enrolls 99 percent of the nation's children between the ages of 2½ and 6, with many adult-child ratios ranging over 1:30 and 1:40 and some as high as 1:60 and 1:64 (487).

Recent U.S. studies show little change in public policy due to careful, research-based attention to school entry legislation (198). Compulsory entrance ages ranged from about five years eight months to eight years, depending in many cases on the child's birth date. In fact, there have been few major changes in entrance age laws during the last decade or two—except to push academic readiness instruction *below* the first grade or to *lower* the mandatory entrance ages. Because of such changes, the appropriate age for beginning structured learning has become even more obscured or confused.

Some wonder whether a child must have developed readiness for school before being subjected to academic instruction (115), or whether formal school training is a prerequisite for broader readiness (580). Rosenthal's findings suggested both circumstances were operating in a group of kindergarten children. In assessing their reading readiness, she found the readiness achievement of younger children related to kindergarten training. For older children, however, who had achieved readiness without kindergarten, maturation was deemed important.

Determining Readiness

The Nature of Readiness
Before school readiness can be determined with any reasonable assurance, it must be clearly defined. Jensen (369) refers to readiness as the achievement of certain subskills along with the developmental maturity to integrate these subskills into a desired skill. If the desired skills are stated in terms of eventual competence in reading and mathematics, for example, what subskills are necessary and when and how are they achieved? For example, the broader and deeper the child's experience, the greater the meaning and skill he brings to reading. The better

he can consistently reason from cause to effect, the greater his skills in arithmetic.

The interaction of all aspects of readiness in successful school achievement was evident in Brenner and Stott's fifteen-year study on children's readiness for school (115). They analyzed sixty-nine variables, including age of children at school entrance and at the time of testing. From the intercorrelations of these variables, they identified factors influencing school readiness. Some were biological and followed a biological timetable. Others were products of experience. But *all* aspects of readiness were the result, in some way, of the interaction between hereditary potential and environmental forces, a balance between maturation and environmental experiences.

Brenner and Stott generalized that the older a child is, the better he will function and structure his environment and the more he will have in experience and understanding of the world. And the greater his body of knowledge *before* he goes to school, the more successful he will be at the beginning and in subsequent school years.

McCarthy (452) examined preentrance variables necessary for school success and concluded that intelligence was only one of many factors. In addition to IQ, he identified such characteristics as social maturity, emotional stability, self-reliance, and physical health. He also found a definite relationship between a secure home environment and school success. As noted in chapter two, parental attachment is a readiness factor deserving far more attention than it typically receives. The total balance or imbalance of development must be considered in determining readiness for school (259).

And in the words of Willard Olson, ". . . children of the same age and the same grade location are regularly found to differ by as much as four or five years in their maturation and their readiness to perform tasks" (523).

Kohlberg (405) presents a similar view. His cognitive-developmental analysis defines readiness as a function of age, IQ, and the general background of experience and stimulation. He notes further that the speeding up of cognitive-structural change is extremely difficult—although a structural change achieved may form a basis for future cognitive development. On the other hand, early learning of specific information (language, captions, etc.) is easy to achieve but not likely to have long-range effects on cognitive development.

Thus, while specific early stimulation and training designed to speed learning seem valuable, Kohlberg finds no justification for teaching things earlier that will come later with less effort. For example, children can be taught with relative ease to recognize letters or names of animals at an early age, but this does not necessarily advance cognitive development. Kohlberg's viewpoint suggests that, although naming and discriminating may cause a temporary rise on an IQ test for preschool children, this information can be acquired during grade school with much greater ease, if it has not already been picked up, and the IQ gain disappears.

The analyses of Kohlberg and of Brenner and Stott imply that readiness for formal schooling must include general age-linked experience and knowledge contributing to certain cognitive-structural changes for conceptual learning. The biological timetable of normal development makes ineffective and unnecessary any attempts to speed up this learning with specific training. On the other hand, a wide range of ordinary life experiences is valuable, and in fact appears fundamental for optimum school readiness.

There has been much conjecture and study of the idea of "conservation," as introduced by Jean Piaget (538), with its implications for abstract reasoning, cause-and-effect relationships, understanding of motivation, and consistency in reasoning and judgment.* The *age-linked* ability to interpret experience appears to enable a child to acquire the ability to conserve (e.g., to recognize that a substance does not change simply because the shape or appearance of an object changes) (621). Kohlberg (405) concludes that this conservation concept is the result, not of maturation only, but also of interactional experience between the individual and the environment.

This acquisition of conservation is not dependent upon linguistic skill, according to Kohlberg. Deaf children with no ver-

*Derived from the well-known principle in physics, the conservation of mass, which suggests that except when subjected to external forces, the mass is constant irrespective of changes in form. Thus Piaget tested the ability of children to reason from cause to effect—to "conserve"—by, for example, taking a given amount of liquid, placing it in different formed glasses (tall and thin, short and wide, etc.) to test concepts of mass.

bal skills of any kind have achieved it (253). A lack of verbal skill seems to deter learning primarily when a child is expected to use a vocabulary foreign to his particular experience (416). If the concept of conservation is also a readiness factor, there probably is little reason to stress formal vocabulary learning early if it can be acquired spontaneously with age and experience.

These findings suggest that experience, supplemented by developmental maturity, produces the cognitive ability to conserve. This ability, along with some verbal skill in the specific language used for learning, normally produces the readiness needed for success in formal school tasks and ensures economy of learning effort.

To support mental readiness for academic achievement, corresponding physical and motor readiness must also exist (150). Simon (628) evaluated the physical maturity of first-grade children and found from a battery of anthropometric indexes that failing students tended to be less mature than successful students. In this study, body maturity proved a sensitive indicator of school readiness.

Neurophysiological readiness (or reasonable maturity of the central nervous system, including the ability to coordinate perceptual processes) is a variable frequently overlooked in evaluating school readiness. If a child appears to have no sensory deficiencies, educators assume he can accomplish the usual school tasks. Morency and Wepman (499) found, however, that the child who enters school perceptually unready (auditorily, visually, intersensorily, etc.) will have difficulty in school achievement. He is not likely to catch up even after his perceptual processing ability is fully developed. They suggest that the full development of perceptual processing ability may be expected by the age of nine. Before that time children learn by whatever perceptual pathways are open, but there is genuine risk that some of them will be closed or still immature. To that extent the child is disadvantaged or learning handicapped.

In studying children's learning through perceptual pathways, McGeoch and Irion (455) observed that relatively young children learned more effectively by auditory presentation than by visual. When Budoff and Quinlan (131) tested these findings with seven- and eight-year-old children, they found that even at this age aural learning was more rapid and efficient than visual learning. This is consistent with Rosner's findings (583) that hearing appears to be more important than vision in learning to read.*

When this perceptual readiness factor is disregarded, normal children may be subjected to unnecessary learning and later to remedial programs which should have been totally unnecessary and are often confusing to children and parents alike. Ilg and Ames (363) say that many so-called reading disability cases result from the attempt to force unready organisms to perform beyond the level for which they were prepared. And Frostig, Lefever, and Whittlesey (251) found that after age ten, with the maturing of visual perception, reading disabilities tended to completely disappear.

From the various aspects of readiness identified by these authors, the nature of school readiness may be summarized as including (1) chronological age that permits the accumulation of some experience, (2) cognitive ability to attach meaning to experience, (3) a body of knowledge acquired through experience (including basic use of language), (4) physical development and anthropometric maturity, (5) perceptual discrimination, and (6) a readiness to read that emerges with the other readiness factors.

Early childhood education, then, must take into account the development of the child's brain, vision, hearing, perception, emotions, sociability, family and school relationships, and physical growth. In terms of these factors the normal child—of gifted or average ability—arrives at a maturity level which implies school readiness at about ages eight to ten, sometimes as late as eleven or twelve. This coming together of developmental maturities has been called the *integrated maturity level* or IML.**

The IML may be as important for school readiness as IQ is for school guidance and counseling; it offers a clear and impressive planning base for parents and teachers. On the basis of the many research findings outlined in this book, we believe that the IML is seldom, if ever, fully achieved before ages eight to ten. Note that the IML is not, like the IQ, determined by mathematical calculation. It simply states that, unless performance or measurements indicate otherwise, a normal child may be considered ready for formal learning experiences within or

*For fuller discussions of neurophysiology and perceptual readiness, please turn to chapters six, eight, and nine.
**While the maturity level idea is hardly new, the concept of integration in

91

outside the home when he has reached these ages. If there is a question about maturity within these years, the later age should be preferred. But, as suggested earlier, when they are then enrolled, it should be with their social-emotional peers.

Effect of Social Class on Readiness

Since school readiness is partly a function of life experience, one might think that many children from low socioeconomic levels fail to achieve in school because they lack necessary experience. Support for this is found in studies examining the effects of preschool experience for disadvantaged children. For example, Bottrill (99) found no difference in the school readiness of children from different socioeconomic levels when the disadvantaged had been provided day-nursery experience. Others, such as Hodges and Spicker (337) have also found that disadvantaged children with preschool experience have increased ability to achieve in the first years of elementary school.

Yet a closer look at other evidence indicates that disadvantaged children may not lack experience *per se* as much as they lack experience with the cultural variables related to formal schooling (620, 55). The Beasleys measured the perceptual language performance of lower-SES black children and middle-SES white children. The middle-class children were more ready for this task in the first grade and performed significantly better than children from the lower socioeconomic level. But by the third grade this difference in readiness was not apparent. All third graders did better than first graders, but there were no dif-

---

the sense described above was stated for the first time by Raymond and Dorothy Moore in the early childhood book, *Better Late Than Early* (492). We include that definition and technical explanation here:

The integrated maturity level is the point at which the developmental variables (affective, psychomotor, perceptual and cognitive) within the child reach an optimum peak of readiness in maturation and cooperative functioning for out-of-home group learning (typical school) experiences.

The IML implies an integration, or cooperative functioning, of the various aspects of human development in a level or degree of coordination that becomes more productive as maturation progresses.

Aspects of human development, or the variables within the person, include the affective, psychomotor, perceptual and cognitive behaviors. As maturation progresses, the degree of coordination among these variables is indicated by a higher level of motivation and an increased ability to learn without undue stress and strain. When all the variables have matured to the point that optimum integration of function is possible, an appropriate state of readiness has been reached for structured school learning experiences.

ferences between social classes when the results were averaged across grade levels. This study suggests that there is a larger perceptual handicap for younger children, regardless of social class.

There are apparently social-class influences that determine how a child functions as well as how his experience-related intellectual abilities develop. Ames and August (17) used the Lowenfeld Mosaic test, which is somewhat free of cultural influences, to compare black and white children from five to ten years of age. With this instrument the responses of black children at five and six years were less mature than those of white children at the same ages. But after age seven the discrepancy decreased so that the black children compared well with white children of the same socioeconomic level and favorably with other white children.

The findings of Wei, Lavatelli, and Jones (699) also suggest that some differences between SES groups narrow as age increases. They found that culturally deprived children made slow progress on classification problems at the kindergarten level, although they were more successful with real objects than with abstract reasoning. But the range of difference between these children and those of middle SES became smaller at the second-grade level, narrowing with increased age.

Gross (299) concluded from a study of middle-class Jewish children that cultural factors have a greater influence on children's school readiness than poverty and related disadvantages. The implication is that the lack of readiness in children from particular SES or ethnic groups relates to a particular way of functioning that becomes less of a handicap after the age of seven or eight. Differences in performance among social classes may disappear by the third grade (approximately age eight), as in the Beasleys' (55) study, or after age seven, as in the study by Ames and August (17), so that the forced elimination of differences a few years earlier may be pointless.

Highly structured and directive preschool programs (such as DISTAR) seem to be more effective in producing cognitive gains in the most disadvantaged low-SES children, while nondirective, less structured preschool programs (such as Home Start) appear to be more effective with the least disadvantaged low-SES children (86). It appears that low-SES children lack the resources to learn by themselves in unstructured programs (see also p. 221). This is consistent with (1) Kagan's (382) findings, indicating that many low-SES homes are not responsive to their children's needs, and (2) Durkin's (199) study, which clearly shows that homes providing for children's intellectual growth are those that reap a desirable harvest.

Kagan (382) lists seven of these notable areas of difference and suggests their rationale:

1. Comprehension and expression of language: Lower-class mothers usually do not converse with their children as often or with as much feeling as middle-class mothers.

2. The child's mental set to activate cognitive structures for solving problems or for understanding discrepant events: A middle-class mother provides a larger variety of conversation, facial expressions, and play, with more surprises.

3. Attachment to an adult, normally the biological mother: The middle-class mother and child more often enjoy a closer attachment, as the mother molds the child with a greater and closer confidence and the child responds.

4. Inhibition and impulsiveness: The lower-class mother often sets an example of impulsive behavior, and the child does not learn to recognize the potential results of conflict.

5. Sense of effectiveness: The middle-class child is more often appreciated and applauded, learns to sustain play longer and persist in solving problems.

6. Motivation: The lower-class child is less motivated because he does not feel friendly to the teacher or care for her praise, partly because he does not admire her skills or temperament. He expects academic failure, so does not try.

7. Expectancy of failure: For the lower-class child, "Failure is less humiliating for he had not expected to succeed and was not convinced that intellectual skills were valuable." This leads to a "combination of inadequate language resources, low motivation, and little faith in success."

A particular need for parent education and encouragement of lower-class mothers may be deduced from Kagan's "differences." This is supported by Geber's study (see chapter two).

While Kagan's analyses of poor and privileged environments reflected primarily SES differences, these categories can be broadened so that "poor" or "deprived" environments are those in which the mother for any reason (such as poverty, illness, or lack of full affection or understanding of her infant) does not give her child the benefits of the "privileged." Thus, a child from a middle- or high-SES background may actually be deprived. Conversely, a low-SES infant may be one who *does* have these benefits because of a mother or surrogate who provides the qualities and experiences that Kagan normally attributes to higher-class families. Longitudinal research is needed to determine what real benefits, if any, accrue over time from intervention designed for early school readiness.

Regulating School Entrance

School Entrance Age

Recognizing the importance of early development and the poor quality of care in many homes, concerned educators have hoped that flexible school entrance policies might improve achievement. Experiments with early admission have yielded a wide range of results. In some instances school entrance at earlier ages than usual (i.e., before age six) appears to have made no difference at all in achievement. Occasionally, with careful screening, younger children seem to have gained an advantage by starting their academic careers early. Yet here far greater objectivity is needed, both for the present and future development of children. The evidence from many studies overwhelmingly suggests that several months to a year or more of additional age throughout elementary school leads to real benefits for most children (399, 290, 187, 126, 305, 239, 447, and others).

Several researchers found no significant difference in the achievement of children who entered school early and those who entered at regular ages: Braga (109, 110), Spaulding and Katzenmeyer (642), and McLeod, Markowsky, and Leong (459). There is some doubt, however, whether these early entrants achieved at the same academic level as their older classmates or whether they performed equally in terms of expected achievement for mental age. If the latter were true, early entrants would be at a disadvantage even though there were no differences in intellectual achievement measures.

Although a difference in intellectual ability may not be apparent, entering school at a younger-than-usual age may have disadvantages in other aspects of life (257, 156). Careful screening for social stability and physical maturity as well as intellectual ability is strongly recommended when considering such early admission (336, 5, 110, 156, 447).

95

Worcester (738) estimated that one year's acceleration of bright children would gain for our country one million years of its best brains in a single generation. Worcester's statement might have some truth if it is assumed that these children were to proceed "lock step" through elementary school, spending a year in each grade. Yet, while such a procedure has been almost sacrosanct in American education, it is hardly realistic in the light of children's varied abilities, experiences, and rates of development.

This is not to deny the viability of acceleration under some circumstances. Much depends on *when* the students are accelerated and on when they start school. In a study of three hundred individuals who started school at about age eight or later, all but four started at second or third grade or later (489). They quickly caught up with their classes and in most cases performed well above the class average. Many were accelerated, but all of these were considered mature for their ages. The four who started at the first grade and were held lock step through all grades were the only students who had strong feelings against school. In each case they felt too old for their grades.

Choppin (152) examined data from Husén's international study (358) of twelve different countries, each with a distinctive educational system. He then concluded that school promotion should depend on the progress of the child and his readiness to join a new class. Schools, he suggested, should be prepared to accept new students on any Monday morning throughout the school year. And the time a child spent in any class or grade should depend on his individual needs and abilities. Thus a bright, mature child could enter school at the regular age, or even later, and still "save" the years referred to by Worcester. This practice has been urged for years by psychologists and psychiatrists on the basis of broad clinical experience (233).

A similar idea was suggested by Klausmeier (403). He found that both learning efficiency and motivation were likely to increase when older, bright children—late starters—were permitted to accelerate their progress instead of remaining with younger, less mature children.

In the absence of this freedom for children's developmental progress through school, careful screening for an early beginning has apparently produced positive effects for some children. The results of a ten-year study in Brookline, Massachusetts, indicated that carefully selected underage children were academically superior and had fewer social and emotional maladjustments than their older classmates (336).

A more recent study in Skokie, Illinois, also yielded positive results for carefully screened early school entrants. Half of these early entrants were considered superior in intellectual performance, and most of the others were average or above in relation to their older peers (5). Ahr concluded, however, that the major advantage in the screening policy for early admission was that it helped detect problems in children who were not ready for school. Through referral services such problems could be prevented or treated before school entrance.

Early screening programs designed for early school entrance also have disadvantages. Mawhinney (447) reports the discontinuation of such testing and enrollment in one of Michigan's wealthiest public school districts. Evaluation of the early entrants at the end of this period showed that nearly one-third of the four- to five-year-old entrants were considered poorly adjusted, while three-fourths were judged entirely lacking in leadership. One-fourth were academically superior, and another fourth were below average. Although the professional evaluation was as reliable as possible, there could be no evaluation of the child's effectiveness in life other than parents' reports. This is a common problem in such studies as those of Mawhinney and Hobson and Ahr.

Furthermore, Mawhinney reported that the testing interview itself—and the unreasoning, negative reactions of parents whose children were not admitted—may well have affected the child's self-image and the relationship between home and school. The costs, which were borne by the community, were highly disproportionate to the benefits achieved. Mawhinney later mentioned that after several years school psychologists had moved to abort the early entrance experiment, but fourteen years were required before parental pressures subsided enough to permit termination.

Apart from the issue of screening is the effect of early entrance on a child's general school progress. From Simmons's comparison (627) of fourth graders' actual school performance and their probable performance had school entry been delayed, Green and Simmons (297) hypothesized that delayed entrance would most likely result in greater achievement in any grade but in lower achievement at a given age. Again, this would be true only in the rigid lock-step pattern of school progress. It need not occur if, as suggested by Anderson (297), the school were designed to fit the individual child (rather than making the child fit the school), advancing him according to his ability and maturity.

Reading and emotional problems and some learning disabilities have also been attributed to early school entrance. Andreas (24), who examined the records of two hundred children for school entrance age range, concluded that many of these problems were either created or worsened by plunging children into learning tasks inappropriate for their ages.

Entering school early usually results in less than optimum achievement (399), but children who enter later are more likely to achieve at a higher level. Shields and Steiner (619) found greater variation in language skills between preschool children with a six-month age difference than between socioeconomic levels in preschool groups. Similarly, Ilika (364) found that even seven or eight additional months of age at the time of entrance to the first grade generally enabled children to achieve faster.

The few months' difference in age that makes the difference in learning is often due to the time of year a child was born. Pidgeon (543) confirmed what has commonly been observed by classroom teachers: that a child born at the "wrong end" of the year—whose birthday comes shortly before he enters school—is at a disadvantage compared to those slightly older.

Unfortunately, as observed earlier, the lower achievement of these earlier entrants tends to persist over the years. Bookbinder (97) noted increased difficulty among slightly younger children in coping with ordinary classes at the age of nine or ten. At this particular time, when conversation and logical thinking should be firmly established, and is so in the older students, the younger ones in the same grade who have not yet acquired it tend to lag behind.

During any given year there is often a chronological difference of nine to eleven months or more between the youngest and oldest children in a kindergarten class or school grade. Gott (290) tested children from the younger and older age extremes at the end of grades two through six. On Stanford Achievement Tests the older groups achieved more than the younger groups in all subjects at all grade levels, except for one zero difference.

This effect of early entrance goes even beyond grade six, according to Forester (239). His study of five hundred pupils whose progress was followed from kindergarten through high school revealed that children who were very bright but very young when they entered school had varying difficulties from junior high on. They were reported physically immature and emotionally unstable. They did not do as well socially, behaviorally, academically, or in leadership as those who were older at school entrance. Forester concluded that early entry could even have an adverse effect later in adult life. Unfortunately, most ECE studies, whatever their findings in the early elementary years, do not move on to measure outcomes during adolescent and later years.

Children who enter school younger are not intellectually deficient, even though they achieve at lower levels and at slower rates. Using standardized tests, Shearer (616) found that summer-born children were not at a disadvantage when age allowances were made. They were not lower in IQ, but teacher assessments of their abilities were typically lower. These teachers expected them to accomplish the same as the slightly older children, even though the younger ones were not as ready.

From a stratified random sampling of fourth graders, Dickinson and Larson (187) found more high IQ's among younger children, but these younger ones were less able to achieve than older fourth graders with lower IQ's. Brown's (126) findings conveyed essentially the same message. When three groups of children (normal, bright, and retarded) were matched for mental age, the older retarded children performed as well as normal children of equal mental age. The younger bright children did less well than their normal mental peers. These bright youngsters performed more like other children of their own chronological age. Brown observed that, even though they were mentally advanced, they were held back by sheer lack of experience. And experience, as suggested earlier, is a prime factor in perception and conceptualization.

School Entrance Rationale

Researchers cannot pinpoint the age when children are ready to begin formal schooling. Hobson (336) and Ahr (5) found that, with screening, some children purportedly achieve early without trauma. But they did not follow these children through school as in Forester's study, and ultimate performances are not known. In their review of school entrance age studies, Halliwell and Stein (306) found substantial agreement among school entrance age researchers that children who enter school later are significantly higher in academic achievement than those who enter earlier.

Unfortunately, recent school entrance laws and regulations are seldom based on developmental needs of children. Anderson (23) summed up the rationale of educators for starting school at age six. Certain educators were saying that by then children have acquired sufficient muscular control and language ability to begin reading. But Anderson questioned this assumption. In reporting an Educational Testing Service study, he noted that a committee of child development experts assessing areas of development necessary for school readiness considered sensorimotor, cognitive-intellectual, and social-personal development of equal importance. Moral judgment and moral conduct were also included as readiness factors. But only 60 percent of a national sample of seven thousand children were ready for school in all or most of these aspects, according to the judgment of their own first-grade teachers. Anderson's conclusion suggests that it would be well to reassess school-entry ages and the purposes of early education.

Jensen (369) observed a need for experimental programs that would actually delay formal instruction until readiness is achieved. He surmised that learning problems might thus be avoided, since forcing instruction on an unready child can result in learning skills with little transfer value or in "turning off" learning altogether. Fisher and Hawley (233), on the basis of clinical experience, strongly agree with Jensen.

There is little rationale for progressively lowering the school entrance age if later school achievement and performance in life are accepted as criteria of school success (574, 576). From an analysis of research in this area, Rohwer questioned whether intellectual competence in early childhood, or even in elementary school, was necessary for competence in later years. He hypothesized that, the longer formal instruction was delayed, up to certain limits, the higher the ultimate achievement. He suggested that formal schooling prior to adolescence should be radically changed, with emphasis on skills performance rather than content retention. Such schooling would be expected to help children adapt to out-of-school tasks, to perform in life.

In evaluating federal programs for compensatory education, Robinson (571) reached a similar conclusion. Since the social environment strongly affects cognitive development, she suggests that delaying academic learning until ages ten to fourteen would give the child the advantage of more fully developed cognitive skills. Fisher (233) agrees. Research is needed to determine more definitely whether, as it appears, such delays would successfully reduce both the frustration and anxiety of so much early learning and the apathy and low achievement of later school years. At this point, from reviews of more than 7,000 ECE studies, we can find no systematic body of evidence to the contrary.

In one study (489), as noted earlier, nearly three hundred individuals who entered school from two to five years later than the customary age of six or seven reported no difficulty in completing elementary school at the usual age or even younger. Apparently these students did not have outstanding intelligence. Some could even have been considered disadvantaged because of living in isolated areas or in countries other than their homelands. The common factor in all cases was later school entrance.

Moore and Moore (492, 493) recommend ages eight to ten for beginning formal school instruction. They suggest normally starting the child with his chronological peers—that is, starting an eight-year-old in the second or third grade. They point out that most late starters, usually without formal training before their first school enrollment, quickly catch up academically and often pass their more school-experienced peers. And the late starters generally excel in behavior, sociality, and leadership. Teachers can easily facilitate such practices if they desire. They can compensate for possible academic needs by using older or stronger students to help the late entrants. Experience has proven, however, that in the long run such late starters bring more joy than trouble to the classroom.

To remedy a lack of achievement in the schools, concerned educators and citizens have proposed lowering school entrance ages, suggesting that it would give children an advantage (566). Others have suggested revamping the curriculum to fit the laws of human development (23, 574). And Jensen (369), Elkind

101

(216), Rohwer (574, 576), Moore and Moore (493), and Robinson (571) have examined the merits of delaying formal academic instruction until the many aspects of readiness enable students to learn rapidly and easily—something rare in mass education today. Such delay would require greater flexibility in school entrance regulations than many states now have. This flexibility should be one of the most urgent subjects for policy reform at local, state, and national levels.

Practical Suggestions for Parents
or Parent Surrogates or Other Care Givers*

(How to encourage academic readiness of their children for eventual schooling)

For Children from Thirty Months to Five Years

1. Gardening teaches your child many concepts of science and economics, besides being exciting and rewarding. It also helps him develop patience, dependability, and similar qualities.
2. Everyday activities provide many opportunities to teach early numbers concepts to your child: counting silverware (when setting the table), rows in the garden, or fruit in the harvest; discovering fractions when quartering an apple or using a measuring cup.

For Children from Four to Seven Years

1. Give your child experience in sorting and arranging household items and goods. He may not yet be able to read words, but he can see patterns.
2. Give him plenty of opportunity for counting, dividing, and measuring in his work and play.
3. As it becomes convenient and helpful, help your child tell time. Use a clock with large numbers or make a paper-plate clock with large numbers and movable hands. He can listen to the radio or telephone to see if the house clock is slow or fast.

---

*These suggestions have been included in this chapter for convenience only. In fact, all the other suggestions given in chapters three, four, and six may be classified under "readiness for school"—which is, after all, one of the primary objectives of the parent educator. At the same time the child's values, self-worth, and so forth are being developed and molded by the home experiences with parents and siblings.

4. Acquaint him with the days of the week by mentioning the name of each day in the morning. Give him a large calendar of his own to mark off the days. Show him how to change the page each month, and draw attention to special days.

5. Your child can learn something about money and its use. He may be given a weekly allowance and helped to budget it.

6. Introduce the study of weather to your child at this age, discussing it with him each day. Listen to the radio or TV weather report and forecast. If possible, secure a large indoor-outdoor thermometer for him to watch. He can record the temperature.

7. Study about the seasons together. Observe the snow and the clouds. Talk about the effects of the seasons on plants, animals, and people.

8. Studying anatomy, physiology, and hygiene informally is invaluable. Your child can begin to understand why we observe health habits and laws.

9. As your child works or plays, he normally will sing or hum many kinds of songs he has learned; so share songs with him. His musical standard will reflect precisely what you teach him.

10. Give him opportunities to respond to the rhythms of various types of music by marching, tiptoeing, clapping, galloping, or swaying. He will still enjoy simple rhythm instruments made from sticks, cans, or other ordinary household items.

11. Teach him the names of the most common musical instruments and help him to identify them by their sounds. However, his eye-hand and ear-hand coordination are not yet well enough established to learn to play an instrument well without undue strain. It is better to delay formal music lessons until he is at least eight or nine. In fact, a poll of 1,500 piano teachers suggested that the optimum age to begin piano is 11.6 years. Few adults realize the complexity of piano playing: decoding the music and translating it into appropriate and accurate action of fingers and feet.

For Children from Six to Eight or Nine Years

1. This may be the time to introduce some simple information about astronomy, locating prominent stars and constellations. Use a child's book on astronomy. If there is a nearby observatory or planetarium, visit it if you can.

2. During this period your child can learn more about the

value of money. You can help him learn to save, to spend his money wisely, and to keep accounts of his income and his spending.

3. Further study of anatomy and physiology is also appropriate at this age. Your child can understand how the health of the body affects the mind and how proper mental attitudes (mental health) affect the body. He needs to know the body is controlled by natural laws. Disobedience of these laws results in illness or a weakened body. He needs to develop pride in a healthy mind and body. He can understand something about reproduction if taught in a natural way.

6
Readiness for Reading*

Synopsis. Those who read easily and early most often come from homes where education is apparently valued and mothers are fairly well educated. However, other important and positive factors are having relatively quiet activities with little or no television, having books available in the home, being read to and "taken places" by adults, having smaller families, being the firstborn or being "taught" by slightly older siblings, having regularly assigned home chores, being able to dress independently, and having sound friendships.

The foregoing conditions, which are generally conducive to reading, can result in spontaneous learning to read before going to school. Yet this early exposure to reading under these circumstances will not likely result in reading problems in school. Young children generally do not push themselves beyond their ability to achieve. On the other hand, overanxious adults who apply pressures for early reading, along with pressures of keeping up with classmates, may cause many so-called reading or learning disabilities. Parents and teachers who care, who respond warmly and consistently, who thus create an environment conducive to reading and support children's efforts, greatly facilitate children's learning to read. Motivation of this kind evidently does more for children's reading than exerting undue pressure to achieve or conducting special early school or other training programs.

*In view of the wealth of research findings on reading readiness, a separate chapter is devoted to this topic. Of all the features of the early childhood curriculum, reading is singled out in this volume because readiness to read has been universally regarded as an important aspect of overall school readiness.

In early childhood, intelligence appears to be less important than social-emotional environment for learning to read. After the third grade, intelligence becomes more important, although even then its effect may be minimal. Age at school entry,* responsiveness to small group instruction, and the child's history of success or failure with reading experiences relate most to progress in reading.

Reading difficulties arising simply from pressured use of immature perceptual processes are often called "disabilities." Yet they may decrease or disappear completely when perceptual abilities improve, usually after the third grade. For children who have functional disabilities—such as visual, auditory, or neuropsychological—early detection is important. Special perceptual training programs have potential value. Still, for normal and gifted children, little is gained from these early training programs. With perceptual integration and maturation, most children have little difficulty with reading.

Children who learn to read words without meaning may also be genuinely handicapped. This problem relates primarily to children who are pressured to read early, before they are able to reason consistently and to comprehend the concepts carried by the printed word. This is common among young children at least through age seven—or the first and second grades.

Given sensory-motor maturity and the ability to conceptualize—usually by the fifth grade or later—reading skill develops rapidly when a child first acquires an interest and then discovers that reading can extend his knowledge about that interest.

A child who reads meaningfully and well does not suddenly learn to read. Acquiring experience, perceptual skills, and symbolic and abstract (cause and effect) understanding is a gradual process. He begins in infancy through play, and reading skills normally can be well developed before he begins to read formally in school.

In a literate culture one of the greatest achievements of early childhood is, of course, learning to read. From the standpoint of structured education this achievement is a major influence on most later learning. The ability to read well is a highly complex function of the central nervous system (36), requiring brain maturation enabling a child to recognize visual symbols and the sounds they represent (172). The sounds, in turn, must form words representing concepts with which a child has had some experience (553). It is not entirely unlike learning to decipher a wartime code

---

*See IML in chapter five for more on academic readiness age.

in which words are at first apparent, but their meanings await the highly skilled decoding officer.

Early Conditioning for Reading

It is not the eye primarily that reads words on the page, but the brain (412)—the brain with all its stored associations and meanings assigned to previous experiences. Children who learn to read easily and early do not come from any distinct background or culture (201), but their experiences and certain environmental characteristics predispose them to an interest in reading.

Durkin found that many children who learned to read at home before going to school came from homes where education was apparently valued. Many of their parents were foreign born, but the mothers tended to have a high level of education. The families were usually smaller than those of other children, which may have provided more opportunities for child-adult communication. The children themselves generally walked and talked earlier than usual, but they were content with relatively quiet activities and had little television, apparently with ample time and freedom to explore for themselves.

The influence of the mother on a child's motivation to read has also been reported by Hess (327) and Hirst (335). Hess identified maternal behavior and cultural background as key factors, and Hirst pointed out the mother's education as a very good predictor of the child's beginning reading achievement in school. In the first grade reading ability has been associated with such home-related variables as having books in the home, being read to by adults, and being "taken places" (479).

Older siblings as well as adults may contribute to a child's interest in reading, especially if a sibling is only two or three years older and likes to play "school" (199). Children learn a great deal from each other, and a sibling may unconsciously teach a younger child. The child absorbs what he is capable of learning without pressure—and sometimes with delight that he is learning what his slightly older peer can do.

The joy of accomplishment is a key factor in building a positive sense of worth. Wattenberg and Clifford (696) found self-concept measures significantly predictive of reading progress. Achievement in nonacademic areas is equally effective in enhancing self-concept and ability to read. Responsibilities for home duties and for self-care, matched to the child's abilities, were found by Milner (479) to be positive factors in learning to read.

Learning to assume responsibility gradually decreases a child's helpless dependence on adults. This may also affect reading success, since excessive dependency has been associated with low achievement in reading among third-grade children (713). And positive correlations with reading achievement were found for third-grade children who dressed independently and performed regularly assigned home chores (339). Being the firstborn and having friends also had positive effects on reading in Hoffman's study. The experiences provided by parents and later directed by teachers form the foundation for reading achievement.

Factors in Reading Success

Children may learn to read spontaneously, with parent or teacher assistance, or with the help of siblings or other children. Creating the conditions conducive to reading can result in spontaneous learning to read before going to school, as noted earlier, with few if any problems in school reading (201). Ilg and Ames (363) found that children may show a marked interest in letters and words at an early age, but they are not likely to push themselves beyond their ability to achieve. Sutton (665) observed that spontaneous reading by kindergarten children did not exceed twenty hours a year, yet resulted in continuous progress. Over-anxious adults are the ones who frequently apply pressures for early reading. But pressuring children to perform at a level for which they are not prepared, including pressures to keep up with peers in the classroom, results in frustration, reading rebellion, and—according to Ilg and Ames (363)—many cases of so-called reading disability. No long-term advantage results from rushing the normal child in reading (638).

Even without a supportive environment and despite poorly trained teachers, many children with severe handicaps learn to read (617). Crosby and Liston (172) strongly suggest that an intelligent child who is neurologically, culturally, and emotionally normal will discover how to read by himself if sufficiently motivated and then left to his own devices. However, parents and teachers who create an environment conducive to reading, and who are supportive of children's efforts without exerting undue pressure to achieve, greatly facilitate children's learning to read.

Weber (697) showed that very poor inner-city children at the third-grade level had met reading success criteria and even exceeded the national norm when certain factors were present. Factors contributing to their motivation, and apparently accounting for their reading achievement, were strong adult leadership, high expectations (which the children were developmentally ready to reach), supportive atmosphere, emphasis placing a high value on reading, and additional personnel for individualization of the program.

The factors identified by Weber as contributing to school reading success of third graders were quite similar to those mentioned by Milner (479) and Durkin (201) as positive *home* influences on reading. This motivation from parents and teachers who care (617, 339) evidently does more for children's reading than pressure (363) or special early training programs (626).

Programs designed to increase children's IQ have little ultimate effect on learning (73). And intelligence as measured by IQ tests is apparently less important than the social-emotional environment for learning to read (200, 40, 149, 588, 335). Durkin (200) found that, regardless of IQ, some children learned to read very well at home.

After the third grade, however, intelligence becomes more important (588), but even then the effect may be minimal. Chansky (149) worked with children eight to fourteen years of age in remedial reading classes, finding no support for the belief that a higher IQ contributed to reading progress. Instead, age, responsiveness to small group instruction, and the child's history of success or failure with reading related most to improvement in reading.

IQ does not seem to be a differentiating factor in the first-grade reading success of boys and girls; yet girls achieve significantly higher than boys (40). The lower reading achievement of boys in Balow's study has been attributed to a lack of psychosocial readiness rather than to maturational factors. For both boys and girls, however, "maturation sensitive" tests (i.e., tests which clearly differentiate the performance of oldest, intermediate, and youngest children) have shown a significant corre-

109

lation of maturation with reading achievement at the end of the second grade (180). And even the relatively rough measure of chronological age at school entry has been positively correlated with progress in reading (24).

Keister (397) reported that normal reading progress was apparently possible for underage children in school, but their reading skills were lost over the summer and were not made up later. Likewise, Freyman (246) found that children with birthdays in the summer, making them a few months younger than their classmates, were frequently assigned to remedial reading groups and received more than their share of low marks. These disadvantages persisted through the primary school years. Starting to school even a few months later can result in greater reading success (311).

Perceptual Abilities for Reading

Although Wepman (208) concedes that use of a neural pathway enhances its development so that complete function occurs at an earlier age, he also points out that a lack of perceptual stimulation is not a correlate of poor perceptual learning. He does say, however, that maturation and development of the neural system are interrelated. Consequently, perceptual processes function more precisely as they mature, and using these processes within the limits imposed by maturation assists their development. (See sections on reading, decoding, and brain development in chapters eight and nine.)

The use of the visual modality, the whole visual system of the brain, for decoding *serial* information—as required in most reading programs—generally develops later than the ability to scan. The young child may follow a moving object—such as an airplane or insect—earlier and more easily than he analyzes ever-changing letters and words—shapes requiring serial decoding. Reading involves both visual-temporal and visual-verbal processing (587).

Reading difficulties arising simply from pressure to use immature perceptual processes are often assumed to be disabilities (363). These maturational "handicaps" may decrease or disappear entirely when perceptual abilities improve, usually after the third grade (588, 651, 250, 498). This assumes that the child has not already become so frustrated that he is inured to reading or turned off altogether. Recognizing the true nature of

110

many reading problems can reduce considerably the pressures and frustrations of remedial reading efforts for youngsters whose primary needs are only (1) time to develop and (2) a supportive environment.

For children who have real disabilities in vision, hearing, or neuropsychological functions, early detection is important so that the problems will not limit normal exploration of their environment any more than necessary. Before they reach the age for formal reading and before they are subject to academic failure, these children need help in learning to use the perceptual abilities they have. Satz and Friel (591) suggest that such children can be identified by an early warning system using a developmental and neuropsychological test battery at the beginning kindergarten age. An assessment of this kind, available as a routine part of children's services, might provide the necessary assistance for handicapped children without subjecting unnecessarily large numbers to remedial pressures that, according to Silberberg and Silberberg (625), have no long-lasting effect on reading levels. There is a great need here for research and development of procedures for assessing and treating perceptual problems.

Cerebral dominance in some cases may not be stabilized until after nine years of age (465); so related reading disabilities may diminish as age increases. Much research in this area is relatively new, and conclusions must be drawn with care. The results of ongoing studies are expected to provide valuable knowledge for understanding the neurophysiological and neuropsychological bases of reading.

Earlier studies (41, 332) showed no significant relationship between cerebral dominance and reading achievement. Hillerich, however, noted a 44 percent decrease in uncertain eye dominance from kindergarten to grade two, indicating some progress in neurological development. Balow and Balow tested second-grade children, and Hillerich studied children longitudinally in kindergarten and again in second grade. The conclusions of Wepman (715) suggest that reading at these ages is probably more perceptual than conceptual in function. Thus, the effects of dominance anomalies observed in these studies may not have been as apparent as they might have been in later conceptual tasks.

Achievement of reading success reflects maturation of perceptual abilities. Many basic reading tasks depend heavily upon auditory processes, according to Flower (237) and Rosner (582, 583). In reviewing research linking auditory skills to reading, Hammill and Larsen (310), however, were less than sure such skills were usefully related to reading. The degree of phonics emphasis may be a variable here. Nevertheless, in the primary grades most children seem to learn more rapidly through hearing than seeing (131). They also pay more attention to auditory materials than to visual (657).

At the same time poorly developed eye movements correlate highly with problems in learning to read (301). Up to age nine or later, visual perception deficits are a contributing factor in reading failure (250). By the end of the third grade visual discrimination of word segments is well underway; it is virtually maximal by the end of the sixth grade (651).

From the third to the fourth grade cross-modal perception—among and between the senses—becomes more important (588), and the perceptual deficiencies of poor readers are not associated primarily with any specific modality (130). The ability to read well requires efficient communication between the visual, auditory and somatosensory systems (36), which most children evidently do not achieve until this cross-modal perception is established *near the end of the primary grades.*

Some children undoubtedly reach perceptual maturation earlier than others and achieve sensory integration at a younger-than-usual age. Yet for most children there is little to be gained from special perceptual training programs. Fortenberry (242) reported no lasting value from visual perceptual training for word recognition in the first grade. Similarly, Klesius (404) found no special benefit for normal children from perceptual-motor development programs to improve reading readiness and achievement. Such structured programs, however, do seem to have potential value in remedial work with learning-disabled children.

With perceptual integration and maturation, the majority of children would have little difficulty reading if conditions and motivation were reasonably conducive to the task. Until then it is probably unrealistic to expect children to read with any degree of success by adult standards, except as they do so spontaneously. Children have their own way of recognizing letters and words—quite different from the complex strategies of adults (729). They employ the same strategies used to master sensory-motor-spatial play. They look for rules and meaning to help establish a conceptual framework for written language—rules they have already absorbed unconsciously for verbal language since early childhood (709).

Early Reading Comprehension and School Achievement

The ability to read becomes functionally useful only when it conveys meaning to the reader. Unfortunately, even children who are considered superior readers and who maintain high reading achievement may have learned to read words without meaning (453). To some extent this can be as real a handicap as other reading problems in general academic learning. Studies identifying this problem relate it primarily to children who were taught to read early, to perform beyond their ability to comprehend (561, 193, 343).

Quigley's (553) assessment of the prereading vocabulary of nursery school children in England showed that most were familiar with less than two-thirds of the words they would soon be expected to recognize in reading books. And Reid's (561) group of five-year-olds, representing a cross-section of socioeconomic levels, had only a hazy notion of what reading was all about. For these children it was not clear whether one read "pictures" or "marks on paper." They were unaware that letters symbolized sounds, and the concept of *word* as spatially ordered letters was difficult to comprehend.

Downing (193) made a further investigation of questions raised by Reid, using children four years eleven months to five years three months, and obtained remarkably similar results. Not a single child's comprehension of a "word" corresponded with the adult's concept of a word. The children had only a vague understanding of abstract terms and of the purpose of written or printed language. For example, some children called pictures or numbers "words," since they had meaning and conveyed ideas.

In the first grade, too, children have been found uncertain of the meaning of "words" and their printed representation (343). The printing idea is difficult for children to understand because printed word units do not always coincide with their own speech patterns. For instance, "an apple" is easy for an older person to decode, but to a small child the concept represented by these two words may have always been "anapple," a single speech unit. According to Holden and MacGinitie, printed speech segmentation is unfamiliar to most children at school-entry age, and they have difficulty comprehending such an idea even when they learn to identify word boundaries in print.

Brekke, Williams, and Harlow (114) suggested that understanding the conservation of substance be an additional measure for beginning reading instruction.* Conservation is not necessarily learned in school (691, 282, 464), but children must have a certain mental age before they can perform adequately in tasks of this nature (395)—in effect demonstrating the ability to extend or develop concepts or abstract thinking from concrete ideas.

Full reading success requires comprehension of both the purpose of reading and the meaning of the material read. In the fifth grade, reading comprehension is associated with the interest level of the reading material, especially for boys (30). Given sensory-motor maturity and the ability to conceptualize, reading skill develops rapidly when a child first acquires an interest and then discovers that reading can extend his knowledge about that interest. This is quite different from purely mechanical decoding—that is, associating printed letters with sounds but with little if any meaning—that usually accompanies a lack of interest in reading.

Heffernan (325) suggested that experiences extending and deepening understanding of the natural and social world, leaving room for creativity, exploration, and expression, are necessary for successful reading. For most five-year-olds, reading is an adult and cultural demand rather than a personally perceived need, and the unready child will often feel inadequate, frustrated, and defeated. Heffernan attributed the rising number of emotionally disturbed children in part to these early pressures for reading.

According to Durkin (202), a child does not learn to read all at once; reading is a gradual process. Much of the recent research in this area suggests that acquiring experience, perceptual skills, and symbolic and abstract understanding is the gradual process. Weininger (709) believes this process begins during the second year of life, through play, with the child's development

*See footnote on conservation, chapter five, and illustrations in chapter seven.

of the concept of "object constancy"—the "ability to carry images in his mind" and to use these images to develop and discover relational qualities among them. He can do this only when he can remember abstract images and no longer is limited to dealing with one concrete object at a time. His mind can sort out his parents, friends, toys, food, rooms, clothes, and so forth, relating them to each other or to the day's events. This concept of object constancy must be developed fully before he is able to read optimally.

A foundation of visual-motor-spatial-linguistic skills should be built up before school entrance. The child should be able to grasp the abstract conceptual definitions of things in the environment. This enables him to use the symbolic approach to problems. Playing and living in his family environment can help him acquire visual and auditory discrimination before he goes to school. Then he can take books and explore reading, with the teacher as catalyst and guiding person. Most reading disabilities result more from a lag in the functional development of the central nervous system than from brain pathology.

Children who are ready enjoy playing with the printed word just as they played earlier with objects and with the spoken word. As reading activities are mastered they ask for more. Parents and teachers will do well to anticipate and prepare for their needs.

Some Practical Suggestions for Parents
or Parent Surrogates or Other Care Givers

(How to facilitate good reading habits and skills)

For Children from Birth to Eighteen Months

1. Language development can be encouraged by responding to the baby's babbling and by talking to him about what you are doing.

2. Your child can enjoy "reading" books with you as early as nine months of age. By using songs, games, finger plays, and repetition you can attract and hold his attention.

3. You can make books yourself, using a simple, familiar picture on each page. Do not use cartoons or puppets. The child needs to learn *reality* in his first years, not be confused with fantasy. He will have enough fantasies of his own to work out.

115

For Children from One to Three Years

1. At eighteen months he is able to enjoy a homemade scrapbook containing pieces of different-textured materials for him to feel. Vary colors and patterns as well.

2. Reading time is learning time, but this is no time for absurd, fantastic tales. Concentrate on true stories about nature, heroes from history, the Bible, Torah, Koran, etc., and stories about the child himself, rather than myths and fairy tales.

3. This is the beginning of the questioning age. Answer his questions as best you can. A reference book will sometimes be great help and will also teach him that we can learn from books. Sometimes you can turn the questions back to him. Don't hesitate to make full use of your local library.

For Children from Thirty Months to Five Years

1. Don't worry about "teaching" him language arts. By being conscious of his needs and being friendly and casual, you will be able to get him to talk freely.

2. Repeating sentences after you can be a game. Keep the sentences simple and correct. Speak clearly. Avoid colloquialisms, slang, and profanity.

3. Use descriptive and action words throughout the day: "the dog is *shaggy*," "the stove is *black*," "*bring* me the book," "*empty* out the garbage."

4. Have a daily story time, and let him tell you about the actions in his picture book.

5. You can teach him to follow simple directions by having him do errands for you.

6. Compliment him and otherwise show appreciation whenever you honestly can.

7. Show affection, holding him and frequently sharing hugs and kisses.

8. If your child has difficulty with a specific sound, make a note of it. At another time, play a game to help him make the sound. Nature provides a good basis for practicing many sounds. Let nature do its own talking. Listen with your child.

9. Learn a variety of appropriate songs to teach him.

10. At this age your child never seems to get enough stories; many have to be repeated again and again. Choose stories that teach honesty, dependability, industry, and concern for others.

Screen out violence. Nature stories are among the best for him now.

11. Stories can be told at any time, not only when reading from a book or sitting down.

For Children from Four to Seven Years

1. Involve your child in nearly all the work you normally do at home, including gardening, sewing, and woodwork. His self-concept and future success in reading and other skills will depend largely on his background experiences and his language development.

2. He has learned to follow directions. Now he should also have opportunities to give directions and to carry simple oral messages to others.

3. Give him opportunities to express himself without interception or correction.

4. Let him dictate a letter, draw a picture to enclose with it, and stamp and mail the letter.

5. If he wants to learn how to write, teach him his name, using a large pencil to write large letters on a big sheet of paper.

6. If he wants to know certain words, labels, or signs, tell him. Whatever he asks about and wishes to learn, teach him in a casual, matter-of-fact way; but do not rush him or push him beyond his capacity.

7. He may teach himself to read. Yet he should not be allowed more than fifteen or twenty minutes at a time with books, in order to avoid eyestrain at this age.

8. When story hour comes, give him opportunities to discuss or repeat portions of the story and to answer questions.

9. He should also have practice in retelling a story or recounting an experience while going about his work with you.

10. Teach him to handle the telephone. Try pretend conversations at first; then call him from another telephone.

11. He should also know how and where to call in case of emergency. He should learn your first and last names, his own phone number, and his address. This will involve recognizing and, perhaps, learning to write numbers. But this should come in his own good time; he needs and wants to know them without pressure from you.

12. Conversations when the family is together at mealtimes can be influential in language development.

13. Help him develop his memory by teaching simple poems or verses. Meaningful verses can be found in such inspirational books as the Bible, the Torah, or the Koran. Avoid silly stories and verses. He generates enough of these on his own.

14. Talk about sounds with your child. Games can also give him an opportunity to hear and identify various sounds.

15. The child's eyes as well as his ears can be trained at this age. He can recognize colors, shapes, sizes, and plant and animal life.

16. In bad weather he can make scrapbooks. Use large pictures to avoid eyestrain. Avoid close work or confinement indoors for long periods of time.

17. He should know how to tie his shoes early in this period. He should also learn to organize himself in dressing, washing, bathing, and putting his things away in an orderly fashion.

For Children Six to Eight or Nine Years

1. He will become aware of auto-driving principles at this time. Your example will be very effective in establishing his future behavior behind the wheel. He can read the pictorial traffic signs and will want to read those with words.

2. This is considered the golden age for memory. He enjoys memorizing such things as the scout pledge and motto, the pledge of allegiance, and children's poems and verses from holy scripture.

3. Books, pictures, and personal experiences will help him understand and appreciate people of other cultures, adding interest to his study of geography.

7

Age and Academic Stimulation

Synopsis. *Since the early sixties, Jean Piaget's theory of cognitive development has been widely accepted by the academic world. Cognitively, children differ from adults in kind more than degree. Cognitive development occurs in sequential stages which never vary in their sequence. Intellectual growth is dependent on appropriate activities at each particular stage. It cannot formally be speeded up through special instruction or training. For a generation research studies have provided scientific support for Piaget's central concepts of intellectual development of the child. Despite inroads by the contrasting theories of such psychologists as Jerome Bruner and Benjamin Bloom, Piaget's guidelines stand out as the practical, common-sense route to sound learning practice.*

The young child's cognitive growth rates vary, with continuous changes in the nature and organization of mental abilities. Learning proceeds rapidly during at least two periods—the preschool years of four to six and the later childhood years of nine to eleven. However, there are maturational differences which determine what can be learned easily and well at these two stages. Primarily, the potential to learn *is being acquired during the early years of life more than learning itself. The need for academic instruction at this stage is open to question since no conclusive evidence suggests lasting effects of preschool instruction. Time provides for the maturation of physical and mental abilities and also permits the accumulation of life experiences on which a child can build. He can then find meaning in academic tasks that he can learn after age seven or eight with much greater efficiency and far less frustration and stress.*

In the preschool years children tend to perceive things globally rather than analytically* and are often confused in sorting out reality from fan-

_____

*These terms, *globally* and *analytically*, refer to the perceptual development of *tasy. Then, sometime around age seven or later, a dramatic acceleration of cognitive growth begins and continues for several years. This is consistent with Piaget's period of concrete operations, in which a child normally develops consistency in cause-and-effect reasoning. At about the fourth grade or later, children achieve almost complete control of their own learning behavior, permitting considerable increase in the efficiency of cognitive production. This correlates with evidence suggesting that, although some aspects of children's ability to make intersensory judgments are well developed by school entrance age, they do not reach full capacity to use them until about the eleventh year.*

Formal training in cognitive tasks during early childhood does sometimes improve intellectual functioning, but such induced learning is likely (1) to be limited in scope, (2) to lack permanence, and (3) to be of little benefit to the child in later learning and achievement. In fact, earlier-than-usual formal learning is often detrimental to later learning (with the exception of handicapped or disadvantaged children—who often need early structural help). Specific training to solve problems does not generally become effective until about the fourth grade (or about age nine or ten). It appears that a child's developmental level places a limit on what he really learns whether or not he receives instruction or training.

During ages seven to eleven (which Piaget calls the "concrete-operational" period) the child is able and eager to make rapid intellectual advancement unless, of course, he has been somehow discouraged. He displays almost complete mastery of common language structures and begins to develop cause-and-effect thinking. Acquiring this kind of thinking ability enables him to recognize and to organize and reason out concepts with facility. This ability, as noted earlier, begins to be used consistently at about age seven or later.

Successful school achievement also appears to be related (1) to attitudes the child develops through interaction with his family, (2) to the age when he enters school, and (3) to his general readiness for school. These factors are all highly correlated with chronological and mental age.

the child. At first he finds it difficult to perceive figures independent of their field or background. He finds it difficult to separate reality from fantasy. He is unable to comprehend underlying motives or perceive relationships and causes for behavior. Then from about age seven or eight to ten or eleven he begins to develop a consistency of reasoning and quality of thinking which differs from the younger child. He is able to understand and appraise motives and is capable of cause-and-effect reasoning. Piaget refers to global perception as "intuitive" or "preoperational" and to analytical perception as "concrete operational" or (later on) "formal operational."

120

Parents may damage rather than promote the personal development of their children by attaching excessive value to academic achievement and by applying pressure on them to "grow up" and achieve earlier.

Cognitive Development of the Child

Cognitive development is a process dependent upon interaction between the individual and his learning environment. Within reason and without strain, the child should be matched with the learning tasks most suitable for him at a given age. We would not expect a child to run before he can walk. In the same manner, we must also know when he is ready to learn various intellectual or cognitive tasks. By understanding the cognitive development of the young child, we can avoid pressuring him to learn something before he is ready or missing the golden moment when he *is* ready.

Gesell (263) was one of the first to show that growth and development occurred in unchanging sequence. He demonstrated that growth took place in stages and that the stages were major periods of change followed by periods of integration. To understand cognitive development, we need to know at what ages the major changes occur and then to identify periods of integration or stabilization.

Piaget's theory of cognitive development revolutionized our understanding of intellectual growth. He visualized mental growth as a process of interaction. Using repeated naturalistic observations of children over long periods of time, he explored and recorded the thinking processes of the human mind.

His theory of developmental stages in cognitive growth suggests that differences in intelligence are not of degree—fast or slow learners—but of quality or kind. These stages of growth differ from one another, each forming a major system of thinking that determines how the child understands and makes sense of his experiences. Educators, then, must consider the intellectual system a child is using at a particular time when providing experiences for him—if they are determined to nurture optimum cognitive development.

For many years Piaget's theories of cognitive development

were generally ignored, partly because they were so revolutionary. But by the early sixties he had accumulated sufficient evidence through repetition and replication (rather than a single critical experiment) to become widely accepted in the academic world. He found consistent systems of thinking patterns in children within certain broad age ranges: sensorimotor (zero to two years), intuitive or preoperational (two to seven years), concrete operational (seven to eleven years), and formal operational (eleven to sixteen years). Each stage also has subcategories. Each is a system of thinking that differs *qualitatively* from the preceding stage, involving major transformations in thought processes compared to the previous stage. Each stage may be compared to a breakthrough or a quantum leap forward.

As noted earlier, these stages are sequential. They follow an invariant sequence. It is thus impossible for children systematically to overcome a developmental lag or to accelerate movement from one stage to the next. They must have sufficient experience in each stage and sufficient time to accommodate (or internalize or stabilize) that experience before moving to the next stage. Although the major substance of each stage identifies that stage, the stages never exist in pure form applying uniformly to all children. There are always some elements of the preceding and future stages mixed in. Like fingerprints, all children have them. They tend to look similar, but all have points of variance.

Before moving to a discussion of related research, it might be well to discuss briefly each of Piaget's four operational stages:

1. The Sensorimotor Stage (Zero to Two Years)

Cognitive activity during the sensorimotor stage is based mainly on immediate experience through the senses. It involves interaction of senses and environment. Lacking language to label or symbolize experiences, children are bound to the immediate things they see, hear, feel, taste, and smell. Learning is a continuous series of peak experiences. They come abruptly and, to a large extent, are promptly forgotten. It is like experiencing each day as if it were the first day of school, the first exam, the first date, the first time being completely alone, the opening night of a show, the first meeting with death, and so on—all in one day.

Visual pursuit—following an object with their eyes—has to be learned before children can learn "object permanence." As they develop intellectually they eventually learn that when an object disappears from sight it still exists even though unseen. This is typical of the economy of effort that time and experience provide in the learning process. In due time they find that the disappearance from sight is only temporary, and they are freed from endless visual pursuit.

Noticing and following objects is the start of recognition. Object permanence is the beginning of simple memory. Thus a rich and responsive sensory environment is the best means of developing the young child's intelligence. It will be shown that this is best provided in the home by the mother. The quality of experience during this first stage prepares the child to move to the next stage.

2. The Intuitive or Preoperational Stage (Two to Seven Years)

During this stage of mental development the *quality* of thinking is transformed. The child is no longer tied to his immediate sensory environment. Whereas he started developing mental images in the first stage—that is, object permanence—he now rapidly expands this ability. At two years a child understands two to three hundred words while at five years this increases tenfold. At two years he talks largely in combinations of one, two, or three words, but a year later he often uses sentences of eight to ten words. Also, the sentences are grammatically correct if his parents or caregivers have provided the right models. At seven to eight years his pronunciation is like that of an adult. Thus, there is a major breakthrough in the use of language during this stage. Parents and other caregivers should take advantage of it.

For the most part the child learns intuitively now. He enjoys imitating sounds and trying out words. Therefore, the richer the verbal environment, the more likely the child is to develop his language. However, formal teaching is normally unnecessary because the child is capable of free associations, fantasies, and unique illogical meanings. Through pretense and imagination the child tries out language for himself. He in fact teaches himself. Because he is intuitive, he is free to try things out, regardless of the real world.

Although at times embarrassing to adults, the spontaneous nature of the child's language is good for practice. And practice will do much to ensure future verbal facility and competency.

123

At this stage the child talks *at* rather than *with* others. Piaget calls this egocentric speech pattern the "collective monologue." In terms of practice, this enables the child to try out words without having to wait his turn.

The intuitive period is truly a golden opportunity for facilitating language development. Verbal deprivation at this stage may result in irreversible developmental lag (111, 701). For this reason nothing can fully replace the one-to-one interaction between parent and child in the home.

Preoperational thought is clearly the predominant mode in the preschool child. That is why, more often than not, he will choose a tall, thin glass of milk or soda pop rather than a short, wide one. Intuitively he thinks it holds more because the taller glass is "bigger" even though it actually holds the same amount (or even less). He will also say that a pile of beans spread out thinly will contain more beans than a smaller, higher pile, because it covers a larger area. It will *not* help to explain why the milk is the same in both glasses or why the beans are the same in number.* The child will repeat the explanation without understanding it at all. His understanding is *qualitatively* different from an adult's.

It can be said, then, that the mental structures of the two- to seven-year-old child are largely intuitive, freewheeling, and highly imaginative. There is a great deal of fantasy. Contrary to common practice, parents do not ordinarily need to supply a fantasy, fairy tale, or mythical dialogue. Although it may seem illogical, the preoperational mode is not necessarily inferior as a way of thinking. Intuition and free association appear to be important components of creative or original problem solving. Intuition frees the thinker from the confines of reality, especially as he is sorting out his structural elements to build eventual stability and consistency.

3. Concrete Operations or Operational Thinking (Seven to Eleven Years)

The next stage in Piaget's scheme represents another major reorganization of mental structure. Whereas the preschool child is a dreamer, with an abundance of magical thoughts and fantasies, the seven- to eleven- or twelve-year-old child becomes *log-*

*(See footnotes, chapters five and six.)

124

ical and *positive.* He understands functional relationships and can test problems because he now is coming to understand the concrete nature of problems. He can measure and calculate the amount of water in the glasses, and he can weigh or count the number of beans on the table. *He understands that there is no change in volume or number even though there may be a change in appearance.* Piaget calls this logical and consistent thinking ability *conservation.*

However, this change in the cognitive mode often leads the child to become almost too literal minded. His ability to understand the world is now as "logical" as it once was illogical. He distinguishes between fantasy and fact yet finds difficulty in separating hypotheses from facts. Five-year-olds usually describe a dream as something which happens in the bedroom, something they watch like a movie, whereas the nine-year-olds describe dreams as mental images inside their heads (541). In addition, it is difficult for a nine-year-old to change his mind once it is made up, even if new information is provided.

In one experiment (217) seven- to ten-year-olds were presented with a number of reasons why Stonehenge, a prehistoric site in England, was a fort rather than a religious center, as commonly conceived. Even when new information seemed to support a rival hypothesis, they refused to consider a different point of view. They confused facts and theories because the idea of a theory was beyond their mental structure. Their thinking was rigid— limited to the facts presented in the first instance.

At this stage we also see evidence of literal-mindedness in the child's humor. For example, he likes slapstick jokes and pie throwing. Although previously they played around with fantasies, during concrete operations children play around with literal-mindedness. They do not yet take readily to figures of speech, common in adult conversation.

Elementary education seems to fit this cognitive stage rather well. Emphasis on skills and activities such as counting, sorting, constructing, and so on promotes cognitive growth. Most teachers and parents should take care not to rush these skills and to keep other activities in balance—such as manual-tactile work and play involving responsibility as well as amusement.

Rule making for activities is also important at this stage. Preschool children will obey rules without understanding them, but elementary school children understand rules because they have functional value (i.e., you cannot play ball without rules). However, their concepts are literal, meaning that the rules are fixed, necessary, and arbitrary.

The elementary school child should no more be taught in terms of the abstract structure of knowledge in various subjects than the preschool child should be expected to "operate" at the "preoperational level." In neither instance does the child have the mental equipment needed to cope with the learnings imposed upon him. The preschool child cannot conserve, and the elementary school child cannot grasp cognitive abstraction such as a hypothesis or a theory.

Children at the concrete-operational stage develop their own manner of understanding the various school subjects in relation to everyday experience. Parents and teachers both sometimes fail to realize how literal children are in their thinking. Not only do they not understand the cognitive limitations of their children, but they also sometimes get annoyed with each other's methods of trying to help children learn. The result is that children are often caught in the middle of two systems of thinking, neither of which they understand.

4. Formal Operations (Eleven to Sixteen Years or Adolescence)

Children now come to employ logical, rational, abstract modes of thinking. They understand symbolism, similes, and metaphors. They can engage in activities which stimulate abstract thinking and thus enhance their cognitive growth at this stage. They enjoy, for example, the use of figures of speech.

Implications of Piaget's Theory for Learning

Piaget's theory of cognitive development has two especially important implications for the education of young children: (1) Cognitive growth in each stage is dependent on activity appropriate to that particular stage. Children must engage in these activities in order to develop fully and effectively (541). (2) The stages of cognitive development cannot be accelerated. We cannot speed up the process of intellectual growth by special training or instruction.

At the same time we cannot expect cognitive growth to take place spontaneously. Piaget (541) emphasized the necessity of an environment responsive to the child: "Present the subject to be taught in forms assimilable to children of different ages in accordance with their mental structure."

Piaget's concept of assimilation and accommodation is as important as his emphasis on appropriate activity at each stage. Assimilation and accommodation form a dual process by means of which children assimilate (or take in) particular kinds of experiences at particular stages and accommodate (or internalize) them. For example, from birth to two years the infant is most able to assimilate sensorimotor experiences, whereas from two to seven years the preschooler can assimilate most fully preoperational experiences. In the same manner, it is impossible for the child to assimilate experiences beyond his level of mental development. Children may memorize information or say they understand when they really do not. According to Piaget, optimum intellectual development occurs when children assimilate experiences from their environment, because only in this manner can they accommodate or internalize these learnings.

Piaget's theory also indicates that thought processes differ dramatically during different stages of growth. It points out the importance of experience and activity in promoting growth and change. Most important of all, it stresses the futility of trying to force inappropriate learning on children before they are developmentally able to benefit.

A discussion of Piaget should not conclude without a reference to the contrasting theory of Jerome Bruner (128). Bruner states in his hypothesis "that any subject can be taught effectively in some intellectually honest form to any child at any stage of development."

Bruner is in a sense right; that is, if all his conditions could be met, children could learn as he says. But since his conditions are often impossible, his theory becomes a fantasy. (It could be said just as well that—if everyone had racial, creedal, and cultural understanding; their own well-furnished homes; their choice of fine automobiles; full employment with adequate incomes; and sound, altruistic mental health and integrity—we could eliminate most delinquency, prisons, inflation, and the national debt.) Because his conditions, generally speaking, simply do not grace our society, Bruner's philosophy is illusory and misleading. It has likely resulted in misdirected educational programs and learning-disabled children whose mental health and school achievement may have been irreversibly marred.

127

Bloom (93), as will be noted shortly, has also offered his now-famed analyses to give comfort to those who would over-stimulate young children. Even though much of what Bloom says is true, the thrust of his theory, as commonly understood, has also brought more disorder than help to early childhood education.

By contrast, Piaget's theory is rational and practical in its conception and possibilities for application. His research is easily replicated. His conclusions jibe with common sense. It is true that some have found his original research hard to understand. Yet, once correctly interpreted in terms common to most psychologists and educators, his findings collectively offer the clearest available explanation of how the young child learns. And ECE research in general systematically and overwhelmingly meshes his thinking.

Explanation of Research Confusion

The conclusion that academic achievement potential increases with age has been commonly accepted by many researchers concerned with children's learning abilities at various ages (51, 53, 243). A look at the composite research picture indeed reveals variable rates in cognitive growth, with continuous changes in the nature and organization of mental abilities (53).

Development of intelligence accelerates rapidly in the early years (51), with some stabilization of mental factors after age three or four (524, 53). Yet changes in cognitive structure and function continue to occur. Bayley (51) found evidence that intelligence is still increasing at age twenty-five.

Bayley also later (53) observed that Bloom's (93) widely accepted definition of intelligence as a unitary mental property was inadequate because it overlooked these continuous cognitive changes so clearly delineated by Piaget and others. Bloom concluded, ". . . in terms of intelligence measured at age 17, from conception to age 4 the individual develops 50% of his mature intelligence" (93). This has led to much confusion in early childhood education. Unfortunately, it has often been interpreted to mean that 50 percent of a person's actual mature or adult intelligence is developed by age four, a conclusion which Jensen (369) showed was "unwarranted and fallacious."

Whatever disagreement there may be over some of Jensen's assertions, his observation that compensatory early education does not produce lasting effects on children's IQ and achievement has strong support in research. Piaget's conception of intelligence for the preschool years, for example, agrees with Jensen's evaluation in this respect. Elkind (215), who has often replicated Piagetian experiments, finds with Piaget that there is no support for formal preschool instruction nor for contrived stimulation of intrinsic motivation.

Elkind (216) makes some further observations on Bloom's conclusions: According to Bloom's analysis, 80 percent of total growth in mental ability takes place by the age of eight, and as formal schooling progresses, the rate of mental growth declines. Indeed, the years before school are particularly important because mental growth is cumulative and depends on what has gone before. Yet children acquire primarily the *potential to learn* during these years, more than learning itself. Educators must question the need for academic instruction at this age since little if any systematic evidence supports any lasting effects of preschool instruction. Elkind (215) suggests, in fact, that a delay of three or four years in formal schooling would enable a child to profit more from instruction because of more fully developed mental abilities.

Palmer's (528) findings agree with Elkind's (216): during the years between four and six (when the children's physical growth stabilizes for awhile), rapid mental development makes this period particularly important for learning readiness. And Bayley (51) identifies yet another period of rapid intellectual development—ages nine to eleven. This later childhood spurt in mental growth has also been recognized in Piaget's theory of cognitive growth (538) and in studies of perceptual and conceptual development (211, 212, 213, 471, 724, 80).

If plasticity of intelligence accompanies a spurt in mental growth, there are at least two periods when learning proceeds rapidly—the preschool ages of four to six and the later childhood years of nine to eleven. Maturational differences, however, determine what can be learned easily and well at these two stages (538, 211, 212, 213).

The Tempo of Cognitive Growth

Achievement, then, derives from a combination of effort, ability, and experience. Quality of *effort* changes according to the child's interest or the relevance of the tasks to his needs. Quality

129

of *ability* may be changed by experience and practice. Experience can also generate interest, making it especially significant in achievement. Harlen (316) reviewed research spanning forty years of investigating development of scientific concepts in young children and concluded that the impact of experience can profoundly affect the development of thought processes. Yet he found that experience does not radically change the rate or order in which thought processes appear.

Time, in relation to cognitive growth, provides an opportunity for the maturation of physical and mental abilities. It also permits the accumulation of life experiences on which a child can build and give meaning to later academic tasks. Piaget (540) makes it clear that maturation alone is not sufficient for a child to realize the full potential of a stage.

But this growth does play a vital part in achieving cognitive abilities. According to Piaget (539), every new problem or experience provokes a disequilibrium requiring a new synthesis of previous knowledge and abilities. In other words, the child's puzzlement at a problem may imply a momentary imbalance or disorganization until he reorganizes his knowledge and experience resources into a new solution. In the regaining of equilibrium, experience can add to both knowledge and ability but not to the extent that maturation permits assimilation of the experience.

Because children in the preschool years tend to perceive things globally rather than analytically (211, 415), they are generally unable to decenter themselves and to comprehend their own motives and the feelings of others (229). They are often confused in sorting out reality and fantasy (670). While such findings are relatively common in child development research, we observe them here because such researchers as Feigenbaum, Geiger, and Crevoshay (229) and Taylor and Howell (670) have each found a definite, age-related progression of conceptual development toward higher levels as children moved out of the preschool years.

Bayley (51) notes that between the ages of five and seven there is a time of relatively stable and quiet mental activity. Then, sometime around the seventh birthday, a dramatic acceleration of cognitive growth usually begins (475), continuing for several years. This is consistent with Piaget's (538) period of concrete operations.

Bigelow (80) found that children's perceptions proceed from global to more analytical styles between the ages of five and ten. In perceiving figures independent of their field or background, elementary school children achieved a small average increase in perceptual performance from ages five to seven, but they showed a highly significant spurt ahead from ages seven to nine, with the sharpest increase at age eight.

L'Abate (415) tested Piaget's prediction of a relatively abrupt change at age seven from the global or intuitive approach to reality to the analytical or logical approach. Using a multiple-choice picture story to determine perceptual style, L'Abate tested children from kindergarten to grade five. He reported that his findings confirmed Piaget's view of cognitive change at age seven. At that age the children began showing a quality of thinking or consistency of reasoning not apparent in younger subjects.

Whiteman (724) also reported finding a significant cognitive change at approximately this same age. Children from two age levels, five to six years of age and eight to nine years of age, were interviewed to determine their conceptions of psychological causality in story situations. There was an important difference between the older and younger children in their comprehension of underlying motivation. The younger children relied on overt feelings expressed in the stories while older children perceived relationships and causes for behavior that were less obvious. The five- and six-year-olds were typically "intuitive," and the eight- and nine-year-olds were "concrete operational," in terms of Piaget's definitions.

Also consistent with these observations is Kendler's evidence (398) that the ability to control learning-related behavior changes between the second and fourth grades. Kendler studied pupils at four developmental levels (kindergarten, second grade, fourth grade, and college) to determine their ability to control their own learning behavior and to produce symbolic (i.e., abstract cause-and-effect) responses to environmental effects. The kindergarten and second-grade groups showed a rapidly rising ability to control behavior but relatively little, if any, change in producing symbolic responses.

A change in the correlation between achievement and motor abilities has also been noticed at this particular stage of development. Chissom (150) found that motor skills and coordination were significantly related to academic aptitude and achievement for first-grade boys but not for third-grade boys. This suggests that motor ability is more indicative of general maturation for younger children. Later, when motor development is less dominant and cognitive growth is in the ascendancy, motor skills became less a criterion of developmental level. After the fourth grade, when the pupils achieve almost complete control of their own learning behavior, efficiency in producing symbolic responses increases considerably (398).

Children are capable of mental tasks *before* the "dramatic acceleration of cognitive growth," which, as noted earlier from Miller (475), begins around age seven. But they appear to learn with much more difficulty and at a slower rate until this transformation occurs. Milgram and Furth (471) compared six-year-olds and nine-year-olds who were expected to conceptualize despite competing or distracting cues such as words, sounds, and actions. Reciting formulas for their work as they proceeded helped somewhat, although the six-year-olds did not profit as much from this as was expected. Nor were explanations and corrective feedback effective with six-year-olds. Nine-year-olds, however, gave clear, consistent performances, regardless of the correction devices to which they were exposed. It had been predicted that six-year-olds would profit more from these devices than the older children, but in general they could not effectively use such help no matter how much they needed it.

As already observed, the interaction of experience and maturation can modify to some extent the tempo of cognitive growth. But these modifications may merely map out different routes to the same objectives. They do not necessarily imply advantages for some and disadvantages for others. For example, in an attempt to measure intersensory communication (in this case, information perceived through seeing and manipulating objects), Conners, Schuette, and Goldman (165) compared children from low-SES and upper-middle-SES backgrounds at ages five, six, nine, and twelve. At age five social-class differences were highly significant. The low-SES children appeared definitely inferior in their perception. By the age of six, children from both social-class levels could communicate quite well a perceived shape, but not size and angle, after feeling an object out of their sight.

In the perception of size and angle there was a gradual rise for low-SES children up to the age of nine, then a leveling off to the age of twelve. There was an even more gradual rise for middle-SES children up to the age of twelve. At that time children from both social classes were again approximately equal in their perception, but the low-SES children had achieved this ability several years sooner. The orientation of low-SES children toward real, sensory-perceived objects rather than logical reasoning (699) may have made possible their more rapid rise in intersensory communication.

Birch and Lefford (84) found that although some aspects of children's ability to make intersensory judgments were well developed by school entrance age, they do not obtain full ability until the eleventh year. They noted that, at each of three age levels between five and eleven years, girls made significantly fewer errors than boys. The extent to which such differences and modifications in the progress of cognitive growth are due to psychosocial factors has not been determined, but cognitive growth does eventually override cultural factors.

Value of Induced Learning

As children's learning abilities mature, appropriate experiences for using these abilities are not always available, so that learning may be only minimal or far below potential. Providing appropriate learning experiences has been a major concern of those responsible for children's welfare.

There is evidence that training, within genetic or biological or other maturation limits, can improve intellectual functioning (52). But in summarizing the ultimate effects of programs designed to induce cognitive growth in early childhood, Bereiter (73) maintains that there really is no answer to the question "How much can the intellectual development of young children be accelerated?" Bereiter says that, although children can be taught specific things, this tells us nothing of their potential abilities.

Efforts to teach specific concepts and skills to children at a younger-than-usual age have at times been successful. Children do not usually perform operations required for logically solving complex problems until later childhood or preadolescence; yet Engelmann (222) gave preschoolers specific instruction and practice in the component skills and logical steps necessary to solve a problem. Although the disadvantaged children in the group

133

never did grasp the problems, the advantaged children learned quickly. Engelmann concluded that the ability to handle such problems was a function of training rather than development.

Similarly, with structured instruction Young (749) caused three- and four-year-olds to learn conservation concepts. Anderson (22) also managed, with bright first graders and individual training sessions, to induce rather complex problem-solving behavior. Towler (674) gave fifteen-minute training sessions for conservation problems to six- and seven-year-old children, finding they often not only learned but also retained and transferred their knowledge.

Brison (117) experimented with five- and six-year-old kindergartners to induce and accelerate acquiring the concept of conservation. With training, half of the subjects were able to understand conservation to some extent, and the induced concept appeared no different from that acquired naturally. The children, however, found it difficult to cope with demands made of them: their cognitive structures were in a state of disequilibrium.

These studies indicate that children can be trained to some extent to learn some concepts at an earlier-than-usual age. Other researchers, however, seriously question the authenticity of such training-induced early learning. Even though learning does take place, they say that it is very likely (1) to be limited in scope (179, 656); (2) to lack permanence (397, 155, 129); and (3) to be of little benefit to the child in total learning achievement (58, 396, 508, 732). Shapiro and O'Brien (613) caution also that such apparent early learning cannot be taken for granted, and Bereiter (73), once closely associated with Engelmann, questions whether the time and effort required to teach them are justified.

Much more research is needed to determine the results of early stimulation, particularly on later school life and adulthood. Additionally, the heavy financial costs, low adult-child ratios, and highly qualified specialists required by most of these early-age academic efforts make them impractical (if not impossible) for the masses—even if they were effective.

The lack of permanence in earlier-than-usual learning at times appears to be a detriment to later learning. Keister (397) found that three groups of children who learned to read before the mental age of six made normal progress during their first year. But their reading skill tended to disappear during the

134

summer months between grades one and two. This loss was *not* made up in succeeding years. The children were permanently retarded in reading after the beginning of the second grade. Mawhinney's findings (447), along with many others, strongly buttress Keister's conclusions. The potential damage of such early formal education may be the most serious deterrent of all.

Clarke (155) attributes the impermanence of early learning to a lack of continuous reinforcement or enduring experience. He suggests that it is not so much age or intensity of training as it is subsequent, consistent, persistent exposure to reinforcement that gives any permanence to early learning. At later ages learning seems to be retained without this constant repetition.

Without adequate experience and cognitive consistency, preschool-age children have often been unable to *use* the information they have been trained to *produce*. Willoughby (732) found that special training for two different methods of solving problems involving choices was not really effective until the fourth grade. Kindergartners with training performed no better than a control group without training. Second graders benefited by training for one of the methods but not the other. In this study it appeared that the manner of presenting stimuli determined the level of performance, but the ability to use information gained through training was a function of increasing age.

This same functional relationship appeared in the findings of Keislar and Stern (396). In this study mental age was a significant variable in second and third grade children's effective use of problem-solving strategies. Children in the highest mental age group were superior when taught a complex strategy. But those with a lower mental age performed better when taught a simple strategy. They lacked the ability to use the more complex strategy effectively, even when carefully taught to do so.

Nelson and Earl (508) likewise found that researchers *could* induce abilities in preschool children, who nevertheless lacked the skill to relate these abilities spontaneously to routine learning tasks. In training trials for using category questions to obtain information, the children seemed to accomplish a task with greater speed, but later testing showed they were no more efficient than children in a control group with no training. Apparently the skills a child learns must match his available conceptual abilities to produce substantial positive change in cognitive performance.

135

Regardless of training or experience, a child's developmental level places a limit on what he really *learns*. Beilin and Franklin (58) found that, in achieving ability to measure length and area, third graders received greater benefit from training and instruction than first graders. With third graders, the influence of training and instruction was minimal only in those areas where few gains were possible because concepts were already in operation. But no first grader, even *with* training and instruction, was able to measure area. The ability to profit from instruction and training in developing measurement concepts correlated with the child's developmental level, supporting the proposal of Piaget, Inhelder, and Szeminska (542) that development limits what is acquired from experience or training.

However, the three-year study of Almy et al. (14), testing the progress of early training in logical thinking, achieved divergent results. Systematic instruction in basic concepts of math and science began in kindergarten for one group of children, in first grade for another group, and in second grade for a third group. Some have conjectured that the groups may not have been comparable in all respects, for children whose prescribed lessons began in second grade performed about as well as those who had been having lessons since kindergarten, and those whose lessons began in the first grade gave the poorest performance.

Yet the second graders instructed in these concepts for the first time may have been approaching an age when they could receive greater benefit from instruction, thus learning the concepts more rapidly. In other words, they were in a state of readiness to learn without undue frustration or stress. Those whose instructions began in kindergarten might have done well because of reinforcement over a three-year period.

The difficulty children have in using what they learn in preschool and early elementary school years indicates their mode of thinking. According to Ausubel (34), elementary school children think intuitively about abstract ideas. This is characteristic of them until early adolescence. Ausubel further asserts there is no validation for the argument that younger learners achieve intellectual skills more easily than older ones. Program structure and continuity, together with diligent effort, can induce early learning skills. Yet these skills are generally not used productively until several years later.

Expanding Abilities in the
Concrete-operational Stage

As the tempo of cognitive growth moves into the seven and eleven-year-old period described by Piaget (538) as concrete operational, the child finds himself able—and eager, if he has not been discouraged—to perform new mental operations with the concepts and symbols he has been accumulating during the early childhood years. While specific training or instruction may have induced some intellectual skills relatively early, the ability to reason or think consistently, to perceive relationships, and to make logical choices appears to be a function of this later development (537). A state of readiness makes learning much easier and more rewarding.

Even verbal ability in a native language, which arises spontaneously in normal child-adult commumication and may be induced in a structured environment, cannot be forced beyond certain cognitive limits of comprehension. Basic language structures are by no means mastered by the age of five or six, as some commonly suppose (151, 526). Chomsky (151) found a surprisingly late acquisition of understanding of sentence structures. The active mastery of common structures was taking place up to the age of nine, perhaps even beyond.

Overall cognitive development is interrelated with the ability to recognize and organize the components of language (sounds, word meanings, etc.) for communication. Gradual consolidation—and therefore maturity—of language structures occurs from kindergarten up to the seventh grade. Abrupt shifts in verbal performance have been noted between kindergarten and first grade and again between grades five and seven (526), but children apparently do not master the phonological system until this later stage.

Hall (303) and Brook (121) concur. Hall found that children's ability to recognize and discriminate between word meanings increases with age, with a near-perfect performance in the fourth grade. And Brook found that children's ability to recognize the origins and arbitrary value of names continues to increase as late as age ten.

In comparing the difference between relatively "primitive" serial or rote learning and paired-associate learning, Jensen and Rohwer (370) observed a very steep gradient for paired-associate learning between the ages of seven and thirteen (for example, associating one object or number with another, such as "knife-fork," "laugh-cry"). Kindergartners learned very little by association; but, as verbal experience enriched the associative network and more verbal mediators—or associates—became available, such learning increased rapidly. Jensen and Rohwer also noted a correlation between paired-associate learning and mental age. The rise in serial learning, on the other hand, was gradual with younger children and almost nonexistent after the fourth grade (age nine). Serial learning was correlated with IQ, but did not require the cognitive development necessary for learning by association.

A similar sequence in learning was found by Williams (730) in testing children's attainment of the concept of number. Kindergarten children could recognize symbols for a number, but number operations such as addition and subtraction were evidently beyond their ability. The recognition of words and numbers is a common preschool accomplishment, but the ability to *use* these symbols in relation to each other depends on cognitive structures that continue to develop throughout the childhood years.

When O'Brien and Shapiro (519) tested the development of logical thinking, they noted the expansion of cognitive abilities, concluding that hypothetical-deductive thinking cannot be assumed until after age eight. Between the ages of six and eight children were quite successful in recognizing logical conclusions. They could identify such conclusions but apparently could not understand why they were necessary. The difficulty with logical thinking prior to this age also applies to cause-and-effect relationships (400), the concept of time (450), the use of problem-solving strategies (520), and the making of choices or decisions (83, 431).

Such a common achievement as differentiating right and left affects the formation of abstract relational concepts, according to Elkind (214), who tested children aged five to eleven for right-left discrimination. In Elkind's study children made no distinction in their concept of right and left before age seven or eight, and full differentiation was not reached until age ten or eleven. Elkind concluded that attaining this abstract concept of discrimination was a developmental measure of cognitive ability. Furth's (252) analysis of data from a nonverbal, part-whole dis-

138

crimination task shows a similar increase in ability to discriminate, with a marked decrease in errors at age ten.

This is also interesting in view of Metcalf's (466) findings that the young child's brain does not lateralize before age eight or nine.* In other words, cerebral dominance—laterality—appears agewise to coincide with Elkind's and Furth's findings on ability to discriminate.

It is the acquisition of logical thinking ability, of course, that enables a child to recognize and to conceptualize, that is, to conserve. In most cultures, for the schooled as well as the unschooled, this begins to occur consistently at about age seven (281). There is, however, some evidence that it appears later in cultures lacking explicit definitions for everyday occurrences, as with the Wolof bush people's tendency to explain changes by "action-magic" (298). In this African culture, school children were eleven or twelve years old before they acquired the ability to conserve. The ability to make appropriate explanations contributes to the development of this concept (532), and the Wolofs' magic orientation limited them.

Such delayed acquisition of conservation emphasizes the impact of experience and mental maturity on the ability to reason abstractly—to conceptualize. But Keasey and Charles (395) make it clear that experience is not a sufficient factor. A child must also reach a certain level of mental functioning before performing these logical operations. For both normal and retarded children, Keasey and Charles found that experience was no advantage without a requisite mental age.

Strauss and Langer (661) sought to induce operational thought and assessed the conservation concepts of five- and six-year-old children, both with and without training. They found a greater trend toward conservation maturity among the older children whether or not they had received the training. Whether experience comes from routine activities or from special training, the level of mental development at the time of the experience determines how easily children attain conservation.

---

*See chapter eight, *"Neuropsychological Factors in Learning,"* for a discussion of lateral dominance and the ages at which dominance for vision, handedness, etc., may be expected.

Adjustment, Attitudes, and Predictors
of School Success

Success in school is commonly associated with the ability to assimilate and use an organized body of knowledge, much of it abstract or academic in nature. Miller (474) identified eight factors in primary school children that correlated with school success. Six contributed to achievement and two detracted from it, but all factors related in some way to the child's adjustment in family interaction. Children who achieved most successfully (1) tended to like school, (2) desired an education, (3) sensed a use for school learning in the demands of some future job, (4) had confidence in themselves, (5) felt free to think and act, and (6) perceived their parents as supportive though not indulgent. Feelings of (1) parental dominance or (2) deprivation led to a lack of achievement.

While many attitudes toward school undoubtedly originate within the family, an international study of mathematics achievement (358) suggests that these attitudes are also related to the age at which a child enters school. The evidence was secured from children of twelve nations (Finland, Germany, Japan, Sweden, Belgium, France, Israel, the Netherlands, Australia, England, Scotland, and the United States). Information was obtained regarding performance in mathematics at age thirteen, attitude toward school, and age of school entry.

Austin (33) commented on the implications of this study and noted that school experience at age five had little effect on later mathematical ability but might be somewhat beneficial. School experience at age six was thought rather important, and the lack of it at age seven was termed detrimental. Rohwer's (574) ranking of the correlations in this study, however, showed that the effects noted by Austin were not statistically significant. What was significant was a strong negative correlation between school-entry age and attitude toward school. Additional years in school did *not* contribute significantly to average performance in mathematics; but the earlier children had started school, the more negative their attitudes toward school.

Huberty and Swan (353) found that predictors of successful achievement in the first grade were different for children with three years of preschool experience and for those without preschool. Without the early education experience, first-grade success depended on general readiness factors (physical and social maturity, age-related experience, etc.). Several years of preschool experience affected behavior variables so that such things as aggressiveness, cooperation, attentiveness, and communication predicted most verbal success. Developmental readiness, however, was still the most important factor for doing arithmetic and understanding paragraph meaning.

Preschool and kindergarten experience have positive effects in helping children overcome weaknesses in specific skills (motor, visual, auditory-language). According to Coffman and Dunlap (159), children who attended nursery school or prekindergarten made greater gains in these skills than those not in school, even when programs were not specifically structured for skill development. No follow-up evidence was provided, however, for the children in their school years.

A number of studies (399, 37, 290, 306, 186, 232, 28) verify, however, that both chronological and mental age relate closely to success in school. Mental age is the greater influence on achievement (232), but the younger a child is when he starts to school, the more chronological age appears to affect this progress throughout his school life (239). King (399) reports that children who entered the first grade before they were six years old failed to realize their optimum academic achievement. Cumulative records over a period of six years revealed a continued disadvantage, even though as a group they had a slightly higher IQ than those who entered school from six to nine months later. Children in the younger group were also more likely to repeat a grade.

Conclusions similar to King's were reached by Halliwell and Stein (306) when they calculated mean IQ and achievement scores in relation to chronological age for fourth graders. From their results they hypothesized that the age effect on achievement would approach zero as tests became reading oriented, and this was partially supported.

Arena (28) found that mental maturity was not only associated with academic achievement, but it also accounted for 55 percent of the total variance in achievement. And Feyberg's results (232) showed that successful school achievement in areas requiring use of concepts—such as numbers, classes, and spatial and casual relationships—correlated highly with mental age. Developing these concepts was especially associated with success in arithmetic, problem solving, and spelling.

141

As a society we attach great value to academic behavior. Parents often rate themselves as parents by the school achievement of their children. And children strive to achieve, not for the sake of learning, but for the approval and recognition of parents and teachers.

Strom (663) observed that the excessive value attached to academic achievement and the pressures to grow up and achieve earlier could be damaging to personal development. He suggests that families who want the very best for their children are often unaware of the frustration of early education: the challenges are too great, too physically taxing, and the personal relationships are based on adult approval rather than on firmly established emotional ties. Strom placed achievement and age in perspective when he observed that the only path to maturity is by way of childhood; that is, the future citizen must be a child before being an adult.

8
Neuropsychological Factors
In Learning

Synopsis. *Although there are gaps in the present state of knowledge of how to relate the research findings of experimental child psychology, education, and clinical psychology with medical findings, many neuropsychologists and neurophysiologists now are aware that structure relates closely to function in the development of the young child's brain.*

We do not yet have clear evidence that brain weight and myelination—sheathing of the nerve fibers—are significantly related to learning; yet other factors, which are more clear, indicate that indeed brain function is closely related to its structural maturation. The great cerebral commissures—connecting bands of nerve tissue—are not complete until after the age of seven. Lateral responses on the EEG in terms of cognitive activity do not stabilize before eight or nine years of age. Normal adult brain-wave patterns are not fully established until about thirteen years. The latency of response to stimulus reaches adult values at about fourteen years. (Note the conclusions of learning specialists such as Robinson, Rohwer, Elkind, and Bereiter, who suggest waiting until ages ten to fourteen, or adolescence, for formal instruction in the basic skills. See chapter thirteen and also chapters four, five, eleven, and twelve.)

Although research indicates certain sequences of brain development, we do not yet know for sure how they affect a child's learning potential in relation to age. Nevertheless, multidisciplinary research analyses in brain-related areas—visual, auditory, tactile-kinesthetic, etc.—provide clues to a relationship between maturity of the brain and learning and behavior. Vision and hearing, for example, are neuropsychological senses or processes which emerge from the brain. The eyes and ears are, in effect, extensions of the brain. Learning activities that overload these senses may therefore also produce stress of the central nervous system (CNS). For example, much close work by young children usually produces nearsightedness. There is also some support for the belief that anxiety level in school children relates to the development of myopia.

Although most children achieve hearing acuity somewhat earlier than visual maturity, the two major modalities, auditory and visual, seem to equalize in perceptual capacity or function by age nine—the age auditory perception specialists suggest for readiness in basic skill learning. Learning difficulties may arise from emphasis on new conceptual learning before a proper sensory-perceptual base is established. Moreover, a child who enters school with inadequate perceptual development may never catch up in achievement even after his perceptual processing ability is fully developed (usually by age nine). The ability to transfer information across sense modalities—vision, hearing, etc.—and to interpret this information is apparently not developed until eight years of age or later.

The weight of evidence in the neuropsychological field points to an optimum time for children's learning academic skills. This does not appear to occur until after age seven. Perceptual training does not appear to speed up this development, with the possible exception of the slow child, whom it may help to reach his highest learning potential.

Limits of Neuropsychological Research

Although research data is obviously limited respecting the bioelectrical and biochemical functions—or more simply, internal functions—of the human brain, enough human response and behavioral or external indicators exist to provide a substantial body of knowledge relating to human learning and behavior. Yet extreme caution must be observed in relating areas of perception, as indicated by externals, to what appears to occur inside the brain. Full understanding of the functions of the nervous system requires, among other factors, comprehensive knowledge of the specific chemistry of single neurons—the fundamental functional unit of nerve tissue—and of the specific connections and their localization on the neurons in various functional systems.

So we must forthrightly acknowledge the many gaps in the present status of knowledge when we attempt to relate the research findings of experimental child psychology, education, and clinical psychology with medical findings (148). This is particularly true when one is searching for evidence on neuropsychological readiness for school tasks.

Yakovlev (740) cautions "against transposing the terms and definitions of biomorphological research into the plane of pedagogical and psychological concepts and definitions"—for example, against drawing direct conclusions for education based upon brain research. Likewise, Metcalf (465) states that "it is not 'legitimate' to make a psychological or 'educational' conclusion from the physiological data." Yet Yakovlev confirms "that structural maturation of the brain appears generally consistent with Piaget's period of concrete operations."

The close relationship of structure and function in the development of the young child's brain now appears to be widely accepted among neuropsychologists and neurophysiologists. It is the interpretation of this concept that is the principal concern of this chapter.

The basic question might be posed in this way: Is there a positive or parallel relationship between the structure, maturation, and development of the brain on the one hand and academic achievement on the other? Or, presented another way, does available knowledge of the maturation and development of the brain at a certain stage in the child's life suggest his readiness to perform the tasks needed for academic learning? With available research, it is not yet safe to draw such conclusions.

Age-related Changes in Brain Development

Most of our knowledge of brain structure and function stems from the experimental study of animals. Scherer (602) concluded in general that the higher centers of young animals seem to be able to receive and treat only a relatively small amount of information per unit of time. Treatment of this small amount of information is processed in nerve circuits that function more slowly than those of adults.

Huttenlocher (360) and Ellingson and Wilcott (219) arrived at similar conclusions while investigating the brain development of kittens. Both studies indicated striking differences between neuronal activity and auditory and visual responses of young kittens and adult animals. A number of other studies are available relating the differences between immature and adult brains.

Bennett et al. (69) and Rosenzweig, Bennett, and Diamond (581) endeavored to answer the question whether experience and training of rats produced any observable anatomical and chemical changes in the brain. Bennett found that increase in weight and thickness of cortical tissue and in chemical activity of the brain related directly to the amount of environmental stimulation (enriched experience) given to the rats.

Rosenzweig and his colleagues obtained similar results but cautioned about predicting, from an experiment with rats under one set of conditions, the behavior of rats under another set of conditions. And it was "much riskier to extrapolate from a rat to a mouse to a monkey to a human." The fundamental processes of lower animals never present the same complexity of systems found in the higher animals (634). Brain changes similar to those in the rats of Bennett and Rosenzweig have been found in several species of rodents, and this appears to have given rise to the assumption that similar results occur in carnivores and primates, including man.

Studies of human development by Robinson and Tizard (572) and Tanner (668) indicate that the brain of a full-term newborn human infant is 25 percent of the weight of the adult brain, compared with a proportion of 5 percent for other organs. Only the eyes of the infant are nearer in size to adult value. By six months brain weight has increased to 50 percent of adult weight; by one year to 60 percent; 5 years, 90 percent; 10 years, 95 percent. The weight of the brain at birth is relatively constant, in spite of much variation in the body weight of infants. Unfortunately, the increase cannot yet be safely interpreted in terms of educational potential. It will be shown in the next chapter that brain weight is not significant among factors regarding mental capabilities.

The neurons are all present by 7½ months after conception, and the subsequent growth of the brain is mostly due to deposition of myelin—the neuronal sheathing—and to a vast elaboration of dendrite processes, along with a considerable increase in vascular tissue, providing for nourishment of the brain by the blood. Myelination continues at least through adolescence, and Yakovlev (740) believes that this development may continue well beyond the ages of thirty or forty. But we do not yet have clear evidence that this development of the myelin is a significant factor in learning.

146

Other factors are more clear, however. Robinson and Tizard (572), as well as Tanner (668), suggest that during the first two years after birth the appearance of function relates closely to maturational structure. Motor development—involving any muscle movement—is in advance of sensory development—vision, hearing, taste, touch, smell, etc. But by two years of age the primary sensory area has caught up with the motor area. Both sensory and motor development continue, however, for a number of years.

The nerve fibers coming from the thalamus in midbrain to the cortex—or higher reasoning centers in the frontal lobe—are not yet complete at seven years of age (741).

The reticular formation, an important arousing system—a neural network through the protoplasm that in turn is often called the physical basis of life—is not fully developed until the tenth year or later. And the great cerebral commissures—the anterior, middle, and posterior, connecting the left and right parts of the brain—are not complete until *after* the age of seven. We have yet much to learn about these and what they represent. Apparently the developmental process continues throughout life.

As development proceeds, there are progressive changes in the rhythm of brain waves (509). In newborn infants the cortical rhythm is poorly developed. As the brain develops, random low-frequency (delta and theta) waves appear, but gradually the basic rhythm becomes more regular. By six years of age the pattern is made up principally of theta waves. By the age of ten, alpha waves, characteristic of the normal adult brain, tend to predominate.

In adolescence some slow-wave activity is not uncommon and may be incorrectly interpreted if adult standards are used. An electroencephalogram (EEG) taken of infants and children is more difficult to interpret than the EEG of adults because of slow rhythms in some normal children. Such slow waves are also characteristic of adults who have become senile or who have reverted to childishness. But in normal adults the higher-frequency waves (alpha, beta, and gamma) are present in the waking state (509).

Metcalf and Jordan (467) have come to similar conclusions about the development of brain waves in children. The course of EEG development is not smooth nor clearly predictable. The rate of development changes throughout the life cycle, being rapid during the first two years and accelerating through adolescence. After adolescence the developmental trend tends to level off. There is increased variability in the individual after ages three to four. No two children are exactly the same.

By age five, according to Tanner (668), the alpha rhythm predominates in the brain waves; then from six through ages eleven to thirteen higher-frequency (alpha) waves appear more and more. This agrees with Nelson (509), who suggests that age ten brings a predominance of adultlike alpha waves. While electrical activity is present early in fetal life, children do not have a normal adult EEG pattern until about thirteen years of age (572).

The latency of the response (or interval between stimulation and response) of a newborn infant is remarkably long compared to an adult, or even to an infant of ten weeks, at which age the adult latency has almost been reached. This sounds much like the animal findings of Sherer, Huttenlocher, and others. The duration of the responses increases throughout childhood, with particularly rapid changes in the first four months. Adult values of response duration are reached at about fourteen years of age (572).

Although EEG responses do show differences with further development and maturation, little is yet known regarding their implications for educators. Any definitive attempt to do so—that is, to overstate our evidence—is likely to confuse rather than clarify the situation.*

The development of laterality, or the performance of cognitive tasks by a specific hemisphere of the brain, is also an age-related function. Metcalf's findings (465, 466) suggest that although lateral changes in the EEG are present very early in life (according to some, during infancy, which Metcalf did not confirm), lateral responses on the EEG in terms of specific cognitive activity do not stabilize until around eight or nine years. Furthermore,

---

*Here we have an illustration of a key ECE principle. The state of the science—ECE—is such that often the synergic effect of the data becomes more informative than any one basic scientific fact. In other words, if we take sound evidence from many ECE areas and interrelate them as objectively as possible, the sum of the evidence will likely be far more accurate and convincing than if we rely on massive evidence from any one area of ECE research alone. This is the essential philosophy of this book. Watch carefully as we attempt to interrelate a number of facets in the otherwise obscure area of neuropsychology and in the next chapter, of neurophysiology.

many aspects of the EEG do not stabilize until after nine years of age, and even during the nine- to fourteen-year-old period there is much EEG instability.

The development of lateral dominance in the brain is evident in perceptual-motor functions. They become more precise as age increases. For example, the eye-hand coordination subtest of the Frostig test yielded scores suggesting this skill is still developing through the teen years (116).

As far as we yet know, no significant relationship exists between the emergence of lateral dominance and intelligence (332). Nor is it clear that the establishment of consistent right- or left-handedness has any beneficial effect on learning to read (41). But while lateral dominance does not seem to affect reading ability, retarded readers do have difficulty in distinguishing right from left in their own bodies and in right-left awareness (82). Such difficulties are more likely a result of poor neurological development (443).

Brain Function and Intellectual Achievement

Tanner (668) suggests that fluctuations in IQ must certainly reflect differences in mental-ability development rates that correlate with differences in rate of brain development. Whether experience or stimulation can accelerate brain maturation, or whether the course of brain development in itself, if speeded up, can result in easier performance of school tasks, are questions no one can answer simply. Metcalf (465) says that they must be "answered in terms of the resultants of complex interactions, of experiential, developmental and maturational factors."

Here again sound research indicates the sequences of brain development. The question is, How does this affect a child's learning potential in relationship to his age? And the answer is, Although some do speculate, we actually do not know. The best answers to this question are probably found from a combination of (1) research and experimentation in learning (including readiness); (2) comparisons of age and achievement (including comparative school entrance age studies); (3) factors relating to vision, hearing, intersensory perception; (4) research in reading; and (5) the child's relation to his parents and others who importantly influence his security and stability. These are more fully discussed elsewhere in this book. The synergic effect resulting from this multidisciplinary approach may offer some clues to the brain's secrets respecting the relationship of its maturity to learning and behavior.

Perceptual training can help a child who is lagging developmentally to perform at his highest potential, but it seems unlikely that perceptual training actually speeds up development (16). General health (618), including nutrition, probably has a great effect on neurological development and resulting intellectual performance. Cravioto, DeLicardie, and Birch (171) have suggested that malnutrition delays neurointegrative development. A delay in mental growth interferes more with achievement in learning than does the general social background of a child, according to Milgram and Ozer (472), who studied the effects of neurological and environmental factors on language development with a group of Head Start children during the summer of 1965.

Visual Perception*

Visual perception is a broad-based neuropsychological process; that is, it involves the brain as well as the eye (412). Even though a single, clear visual image may be received by the eye, a child still may not be able to decode printed material because of deficiencies in organization and interpretation in the central nervous system (CNS) due to lack of maturation. Though it is generally accepted that the human eye is as fully functional as the adult's at birth, many other factors affect overall vision— from the differences in plasticity due to age and the developmental advancement of the visual cortex and other related CNS factors.

Development of the eye itself corresponds somewhat with that of the nervous system as a whole. During the first three years of life the eye increases in size (572), but there is no drastic change in refraction (752). Then there is a clear visual progression from 3 to 7½ years of age, with visual perception disabilities virtually disappearing after the age of ten (251). By the age of thirteen or fourteen the eye has reached its maximum growth (752).

---

*When we are dealing with the perception senses (visual, auditory, etc.) we do not only refer to seeing and hearing as such, but also and more largely to visual and auditory *perception*—the child's relating to his environment what he sees and hears or the meaning he brings to what he sees and hears, as well as how these meanings in turn enrich his life through the concepts they afford as he develops.

Animal studies indicate that the visual system of the brain develops later than the auditory (219). Work with young children seems to bear this out. The results of a study by Stevenson and Siegel (657) suggest that children in the primary grades are more responsive to auditory materials. At the time when most children enter school, the visual-perceptive mechanisms are still incomplete, compared to the development of adult mechanisms (203).

Nearsightedness (myopia) is frequently the result of prolonged looking at near objects at an early age (752). Young children and young monkeys are normally distant-vision creatures. In studies with monkeys, Young (750, 751) found they developed myopia when kept in a restricted visual environment. Young et al. (753) reported a study of Eskimo families in Barrow, Alaska, after Alaska became a state and required schooling for its children. Up to 58 percent of these children had myopia, whereas both parents and grandparents showed virtually no myopia. It might be concluded that the children's myopia relates to the closed-in environment characteristic of school attendance, since other conditions remained virtually constant and education in Alaska had *not* been compulsory for the older generations. Ludlam (437) concurs with Young's findings on early myopia. He found that while the cornea is fully developed at birth, growth of other parts of the human eye continues to the age of nine to eleven. He strongly suggests that reading earlier than the sixth or seventh year is often responsible.

The hypothesis that the development of myopia is related to anxiety level also has some support (662). In a study of visual changes occurring in public school children, the incidence of myopia decreased as desirable changes were made in the school program. These program changes related to developmental placement of children and tended to reduce stress, since the children were developmentally ready to do the work expected. In 1970, at the start of the study, 19 percent of the sixth graders in this school were myopic; in 1971, 27 percent were myopic. In 1974 sixth graders who had enjoyed the advantages of the program changes showed a significant decrease in myopia.

These studies show that myopia cannot be ascribed to heredity. It is more a matter of adjusting vision to near objects over a period of time. It can occur in later life as well as childhood, but with adults the strain is on the lens, not the immature and plastic eyeball as in childhood. A U.S. Navy study (457) found that experienced submariners had more myopia than submarine school candidates or Navy divers or similar groups, ascribing it to the fact that the submariners had to accommodate or adjust their vision to shorter distances for longer periods than the other groups.

These recent findings support the observations that Hilgartner (330, 331), an opthalmologist, made from clinical data he and his father accumulated in Texas over more than fifty years. His records show that in 1910 there were 7.7 cases of farsighted children to 1 nearsighted child. By 1935 this ratio was 1.8 normal farsighted children to 1 nearsighted child. By the mid-1950s, before television was common to most homes, there were about two abnormal-visioned children to each normal-sighted child. And by 1962 Hilgartner reported a ratio of one farsighted child to five nearsighted children! He recently reported to us that in recent years he was having difficulty finding any normal-visioned school children around the ages of ten to twelve.

These changes in ratio of hyperopes (farsighted) to myopes (nearsighted) correspond to the progressive lowering of school entrance age laws in Texas since 1910—shortly after Texas lowered its school entrance age from eight to seven. About 1930 the age was further lowered to six. Hilgartner suggested that the accommodation, or adjustment of the eyes to restricted areas in schoolwork and more recently to television, may have been a factor in these changes. Newton (511) supported Hilgartner's findings and noted that myopia still seems to be increasing. It is so serious, in fact, that some eye specialists, resigned to earlier schooling, are refracting preschoolers to prevent myopia!

Visual and visual-perceptual deficits are frequent among elementary school children. Coleman (161) reported that half of the children in a sample from grades one through six had visual, visual-perceptual, or refractive errors, with 70 percent of these visual problems among boys—who are generally considered to lag behind girls in developmental maturity.

Buktenica (132) concluded that the child's development of visual skills is directly influenced by inborn tendencies, physical characteristics, and environmental factors. Both environmental and developmental factors were emphasized by Frostig, Lefever, and Whittlesey (251), who pointed out a connection between

152

disabilities in visual perception and poor classroom adjustment at lower age levels.

Further study is needed to determine what relationship actually exists between developmental age, visual demands made on children, and concomitant vision problems. Yet enough is now known to suggest caution about placing young children in programs requiring formal study before the ages of eight or nine.

Auditory Acuity and Perception

Auditory perception is similarly a broad-based neuropsychological process. The development of auditory perception is also a function of age, but most children evidently achieve it somewhat earlier than visual maturity (445, 657). While the development of visual perception proceeds through later childhood and into early adolescence, satisfactory auditory perception and discrimination of sounds is usually acquired by the eighth birthday (714).

From five to eight years of age, Impellizzeri (365) noted a consistent increase in auditory perceptual ability, along with an apparent relationship between physical maturation and success on the auditory perception test. Similarly, third graders could interpret and order auditory stimuli more readily than first graders (567). The younger children could distinguish amplitude, or loudness and softness, but had difficulty in the discrimination of frequencies, or high and low pitch.

Riley et al. (568) observed that first graders did not respond to frequency of sound in the same sense as they did to amplitude, nor in the same sense as did older children. All the children performed more accurately with amplitude problems than with frequency problems, but the older children were superior to the younger children.

According to the developmental capacities of children, training in perceptual discrimination has also been productive. Although some deprived children have very low auditory discrimination ability, specific training along with social and verbal interaction effectively improved this ability (660). More on auditory perception follows in the discussion of intersensory factors below.

153

Intersensory Perception and Integration

Birch and Lefford (84) studied the relationships among visual, haptic, and kinesthetic sense modalities. For geometric-form recognition, they found the ability to make various intersensory judgments well developed by school entrance age—which for most of the United States is officially age seven, but in practice age six. However, full effectiveness in using intersensory information comes later.

Wepman (715) examined the early progress of children as they developed the capacity to utilize their maturing neurological systems, concluding that maturation and development of the neural system is "hierarchical, yet interrelated." He defined *maturation* as the establishment of the neural components necessary for sensory transmission and integration, as well as for motor transmission of signals within the nervous system. He defined *development* as the functional adaptation of an established neural pathway. In a time-bound progression the neural system builds each succeeding layer upon previously developed layers, both in the sense of maturation and of development. Insofar as we know, it parallels the physiological maturation of the central nervous system. Here we have an example of function moving with structure.

Wepman's findings may be summarized in this way: Each person has a particular modality of choice in learning—auditory, tactile, or visual. Thus, different children use separate input pathways. In effect the child chooses one of the senses as his own principal learning agent. Take, for example, the one who subconsciously chooses his sense of hearing as the primary pathway: such an audile child not only matures earlier in an auditory sense, but also develops his mature auditory pathway with greater ease than other children. This modality distinction seems more a result of innate capacity than environmental factors. Wepman found no specific lack of stimulation in the homes or environments of children with poor auditory learning or, for that matter, poor visual or tactile-kinesthetic learning. The children came from all types of homes.

Wepman further indicated that constructive use of a neural pathway helps it develop and become completely functional at an earlier age than it otherwise could. Usually, the modality showing the most rapid development indicates the child's pre-

154

dilection, or "choice." Thus some children are predominantly hearers, some seers. But the two major modalities—auditory and visual—seem to equalize in function by the age of nine. By then children overcome whatever sensory developmental lags have been present.

Many children with learning problems use one such pathway more easily than another. For example, their transmission of auditory signals may be good while visual or tactile signals are poorly transmitted. To ascertain the effect of this modality preference on learning, researchers must isolate the preferred modality (auditory or visual) to assess the level of achievement and the potential for special training of whatever modality is developmentally delayed. Visual-motor and motor-kinesthetic pathways need equal attention, according to Wepman. Children who are slow at developing any of their perceptual skills, regardless of modality, will find learning difficult. For these are the principal avenues open for learning.

Wepman distinguishes between two kinds of learning: the perceptual, prelinguistic, preoperational learning (sensory-motor) and the more complex, conceptualizing learning, with comprehension and intent. However, *learning difficulties may arise from emphasis on new learning at the conceptual level before a proper perceptual base has been established.* This is a serious, common danger in primary schools, kindergarten, or other preschool. At the beginning stages of learning, teachers must give attention to the perceptual level in order to develop a basic structure for later learning at the conceptual level—if optimum achievement is expected.

Most of us would agree that problems cannot normally be solved without basic facts. Yet children are often expected to do exactly this: to learn conceptually (with comprehension and intent, reasoning from cause to effect, etc.) before they have developed the modalities or agents of perception (auditory, visual, and tactile-kinesthetic) necessary for comprehension. Educators can identify maturing perceptual levels by the progressive achievement of skills such as discrimination, retention, recall of sounds and letters, sequential ordering of phonemes and graphemes, and the ability to interrelate one thing with another. Wepman concludes that this ability to form minimal contrasts is still developing in most children through the eighth year.

Morency (498) observed that perceptual abilities develop significantly during the first three years of schooling, progressing individually along lines of the sensory (auditory, visual, tactile-kinesthetic) preference at differing rates in the same individual. Improvement continues to occur in both auditory and visual perceptual ability from the first to the third grade. If the child has perceptual difficulties at the beginning of school, they will likely influence the level of school achievement somewhat for the next three years. Wepman (715) came to a similar conclusion.

Morency (498) also noted that the developmental level of the various senses is crucial for successful early learning and school achievement. She and Wepman observed that perceptual readiness strongly influences later school achievement (499). And generally the child who enters school with inadequate perceptual development never catches up in achievement even *after* his perceptual processing ability is fully developed, which usually occurs by the age of nine.

According to Morency (498), most children in elementary school learn by any method that is used. But there are always a few children who may not be ready for academic learning because one or more of the perceptual pathways is not sufficiently developed. With such perceptual deficits, she notes, learning is difficult. Grouping children into "hearers" and "seers" can result in more efficient teaching and less frustrated learning, since the modality that functions most adequately may be used to support cognitive learning (499).

A poorly developed modality may be improved through special training if its function is less than its developmental potential (16). However, by age eight or nine, hearing (498, 715) and, between ages ten and fourteen, vision (251) have reached their full development. Then both training and learning can proceed unimpeded by developmental deficits.

When a child has lacked opportunities to use his perceptual capacities or has become apathetic, stimulation and training can arouse his latent abilities. Rosner (582) identified the perceptual skills needed to prepare for reading and arithmetic, concluding that they can be taught to young children. Such training can be most rewarding for a child when he learns to use perceptual skills of which he is developmentally capable. But struggling to acquire skills beyond his developmental level can be extremely frustrating and discouraging.

156

Rosner suggested that, for competent school performance, visual-motor skills should indicate an ability to analyze and organize visual data according to spatial attributes, to see specific visual patterns against larger and more complex patterns. Auditory-motor skills should indicate an ability to hear specific sounds and accoustical patterns extracted from the larger auditory environment. Rosner (583) found highly significant relationships between auditory perception and primary reading achievement, as well as between visual perception and primary arithmetic achievement. He concluded that auditory perception may be more important than visual perception for learning to read.

Other researchers have noted increased learning abilities when cross-modal communication develops (261, 57, 588). The ability to experience an object through seeing or feeling precedes the ability to speak the name of the object. Then, after experiencing the object through the senses and hearing the sound of the name, a child can more easily decode the printed word (261).

This ability to transfer information across sense modalities apparently is inadequately developed in preschool and kindergarten children. Jessen and Kaess (376) gave three- and five-year-old children visual and visual-haptic (eye-hand) experiences with various complex shapes, then requiring them to identify the shapes by sight or feel. The children performed more accurately on visual tests than on haptic, but they gave almost no evidence of cross-modal matching.

By the age of six this development of haptic-visual transfer seems to be relatively complete for identification of shape. However, the ability to interpret information about the size and orientation of figures develops more gradually (165). By age eight children achieve a highly differentiated sense of touch and are able to judge the sensory quality of a multidimensional object (410).

Thus, maturity in intersensory integration is a distinct advantage in learning. Yet it is evidently not the only or even the primary skill responsible for improved achievement with increasing age (689). Instead, total readiness—physical, social, and mental—maximizes and strengthens learning achievement involving perceptual processes.*

*See chapter five on the integrated maturity level (IML).

9
Neurophysiology: Development of the Brain and Learning

Synopsis. Even with much research over the past half-century, there is yet a great deal to understand about the development and function of the central nervous system (CNS). Learning must not be confused with physiological development; nevertheless, we know and can clearly state some facts helpful to the parent, psychologist, and educator.

The CNS is not structured to mature as a single unit or organ, but rather as a complex interworking of many highly sophisticated lesser elements. Each separate functional area has its own timing and sequence of development. Furthermore, and importantly, the structure and the function of the human brain appear to move along together in the developmental process. Yet the sheer limitations of brain research suggest caution, as, for example, in relating increased brain weight to increased mental capacity and in relating other brain development sequences, such as myelination—or sheathing of the nerve fibers—to learning and education.

At birth the brain is about one-quarter of the adult weight, possessing virtually all its brain cells and all major brain regions. By six months its weight has doubled, but hereafter growth slows down; from two years until adolescence it is relatively uniform. The posterior area (visual-sensory function) appears more developed than the anterior area (emotional and cognitive functions), but after age two the frontal lobe accelerates in its growth and by age six is equal in area to that of an adult. The brain continues to grow in mass until twenty-five years of age, but maturation of the parts of the nervous system is not necessarily uniform throughout this growth period.

The maturation of the central nervous system at the cellular level is not clearly understood. We do know that the motor system develops first, fol-

159

lowed by the sensory system, but the precise mechanisms controlling developmental sequence are not known.

Progression in the bioelectrical activity of the brain is similar. Functional capabilities are staggered along maturation lines of development. Thus, the anatomic or structural state of maturation dictates in part the emergence of brain function. Studies relating to development of brain bioelectrical activity are important because they provide significant correlates with brain maturation and behavioral development.

Specific developmental differences are noticeable between the varying conscious states of the child and the adult. It is known that at about the ninth year the electroencephalograph (EEG) record in the posterior brain region is essentially like that of an adult. The frontal region reaches the adult level at about the fourteenth year, and all cortical areas reach it after nineteen years. Yet more longitudinal studies involving electrical patterns of developing children are obviously needed.

Some suggest that simple reflexes provide the behavioral substrate for all our activities. This is simplistic, to say the least. The orderliness and careful time sequences during neural development, together with complex biochemical influences, produce an immensely complex brain capable of diverse actions throughout the body.

The duration of neural development is variable. Often it does not appear to proceed in a smooth fashion. Eventually neural linkage occurs between the major brain systems; once maturation of the neurons is complete, brain "plasticity" emerges. Learning is one aspect of this so-called plasticity. But we now know only a little about the brain mechanisms involved in learning or memory storage. Perhaps the brain is more modifiable by environmental conditions than previously thought; considerable evidence shows that the effects of learning can last a long time. There is doubt, however, that much learning can occur without motivation and reward. And in brain development it is difficult to separate the nature and extent of genetic control from behavioral-cultural influence.

Based upon the neurobiological framework of brain development as presently known, it would be wrong to establish some precise cut-off point defining the brain as fit or unfit for learning.

We are only at the threshold of understanding brain growth and maturation. Yet it is apparent both from educational studies on how children learn and from our understanding of brain maturation that improved technology may not necessarily improve or accelerate intellectual growth. First, the child must achieve brain maturation appropriate to the learning task.

Since CNS structure and function move along pretty much together, it is tempting to guess at developmental ratios between brain development and

160

academic educability. But research generally cannot yet verify such conclusions. However, sufficient available data exist to suggest caution in mandating academic or academic-readiness schooling for children under eight years of age.

There are qualitative breaks in the unfolding of intelligence and conscious experience. From our current understanding of brain development, these follow the growing capacity to process simultaneously multisensory information. Replicable research evidence suggests this capacity is not fully accomplished until about eight to ten years of age or even later (See chapters seven, eight, and eleven.)

Limits of Neurophysiological Research

Few intellectual problems we face are as important or baffling as understanding the human brain. Some consider it the ultimate scientific challenge confronting mankind (207). Although we have many remarkable treatments for behavioral distortions and defects and malfunctions by the brain, we still face many unknowns about this incredibly complex base of our central nervous system. Yet generally we have given inadequate attention to neurophysiological immaturity—uneven maturation of perceptual motor activity—so that we have not fully been aware of the handicaps these visual, auditory, and intersensory lags pose to the young learner.

As the neurosciences expand, many problems are solved but many more questions press forward on this overwhelming intellectual frontier. New scientific approaches and disciplines emerge to challenge these questions. The neurosciences have grown vigorously in the last hundred years. Despite this growth, the origin of the nervous system and each developing sequence is a dramatic mystery. Influences promoting the wiring and interactions of brain cells during the span of life are beyond our direct observations. Research provides only a glance or a small window to view these events. Because researchers must often investigate animal species other than man, their results can relate only tentatively to what we know about our own capabilities for brain performance.

Neurophysiologist Paul Yakovlev concurs with psychologist Jean Piaget in stating that *"learning* should not be confused with

161

development." Development to them is a universal property to all species, whereas learning is a "species specific, yet highly individual, particular function, which is in constant change and evolution"(740).

Yakovlev also agrees with other neuroscience specialists (neruophysiology, neurochemistry, neuropathology, neuropsychology, etc.) in saying that the state of the art allows only the most limited application of neurophysiological research to education and related behavior. Says Yakovlev, as noted in the last chapter, "In all due candor, I would caution against transposing the terms and definitions of biomorphological research into the plane of pedagogical and psychological concepts and definitions" (740).

On the other hand, there are some things we do know and can state clearly regarding the human brain—many of them taken from experimental research on humans and many from those animals which have characteristics similar to specific human structure and/or functioning.

Neurophysiologists appear reasonably certain, for instance, that the human brain is not structured to mature as a single unit or organ, but rather as a complex interworking of many highly sophisticated lesser elements, each separate area of functioning having its own timing and sequence of development. Overall maturation progresses according to this sequence from conception throughout life. Yakovlev says that it has "an arbitrary 'beginning,' but no definable end ... and is *never* complete" (740).

Also, the development of structure and of function in the human brain appears to move along together. The two are quite directly related. It seems, then, that functions must develop and mature as the basic necessary structures mature. For example, the learning of reading at first involves a distinct process of decoding. This, in turn, requires the child to establish visual-verbal association, as Rudel and Denckla (587) point out, in one (or both) of the following ways: (1) assigning speech sound equivalents to each letter or diphthong and framing these into a word with which the child is familiar or (2) using whole sight words which are matched with spoken words. These visual-spoken language processes or pathways from visual areas to language areas of the brain are usually relatively late in maturing, although timing varies widely from individual to individual (262). See also chapter six on "Readiness for Reading."

Limitations of brain research suggest a further cautionary note: It is neither appropriate nor accurate to think of increases in brain weight as indicators of increased mental capacity. Similarly, other brain development sequences (that to the behaviorist and the educator might appear to relate brain development and maturation directly to learning and education) are also inappropriate and misleading. An example of such a sequence is the progression of myelination.

In spite of these restrictions and lack of knowledge, some achievements are exciting to the student who attempts to understand the neurophysiological bases of learning. It is the objective of this chapter to briefly recapitulate some of these research findings. This chapter will attempt to answer these questions: How does the human brain mature in structure, or neuromorphology, and in functional capabilities? Can we identify in the life of a child (a period of dramatic brain maturation) optimal time frames for academic achievements related to the neurophysiological substrates of development?

Gross Changes in the Brain during Maturation

At birth the average brain weight for a full-term infant is less than one pound (340 grams), or about one-quarter of the adult weight. All major brain regions—such as frontal, parietal, temporal, and occipital lobes that will later support sensory, motor, and other complex functions—are apparent. But the posterior aspects (visual-sensory function, visual projection area) appear more developed than the anterior ones (prefrontal areas concerned with emotional control and other cognitive functions—related to limbic lobe involved in the basic patterns of behavior). At birth the brain also possesses virtually all of its brain cells, or neurons. With development and growth the neurons enlarge, becoming more expansive in their connections, and supporting elements multiply.

By six months the weight has about doubled (660 grams) in mass, and the convolutions are deepening toward the mature state. The frontal lobe has enlarged somewhat from birth by this time, but major growth is still taking place at the posterior or occipital brain areas. The white zone below the cortical mantle has become more distinct. At twelve months the brain

163

weighs an average of 925 grams and shows considerable depth and enlargements of the cerebral convolutions. Thereafter, the brain mass shows a slower growth rate. For instance, the average brain of a two-year-old child weighs about 1064 grams. At this period of maturation (two years) the brain is much firmer than in preceding stages and the color of the cortical mantle is darker.

From age two until adolescence the growth of the brain is relatively uniform and without dramatic spurts, although girls gain slightly more brain mass than boys for the first three years of life (3). After about two years of age the frontal lobe begins to accelerate in growth, and by the age of six this area is about equal to that of adults (554). The brain continues to grow in mass until the age of twenty-five years; but, as indicated above, the maturation of the nervous system is not uniform in all brain parts throughout this growth period. For example, the brain stem is one of the first parts of the nervous system in the human embryo to begin proliferation. The cerebellum develops later.

The brain stem supports vital functions, such as heart and respiration, while the cerebellum, or little brain, is involved in coordinating skilled motor movements. Also, within the brain cortex variations of development exist from birth throughout the formative periods. In general, areas concerned with body sensations, vision, hearing, and volitional motor control mature early. But frontal and temporal aspects involving speech, complex recognition of sensory patterns, and so on are later to mature.

Even when a child is born premature by several months, he must await an elapsed CNS development time equal to his prematurity. Premature birth does *not* accelerate brain development. As there is no multiplication of neurons after birth, the increasing brain is the result of progressive enlargement of existing structures and other cellular supportive elements.

Microscopic Changes Associated with Brain Development

The progressive maturation of the nervous system at the cellular level is relatively poorly understood. The process begins at about the fourth week after conception by neuroblasts located in the neural tube. By the eighth week of gestation simple somatic or body movements begin, but by this time the basic organization of the reflex arc has been present for one or more weeks.

In general, the intrinsic nervous elements are laid down in the embryo in a precise manner, and the sequence of development follows the pattern revealed by functional capabilities—namely, the motor or *efferent* system develops first, followed slightly later by the sensory or *afferent* systems. Intrinsic connections between the frontal lobes and deeper brain structures, for example in the brain stem, are only beginning to emerge when the human embryo first shows reflex motions such as avoidance reactions (355). The order of development is rigorously controlled by the order and sequence of migrating and forming elements of the brain. These precise controlling mechanisms are not known. However, cells in the reticular—neural network—formation appear reasonably mature at birth.

In the postnatal period there is progressive elaboration of the axonic and dendritic trees—trunk and branches—of the growing neurons. These expanding processes are very important in establishing the neuron connections for handling electrical events in the nervous system at a later time. They have been examined in man (551) and in other animal species (516). The results are as follows: Apical growth—apex or tip—of the dendrite precedes basal dendritic growth. Synapses, the interfaces from one neuron to another, are established first on the apical dendrites (604), followed later by synapses being established on basal dendrites and the cell soma, or body. Apparently it is important in the sequence of developing synaptic contacts between neurons that apical dendrites appear first, followed later by the growth and elaboration of the basal dendrites.

In some cell structures, such as the caudate or taillike nucleus, it is rare to observe synaptic contacts with neuron regions close to the cell soma even in the adult. Furthermore, neurons in deep structures of the brain mature earlier than superficial neurons of the cortex, so that one can describe the maturation of the brain as it procedes up the neural axis. The dendrite pattern of the neurons begins to approach that of the adult by about two years of age, but the numbers and complexities of these patterns are still considerably fewer than in the adult.

Only a few axons are present at birth. Those that are course tangentially to the cortical surface. The great bridge of connecting fibers between the cerebral hemispheres in the corpus callosum—or body of the brain—are only partially developed at birth. As development continues, myelination of the axons fol-

165

lows the ontogenetic—or life history—course of brain maturation. The greatest degree of lipid formation is in the brain stem, followed by the cerebral hemispheres, with the cerebellum coming in near the last (333). Prior to myelination the immature axons are ensheathed by an outer sleeve of Schwann cells encompassing the bundle of naked axons (534).

As the axons enlarge in diameter, they conduct action potentials at higher velocities from one place to another in the nervous system. Finally, the axon diameter increases beyond a critical level; then myelin is formed around the individual axons with greater cellular industry.

The formation of central myelin is complex, but the effect of myelination is to benefit conduction of electrical impulses more efficiently and with greater speed and reliability. The general morphological features in the immature brain can be substantiated by concordant bioelectrical activity. In fact, most early research on the maturation of the nervous system originated in searching for ontogenesis—or origin and operational development—of electrical activity in the early brain.

Bioelectricity in the Immature Brain

Histological development of the brain can be closely followed by significant changes in cortical electrical changes. In the kitten brain, for example, cortical activation by peripheral nerve stimulation results in a surface-negative evoked response. (The surface of the brain is negative; deep, it is positive.) Apparently this results from synaptic activation of apical dendrites in the cortex, of neurons that do not have well-formed basal dendrites (601, 552). Correlative studies are necessary before more intimate understanding between maturation processes and physiological functions is available. However, immature neurons, in contrast to adult cells, generally have lower firing frequencies (209, 362, 633), have longer-lasting hyperpolarization (inhibition) (209), are slower to conduct impulses (634), and have longer latency responses (602). All of these electrical properties have the effect of *reducing* the amount and velocity of impulse traffic in the central nervous system.

Functional capabilities in the brain are staggered along maturation lines of development. For instance, Marty and Scherer (445) have demonstrated in the cat that somesthetic (tactile) sensibility in the forelimb (e.g., sense of touch in the paw) precedes the auditory system, which precedes functional maturation of the visual system. Presumably the same phenomenon is true also for man, since cortical development in man essentially follows these same patterns. *In other words, the anatomic state of maturation dictates the functional emergence of brain function.* For instance, the long latency for response in the immature brain is largely explained by the smaller diameter of the nerve fiber and general absence of myelination.

Other factors may also play a role in slowing the response time in the immature brain. *The consequence is that the sensory message to the brain, as well as the motor reaction over a reflex pathway, will take longer in a very young person than in an adult.* If the cerebral cortex is involved in any part of this reaction, the process will take even longer. Therefore, a young person does not possess a nervous system ensuring rapid response to many events within his sensory world—in contrast to the adult. As brain maturation takes place, these differences become less observable.

Other electrical aspects may also be important. Cortical-evoked responses in neonatal animals show pronounced fatigability (602). While the term is not very precise in identifying possible cortical mechanisms, it essentially means that there is a reduction in cortical response when afferent—sensory—stimulations are repeated often over short intervals. We do know that the efficiency of energy metabolism in the neonate—newborn or less than a month old—is smaller than in the adult (334), and undoubtedly the supply of energy sets the upper limits for conducting repeated stimulations to the brain.

Refractory periods—the time intervals between successes in transmitting impulses in the neuron chains—are also considerably longer in the immature brain than in the adult, or they are essentially less able to process neural events or input and output at higher speeds. These factors probably account for age changes in functional capabilities and in spontaneous electroencephalographic activity of the maturing brain. *Studies relating the ontogenesis of brain bioelectrical activity are important because they provide significant correlates with brain maturation and behavioral development.*

The Electroencephalogram of the Developing Brain

Considerable evidence exists that immature fibers can conduct electrical impulses before they are ensheathed by myelin. Some suppose, in fact, that the additional CNS processing capabilities acquired through development of various motor and sensory skills constitute no small demand for myelination to take place. As the progress of maturation marches on, with proliferation of neuron processes and synaptic interconnections, cerebral functions become increasingly complex. With this maturation, the emergence and differentiation of the electroencephalogram (EEG) seem to reflect the complex maturation changes taking place in underlying brain tissue.

Some of the earliest studies of brain development focused on the ontogenesis of electrical activity. One of the first EEG recordings from the immature brain was made by Hans Berger (78). Since then extensive literature has been directed to understanding the developmental EEG in childhood (271).

At birth the EEG consists of irregular low-voltage waves alternating with periods of isoelectricity—of generally equal potential—when very little or no activity occurs. At this early stage it is very difficult to observe sleep-wakefulness EEG patterns that emerge later in life and are so distinct to various conscious states (218). For example, the problem of identifying sleep or wakefulness in the neonate is considerably more difficult than in the adult. Spindle-burst activity—sharp, spindlelike tracing on the EEG—that occurs just before and during slow-wave sleep does not begin until about the second month after birth.

During this early period the altered states of consciousness also seem much different in comparison to those of the adult because the cycling mechanisms in the brain stem for awake and asleep are not as well developed. A rapid-eye-movement (REM) type of sleep is almost continuous and uninterrupted during the first few months after birth, even when the child is crying or engaging in other activities (220).

With each passing week during the early part of the infant's life, the EEG changes. These changes are irregular and diverse in the same person, as well as across individuals related by age. For example, at birth the parietal area is more active than other parts of the brain,* but by the sixth month the posterior or occipital lobe is usually more active than other brain areas (635).

The irregular slow-wave activity in the neonate increases in

*The complete significance of this is not clear, but it does show that development occurs from the core of the brain stem outwards.

frequency until by the first year the EEG is typically 5 to 8 Hertz (Hz.). At this time the EEG arousal pattern is clearly different from the asleep pattern. The frequencies steadily increase each year until the fourth, when the occipital record is 7 to 8 Hz.

By about the ninth year the EEG record in the posterior brain region (occipital pole or visual cortex) is essentially like that of the adult. The trend toward higher frequencies is still progressing in the frontal aspects (concerned with emotional control and other cognitive function), and it is not until about the age of fourteen that adult records are established with consistency. After nineteen years most individuals have normal adult EEG activity in all cortical areas (167, 271, 509).

In the awake individual, developmental EEG changes are generally from slower frequencies and higher voltages to faster and more complex wave-form patterns. The prognostic value of the EEG in early life is relatively limited in identifying subtle abnormal brain development. Persisting isoelectric EEGs in children beyond a few weeks old indicate a very serious clinical problem, and hyperactive tracings may herald major malformations of the cortex (485).

So-called moderately abnormal EEG in children is not reliable for diagnostic purposes since many normal children show certain types of paroxysmal activity in the form of sharp waves and spikes during childhood. These intermittent electric phenomena generally tail off after the age of fourteen years (535).

Longitudinal studies involving electric patterns in developing children across time together with increased penetration into the meaning of brain electrical activity, are obviously needed. Also, researchers need to relate structural counterparts of electrophysiology more tightly to these broadly defined neuroelectric data. Until the EEG is better defined, information from complex neuronal systems is elusive. The statistical methods involving pattern recognition have not in general been applied to analyzing or validating the developmental patterns observed in the maturing brain (690).

Determinants of Neural Plasticity

Many experts believe that some kind of functional pressure determines the shaping of neural ensembles that will eventually form the adult's organization and behavioral constructs. Also, formation of the neural nets supporting a behavioral task seems to start as a fundamental reflex and expand as the elementary response emerges and encompasses more and more complexities. In other words, simple reflexes provide the behavioral substrate of all our activities.

On the surface this postulate seems plausible, but it is too simplistic. It is true that commitment of the neural mass in the developing nervous system is not only intrinsically determined, but is also influenced by demands from peripheral devices that the brain cells will innervate. To isolate the genetic influences—heredity—from the periphery adaptation—environment—is an incredibly complex task as far as reconstructing the interplay between these two influences. The orderliness and careful time sequencing of these proliferating events during development are fascinating and astonishing. In addition, though they will not be discussed here, complex biochemical influences (i.e., hormones and nerve growth factors) are brought to bear in the developing brain (548). The end product is an immense and complex brain capable of incredibly diverse actions throughout the body.

The duration of neural development is variable. And apparently the ordered time sequence from one brain system to another is only partly coupled with other systems. Thus the rate of development may accelerate or slow down within the same species (407). Often it does not proceed in a smooth fashion. Also the synchrony—or concurrent happenings—between the periphery and central nervous system suggests that the two developmental processes are interacting during maturation.

At other times brain development appears isolated from other nervous system elements. For instance, the motor system can develop in the absence of sensory input (205). Consequently, the motor system is capable of initiating and sustaining motor actions without sensory influences. Eventually, however, there is neuronal linkage between brain systems via differentiating populations of interneurons.

Once the bridge is established and neuron maturation is completed, the brain continues progressive refinement of cerebral signals. This maturation is variously defined but is essentially associated with brain plasticity. The complex phenomenon called learning is one aspect of brain plasticity. But so far only a few phenomena have emerged that shed some light on brain mecha-

170

nisms involved in learning or memory storage. Most of the work gives only indirect evidences of how learning occurs.

As noted earlier, Bennett, Rosenzweig, and Diamond (70) have shown that litter-mate rats exposed to so-called impoverished or enriched environments have significant cerebral cortical effects. The "enriched" animals have thicker cortexes, increased enzyme acetylcholinesterase activity, more glial elements, and neuron cell somas of greater diameter in comparison to the animals reared in "impoverished" conditions. However, this does not necessarily indicate increases in mental capability in rats or humans.

Attempts to extrapolate such animal studies to man are not easy because of many unknown factors that might affect the results. The results do point up the interesting prospect that environment and learning may modify the brain more than previously thought. Clearly, the functional architecture of the brain must be capable of plastic and dynamic change. Otherwise how do we support memory or learning abilities?

Then, synapse is often considered one location in the nervous system where possible alterations may play a key role in neuronal plasticity. Other speculations involve changes in brain proteins or other macromolecules (361). The issues are not resolved, though in the first case the problem is reduced to a statement that repeated synaptic usage strengthens or modifies synaptic connections (206)—that is, the repetition of a thought or act tends to strengthen retention or skill. In the second case learning brings about chemical changes or synthesis in the neuron or glial. Support for either concept is largely derived from disuse experiments in which synaptic input is effectively reduced by dissection, lesions, or chemical methods. At this time no compelling evidence supports the idea that only one mechanism underlies plasticity in the brain.

It is currently fashionable to view the brain as an information-processing system having a memory-storage element with communications over input and output lines. Electrical events in this system are relatively short, lasting only a few milliseconds, and are responsible for managing sensory and motor actions along with many other functions. The spike events (EEG movements or action potentials) are not durable in the same context as is a learned experience. Considerable evidence exists that the effects of learning can last a long time. The efficacy of the learning process is n)t entirely known, but there has been a flowering of concepts within the last few decades. Briefly, the ideas center around (1) an increase in the size of synaptic contacts, (2) an increase in sensitivity of the nerve membrane, or (3) alterations in transmitter neurochemistry released at the junctions. These changes are thought to involve large populations of neurons, and somehow the brain retrieves learned events from these ensembles of many neurons (254). Various factors can tone or affect learning. For example, learning is more efficient if motivations and rewards are clear and identifiable.

In fact, some researchers doubt that learning can occur in complete absence of motivation and reward. We are doomed if our objective is to learn without reinforcement in which some reasoning sensory selection helps sort out significant events by the central connections. Otherwise a phenomenon called "extinction" occurs, and correct responses to unmeaningful and repetitious events become less likely.

Attention and motivation are critical in the learning scheme and conceivably could help or hinder learning consolidation. The point is that the details for understanding such a simple nervous system action as memory are obscure; we can only hypothesize possible neurophysiological mechanisms. Various elements in the neuron chain can distort or render our learning useless. In the context of brain maturation, it is difficult to separate the nature and extent of genetic control from behavioral and cultural overlays. Both of these factors can thrust effects upon the molecular level of the brain, as evidenced by the maturation pattern of developing neurons and the fact that the learning process involves some durable changes in biochemistry, electrophysiology, or anatomy of the brain. Genetics may also have an influence later in childhood by switching in effects during behavioral adaptation.

Implications for Psychology and Education

Obviously, not all of the developing aspects of brain growth and maturation are summarized in this chapter. Even with the power of the scientific enterprise, only a few facts have endured over the last fifty years. Says Weiss (710), "We are at the beginning, and not near the end, of the process of understanding development. This is not the time to summarize, but a time to prospect and project into the future; and the best thing is to turn for guidance to the living object which teaches us the lessons and also teaches us the real problems to which we are to direct our questions."

It is apparent both from educational studies on how children learn and from insights on brain maturation that improved technology may not improve or potentiate intellectual growth. *First, the child must achieve maturation of the brain.* This comes about through neurobiological strategies and mechanisms in brain cells during development. Based upon the neurobiological framework of brain development, it would be wrong to establish some precise cut-off point defining the brain as fit or unfit for learning. But there are sensory-motor precursors for symbolic intellectual activities. When language is acquired, new brain functions emerge. Verbal reasoning does not begin before that time (224). Qualitative breaks in the unfolding of intelligence and conscious experience exist, but from our current understanding of brain development these seem to follow the growing capacity to process simultaneously multisensory information. These maturing processes are very deeply neurobiological (728).

10
Sex-Difference Effects

Synopsis. The development of sex differences in gender roles and behavior patterns of young children appears to result from complex interactions among genetic, hormonal, and environmental factors (including psychosocial effects) and possibly from structural development of the brain. By the age of three children are usually aware of the expectations associated with their sex in their culture. These sex differences are, in fact, a function of the socializing process and of the environment. Although expectations are not the same in all cultures, males are generally expected to perform tasks demanding physical strength, to achieve, and to be self-reliant. Females are generally expected to be nurturant and trained in home responsibilities.

Physically, boys are about four weeks behind girls in skeletal maturity at birth and often nearly a year behind by school age. This generally increases to approximately eighteen months at nine years of age and on to two years at adolescence. Normally no significant differences exist in inherent intellectual abilities of boys and girls, but physically and emotionally young boys are more vulnerable to the environmental hazards of home and school, and this may affect their mental development. However, as they grow older this vulnerability diminishes. During primary school girls seem more dependent on, and more greatly influenced by, their parents and other adults.

Generally girls in the Western world acquire language, motor, and perceptual skills earlier than boys; they can acquire these skills with maturation and out-of-school experience. Because of slower physical maturation rates, greater emotional vulnerability, less realistic cultural expectations, and psychosocial interactions in the early years, boys are more likely than girls to experience learning and behavior problems.

Educators seldom make allowances for boys' limitations in early learn-
ing situations; so their abilities are frequently masked by aggression, nega-
tivism, and lower teacher ratings. Findings that boys are more negatively
affected by early school entry than girls are therefore not surprising. How-
ever, when boys are given an opportunity to mature until about eight to
ten years of age before starting school, they usually do as well as girls.

In Western societies, entrance age laws requiring boys and girls to enter
school at the same time are seldom in the interests of little children. In
fact, they tend specifically to work against little boys. Such legislation
should be flexible enough to accommodate the young child's developmental
needs and abilities, including boys' later maturity.

Biological and Environmental Bases

The earliest observable differences in the behavior of boys and
girls are apparently of biochemical origin (309). Although the
implications are not clear, for the first three years of life, as
noted in the previous chapter, girls gain slightly more in brain
mass than boys (3). Yet usually cultural shaping also begins almost immediately after birth, setting the stage for gender-deter-
mined responses to the newborn. The subsequent development
of sex differences appears to result from complex interactions
among genetic, hormonal, and environmental factors.

That sex differences may be due in part to environmental factors is borne out by the Stanford CAI (Computer-Assisted Instruction) Project. Most agree that in Western societies girls generally do better than boys in reading; yet there was no
difference between first-grade boys and girls in rate of progress
and accuracy of performance (31). Evaluation of the program
after seven years showed that both boys and girls benefited from
computer-assisted instruction—with less-than-usual teacher influence—but that it was relatively more effective for the boys
(32, 235). Thus, when teachers and their gender bias are mostly
eliminated—that is, by computer teaching—boys reflect greater
benefits than girls.

It is often difficult to determine whether sex differences result
from biological predisposition or from psychosocial reinforcement of maleness or femaleness. Sex differences in the behavior

of human newborns, however, appear to be of biological origin since at birth environmental factors have not yet exerted notable influence.* Several examples of such early differences in behavior have been observed. For instance, Bell and Darling (60) found that newborn males gave evidence of greater muscular strength than females in their ability to raise their heads higher. And female infants seemed more sensitive to skin exposure and more responsive to tactile stimulation than males (59, 711). This was still true at the age of two or three months (736).

These neonatal—or newborn—behaviors begin to interact very soon with environmental factors, exerting a definite influence on development of further sex differences. Moss (505) found that, as early as three weeks of age, infants were shaping their own environment to some extent by the behavior they elicited from their mothers (e.g., through crying and other demands for attention). He reported that male babies at this early age were less easily soothed than females, and an interaction pattern was established accordingly. The common assumption that boys are more difficult to socialize than girls could very well be true because of basic differences in the biology and temperament of children and adults, together with resulting interaction effects.

Hamburg and Lunde (309) suggested a possible source of sex differences in neonatal behavior, concluding that androgenic—that is, male-producing—hormones probably affected the central nervous system during prenatal development. Postnatally, not only biochemical but also neurophysiological and behavioral evidence exists that sex hormones, especially progesterone, enter the brain and affect its activity (308). Hamburg and Lunde (309) have proposed that the sex differences apparent in early infant behavior might ultimately affect (1) the orientation of an infant to his environment, (2) his readiness for learning experiences, and (3) his relationships with other people.

Some Characteristics of Gender Roles

While hormonal chemistry may initially give rise to particular behaviors that generate "boy" or "girl" responses, the child's learning of a sex role, and the behavior related to it, appears

*This, of course, does not question or deny the probability of variables in the embryo before birth, some of which almost certainly have psychosocial implications after the child is born, especially relating to the mother's security and personal life-style—eating, drinking, smoking, using drugs, etc.

quite independent of his biochemical functioning (483, 313). Culture and environment determine expectations of males and females (175); these expectations are learned during the first few years of life (309). Probably, the critical period for learning a gender role is roughly between eighteen months and three years of age (312, 484, 483), although such role learning does extend beyond this period.

An American study by the Joint Commission on Mental Health of Children (379) indicated that sex differences are in part a function of the socializing process and of the environment in which it occurs. The trends of the times, the values of various subcultures, and the psychological climate of schools or other learning environments are largely responsible for specific sex alignment of such behaviors as aggression, conformity, etc.

Although specific tasks assigned to the sexes may vary from culture to culture, most cultures tend to expect males to perform those tasks demanding the most physical strength. In a study of 110 primarily nonliterate cultures, Barry, Bacon, and Child (47) found that boys were under greater pressure to achieve in 87 percent of the cultures and to be self-reliant in 85 percent. Girls, on the other hand, were expected to be more nurturant in 82 percent of the cultures and more trained in home responsibilities in 61 percent of them.

Whiting and Edwards (725) made a cross-cultural analysis of sex differences in six cultures: Kenya, Okinawa, India, the Philippines, Mexico, and New England. They found universal sex differences in the behavior of children aged three through eleven. The differences within some cultures, however, were not as great as those in the United States and western Europe. In certain East African societies—for example, Kenya—where boys took care of infants and assisted with domestic chores, there were fewer sex differences between boys and girls. The boys were less egoistically dominant, less aggressive, and less attention seeking than in societies expecting more "masculine" behavior. Researchers noticed less pressure on these East African boys to "prove" themselves in more aggressive ways.

Whiting and Edwards also reported that in Orchard Town, a New England community where girls had very little contact with infants and were assigned less "feminine" work, the differences between boys and girls were not as great as in other American societies. The nature of tasks assigned to children seems to be among the best predictors of gender-role behavior.

Pressures on boys to achieve and to be self-reliant are by no means limited to nonliterate cultures. In the United States, Bledsoe (91) studied fourth and sixth grade boys and girls in Georgia and found that achievement was significantly related to self-esteem for boys, but not for girls. Achievement is evidently such an integral part of the male role that without it male self-esteem deteriorates (234).

These pressures exist even in the early preschool years, according to Tyler, Rafferty, and Tyler (681). In their study of children in a college campus nursery school, boys were expected to be more independent than girls. The later physical development of boys (668), coupled with cultural sex-role pressures, possibly explains some of the vulnerability in the male role during early childhood.

Boys' problems seem especially difficult in literate cultures where achievement depends largely on school-related tasks (438, 442). Data from 525 mental health clinics in twenty-four states indicated that more than twice as many boys than girls were brought to these clinics (578). Boys' needs for such psychiatric help during the elementary school years peaked around the fourth grade.

The real discrepancy between boys' gender-role expectations and their ability to achieve suggests that, in those societies where they trail girls in maturation, schooling practices may increase their difficulties (423). Since achievement is not so crucial for girls, who are often more advanced for their ages developmentally, they have fewer school-related problems in early childhood.

Sex Differences in Physical Maturation

Skeletal growth is commonly considered one of the most reliable indicators of maturity—more so, for example, than chronological age (236). In physical development, sex differences exist even before birth in the rate of skeletal growth, and later differences occur in permanent dentition rate (668). Tanner noted a curious lack of difference between boys and girls in primary dentition, but in skeletal age he found boys approximately four weeks behind girls at birth, and until adulthood the skeletal age of boys remained about 80 percent that of girls.

At the average age of school entry, girls were approximately a

179

year ahead of boys in skeletal maturity, according to an assessment using the osseous development of the hand, including the wrist (the carpals, metacarpals, and phylanges) as an index (236). Flory notes that for some years males continue to widen this gap, not catching up with females in maturity of bone structure until about age nineteen. In fact, by age nine boys lag eighteen months behind girls, and they extend this maturity difference to approximately two years during adolescence.

From birth girls also appear more robust. Data indicate that fewer girls suffer brain damage at birth, and they have more resistance to disease in early childhood (190, 195, 695). Jersild (372) concluded that boys have more congenital defects, more physical and emotional vulnerability, greater damage from malnutrition and disease, and shorter life expectancies.

In spite of the differences in skeletal maturation, however, Girai and Scheinfeld (255) found no significant sex differences in motor skills when boys and girls were given equal training, equipment, encouragement, and opportunity for practice. Although motor skill differences in the sexes appeared at kindergarten age, they seemed to result from cultural pressures.

An important development in physical maturation is the sudden increase of hormonal activity that occurs, for both boys and girls, about the same time as maturation of perceptual processes at age eight to ten (505, 669). It is not yet possible to say how hormonal activity relates to the expanding cognitive abilities at this age, but Brenner and Stott (115) consider it a reliable indicator of development, including the brain and nervous system.

For both sexes Tanner (669) noted negligible amounts of androgenic hormones up to age eight or ten. Then a sharp increase occurred, with boys reaching a level of absolute values about twice that of girls. Similarly, Nathanson, Towne, and Aub (505) observed very low levels of estrogenic (i.e., female-producing) activity in both sexes until age eight or nine. After that, estrogenic activity increased for girls, accelerating around age eleven. These concurrent developments—increased hormonal activity and increased perceptual and cognitive abilities in later childhood—deserve exploration.

Sex Differences in Affective Relationships

The emotional climate of early childhood usually relates to parent-child interaction, and sex differences are highly evident

(500). Boys seem to need greater maternal warmth and protectiveness during their first few years, while girls indicate an earlier need for a certain amount of freedom to explore (501, 54). Bayley and Schaefer suggested that girls possess a measure of genetic control in intellectual performance, while boys are more responsive to environment and particularly to interaction with their parents. Bayley (53) concluded that, for mental growth, boys depended more than girls on emotional climate.

As development progresses, however, boys become more emotionally secure. Moss and Kagan (501) found that the positive effect of maternal encouragement and concern on intellectual development of boys diminished from age three to six. By the age of eight to eleven mothers' concern affected boys' achievement in only a small way (210). By then achievement was apparently more related to the culturally assigned independence of the male role.

In their analyses of six cultures, Whiting and Edwards (725) similarly found that (1) in five of the six societies girls aged three to six seek more help than boys of that age (leveling out between ages seven and eleven); (2) boys aged three to six seek more attention, but girls seek more physical contact; (3) boys three to six are more egoistic than girls; (4) girls of this age offer more responsible suggestions than boys, but by seven to eleven there are no significant differences; (5) girls seven to eleven are more compliant with mothers' orders, offering help and support more often than boys; (6) boys of this age react more frequently with counteraggression; and (7) there is very little difference between the sexes in seeking or offering friendly interaction.

Grossman (300) observed sex differences in first-grade children in relation to contact with parents and desire for success. Girls who had a close and affectionate relationship with their parents were anxious to do well, but boys generally proved less cooperative. Even with a similar quality of parent contact, they responded at a lower rate. This might be expected in view of boys' one-year lag in maturation.

Among primary school children, relationships between academic performance and parental attitudes and behaviors have revealed further sex differences (170, 391, 392). Parents' reactions to their children's achievement in grades one and three were significant for daughters only. As in the studies by Moss and Kagan (501) and Eklund (210), boys' academic performance at this age was independent of—or indifferent to—parental behavior. Some evidence exists, however, that earlier parent-child interactions influence boys' behavior in these primary school years (54).

Boys may be more dependent in the first few years of life (429, 53), but by preschool age there is little difference between boys and girls (169, 681, 406). From school age on, however, girls appear more dependent than boys (169, 68)—perhaps, as suggested by Mischel (482), because of the greater accommodation in our culture of female dependency.

School-age girls are also more greatly influenced than boys in acquiring moral concepts from their mothers (208) and in conforming to adult moral standards (185). While parents do have an influence on boys' moral development, it is less evident than with girls. Devereau concluded that inadequate parenting often produced peer conformity in boys, with such traits as irresponsibility, childishness, anxiety, and resistance to authority.

The exploration of sex differences in parent-child interaction also correlates sex of parent with development of verbal and math abilities. But since the variable of independence or self-reliance is also involved here, sex of parent may be only an indirect influence. Carlsmith (142) investigated the effects of father absence during World War II on children from intact families. Father absence was consistently related to differences between mathematical and verbal abilities. The longer the father was absent and the younger the child during the absence, the greater the relative superiority of verbal to mathematical aptitude. This effect was greatest for children whose fathers were absent at birth or were away longer than thirty months. Mathematical ability increased relatively when the father's absence was brief or occurred later in the child's life.

Bing (81) explains this phenomenon thus: Developing number ability requires independent concentration and capacity to carry through a task by oneself. Early verbal ability, on the other hand, is generally fostered by close relationship with a demanding and somewhat intrusive mother. Carlsmith's results may reflect this intrusive maternal behavior, which is perhaps more likely in the father's absence. But no one knows whether these effects depend upon differences in parental expectations, developmental maturity of boys and girls, or some other factor.

Child-adult interactions can, of course, include adults out of the home as well as parents and other adults in the home. Even for very young children, there are sex differences in response to nonfamily adults. As early as age two, boys appear more aggressive toward adults other than parents, while girls are more compliant with adult demands and initiate more interactions with their teachers (624).

The variables of sex are very complex. Not only does the teacher's sex affect the child's behavior, but also the child's sex appears to affect teacher attitudes. Lee and Wolinsky (423) noted differences in children's self-concept development as possibly resulting from effects of male and female teachers in early school experiences.

Feshbach (231) found that student teachers tended to respond to boys and girls according to preferences they considered appropriate for each sex. For example, they gave higher ratings to the most rigid and conforming children—unlikely behavior for boys far more than girls. And Brenner and Stott (115) observed dynamic interaction patterns between female teachers and boys that produced lower teacher ratings for the boys.

Teachers also appear more threatening in the preschool to boys than to girls (241). The predominance of female teachers, interacting with boys showing expected aggression, results in different behavior patterns for boys and girls, with apparently far-reaching effects.

In early schooling the sex of a child has proved an important monitor of the effect the school experience will have (67). Mason and Prater (446) recommended separate reading instruction for boys and girls because of the psychosocial effects of reading instruction at the kindergarten level. In this particular instance, boys' behavior changed significantly in a negative direction because of reading instruction. Boys and girls do not seem to differ significantly in nonverbal cognitive abilities (252, 115), but rather in certain skills such as verbal (53, 563) and analytic abilities (734, 384)—apparently influenced, in part at least, by psychosocial factors. The sex differences found by Brenner and Stott (115) indicated that in kindergarten and first grade boys may be more ready for problem solving and risk taking, but girls usually achieve better where traditional learning-obeying-conforming attitudes are required.

Sex Differences in School Readiness

Even when boys and girls are very similar in IQ, social class, school readiness, and perceptual measures, they are still different in early reading achievement, with the girls evidencing superior average reading ability over the boys (579). The girls' advantage may be due to earlier stabilization of verbal ability (53, 438), earlier mastery of vocabulary and reading comprehension, and earlier *integration* of audio and visual skills (563). Boys seem to have more difficulty with visual perception in their attempts to read (161).

Carroll (144) and Hall (304) also observed reading problems in boys. Carroll's data suggested that younger children especially had problems. Hall found that boys not only achieved at a lower level than girls, but also three times as many boys were among underaged children at the time of first-grade entrance. It was recommended that beginning instruction in language arts and reading be postponed, especially for boys. Or, Hall concluded, if achievement standards remained rigid, the school entrance age of boys should be delayed from six months to a year.

The same pattern appears in studies of boys and girls below elementary school age. Sex differences in school readiness due to kindergarten attendance were compared with the effects of a year of maturation and incidental out-of-school learning for boys and girls of the same chronological age (586). The effects of kindergarten attendance were negligible for the girls; maturation and out-of-school learning had increased their readiness skills as much as kindergarten. The boys, however, did show some benefit from kindergarten.

Rubin concluded that the girls had already passed the stage for developing the readiness skills measured; so kindergarten had little effect on them. But the boys, who matured more slowly, were developing these skills in their kindergarten year. Boys exposed to kindergarten activities developed readiness skills in language, numbers, visual decoding, and copying to a greater degree than boys who remained at home. Since the girls appeared to develop most of these skills prior to kindergarten, we need further comparison to determine whether the boys would reach the same readiness level after time for sufficient maturation and out-of-school experiences, accommodating their apparent developmental lag.

184

Rubin's findings are supported by Coffman and Dunlap (159) and by Marshall P. Smith (637). These studies involved pre-kindergarten children at an age slightly younger than Rubin's kindergartners. At this younger age, Coffman and Dunlap found that girls were better able than boys to profit from training in motor, visual, and auditory-language skills. Smith reported similar results in intellectual performance. He supposed that these differences between boys and girls were most likely a function of girls' greater psychosocial readiness.

Generally, in the Western world girls acquire language, motor, and perceptual skills from several months to a year earlier than boys, and they can acquire these skills with maturation and out-of-school experience. The differences in the school readiness of boys and girls, however, involve much more than a mere time differential for a single aspect of development (115, 586).

Effects of Early Learning and School Success

Certain aspects of intellectual development cannot occur until relevant physical structures are complete (438). Since girls mature physically earlier than boys (668) and stabilize their verbal skills sooner (53), they seem to possess an advantage in learning. Girls also acquire an IQ similar to their natural parents' earlier than boys (348, 501, 54). But by the age of six the correlations between parent and child IQ are similar for both boys and girls (501), and almost no sex differences in IQ exist during the school years (256).

Very likely because of inherent physical differences and developmental rates of the sexes, school entrance age studies have often found that boys are more negatively affected by early entry (399, 145, 186) or that boys are more likely to repeat a grade, especially in primary school (399, 304, 442). These sex differences in development, plus premature expectations of performance for boys (71), may account for the facts that 70 percent of all children in special education are boys (503), and boys are involved in more behavior problems (174).

Maturational factors strongly influence learning and school success, and the sexes usually do equally well when children have reached about eight to ten and have matured neurophysiologically, visually, auditorially, etc. (496, 486). By the age of six sex differences in vocabulary have largely disappeared, and by age ten boys have caught up with girls in reading skills (438). Sometimes boys even forge ahead of girls at the eight- to ten-year maturation period in tests of analytic ability. Witkin et al. (734) found school-age boys higher than girls in this ability, while Kagan, Moss, and Sigel (384) found clear sex differences, with boys using analytic groupings of objects more often than girls in the second to fourth grades. Yet at the earlier ages of four and five, boys and girls had equal analytic abilities (622, 439).

Aggression, accepted as an integral component of male behavior in many cultures (726), complicates boys' learning problems, since aggression appears to have a negative effect on intellectual performance for boys (65, 383). For girls, however, some aggression has been found conducive to learning and school success (383).

Evidence related to effects of sex differences on learning, then, indicates that boys are more likely than girls to have learning and behavior problems because of slower physical maturation rates, less realistic cultural expectations, and psychosocial interactions in the early school years (379). Educators seldom make allowances for boys' limitations in early learning situations; so their abilities are frequently masked by aggressive behavior (678), negativism (238), and low teacher ratings (115, 423).

Since relevant physical structures are necessary to support intellectual activities, findings reporting boys more negatively affected than girls by early school entry are not surprising. With maturation, however, boys do as well as girls. So, at least in Western societies, inflexible school entrance age laws mandating the same treatment for boys and girls are hardly fair to little boys. They are not in the interests of children or teachers or parents—particularly because they tempt the teachers to tag the boys as underachievers, a stigma they often carry for life. Laws and school policies should be flexible enough to accommodate the later maturity of boys.

Willard Olson (523) points out that "children of the same grade location are regularly found to differ by as much as four or five years in their maturation and their readiness to perform tasks." This, of course, includes both boys and girls, but it is especially poignant—and ominous—for little boys.

11
Effectiveness of Early Schooling

Synopsis. *When viewed systematically, research related to early school-ing effectiveness suggests that early childhood is the best time for pre-venting the effects of environmental deprivation. It is the time to establish a firm base for effective learning in later years. There is some confusion, however, about what experiences are crucial for these outcomes.*

Compensatory education—the privilege of catching up—is needed, of course, at some time by some children—particularly the disadvantaged. Many experimenters claim desirable short-term *outcomes from such edu-cation. Yet there is no conclusive evidence that, in general, early schooling programs provide* long-range *benefits. In fact, research findings generally support the opposite conclusion. For example, although preschool expe-rience has sometimes resulted in short-term intellectual and social benefits for disadvantaged children, there is little, if any, reason for such optimism over the long term.*

Parent participation often improves parents' attitudes toward school but fails to improve their attitudes about themselves. It is commonly assumed that the family does not provide adequate positive socialization for the young child but that early schooling does this very well. Here, again, hu-man intuition and conventional practice have little basis in fact. It is true that children from disorganized family systems do not develop optimum in-ternal control and motivation for normal learning. So external control in a carefully structured school environment may benefit them. Although this leads to some desired cognitive gains, it does not provide the necessary in-ternal motivation for self-initiated learning.

Gains are almost inevitably lost unless this external structure is contin-uously maintained. And few school districts have the finances or personnel to even approach an adequate job. Small group instruction with the same teacher on an adult-child ratio of around 1 to 5—depending on the age of the children—may help build motivation. But continuity is also required here, and school programs seldom provide the necessary continuous, long-range relationships.

IQ gains achieved by preschoolers appear to have questionable authenticity. The lower a child's initial IQ, the greater gains he is likely to make after sufficient experience in a preschool program. However, such IQ gains may really reflect a greater ability to use what was already there. These dramatic gains are not usually continued in early grade school. In fact, a steady decline in IQ, self-concept, language, and achievement follows for several years after these preschoolers enter elementary school. It appears that even the best intervention programs cannot make up for an inadequate home or inappropriate school experience.

From World War I through the 1950s traditional nursery school programs with a relaxed structure have been of little value in promoting cognitive gains—whether or not the children were disadvantaged. The emphasis of these schools was typically social and developmental, with no special efforts to hurry intellectual attainments. Still, attending early nursery school then and continuing several years was not generally of significant help in children's social and emotional adjustment. Later preschools, more oriented to academic readiness, did no better.

Most intensive efforts to develop academic skills in the preschool years may be dangerous and shortsighted, correlating with frustration, anxiety, and apathy in later school years. Even, as noted earlier, when early schooling does appear to enhance school performance, these gains are not usually carried through later school life. Emphasis on parenthood education and family rehabilitation appears far more logical than early schooling if we are to insure the child's optimum learning and personal development—which is his right.

Research Variables

Rohwer (574), after a review of research related to early schooling, concluded that an effective school program must relate to children's present experiences and tasks. The quality of schooling should be judged by how well it helps the student adapt to out-of-school tasks *now*. Activities and learnings focused toward some nebulous success in the future tend to make school ineffective, especially for younger children. Yet, educators must consider the outcomes their efforts will bring as the child matures.

Many studies have been designed to test the effectiveness of instructional strategies and environmental factors on the learning of young children. The results have shown that children *can* learn at early ages, they *can* be trained to perform fairly complex problem-solving operations, and they *can* achieve IQ gains after participation in school programs (see chapter seven).

To make a valid appraisal of the effectiveness of early schooling, however, we must determine what outcomes are most important, with least risk in the total development of children through the years. Special care should be taken in analyzing these studies to determine whether or not they involved *disadvantaged* children. Such youngsters often respond differently from those who are not disadvantaged.

The senior staff of the Harvard Pre-School Project and the Public Education staff of the Ford Foundation (417) strongly suggested, from available research, that childhood was the best time for preventing the stunting effects of environmental deprivation. They were still uncertain which crucial experiences would foster the development necessary for *later* success in school.

This study further suggested that early learning experiences (whether in or out of school) should provide a firm base that would make later schooling more effective. Preschool and primary programs throughout the country have sought to provide such a learning base. Yet, after all the special methods of instruction and well-planned techniques, massive numbers of preschooled children still do not learn adequately in elementary school (575).

Some children *need* compensatory education at some stage of the learning process. Yet many disagree on the effectiveness of many early schooling programs (417) and on the age-appropriateness of present education practices (417, 215, 216, 574, 575). Perhaps frequent segregation of children into age groups, largely isolated from adult activities, tends to limit experience with the real world, and it may weaken motivation as well. Certainly age-based segregation needs further investigation (454).

The desired outcomes of early childhood education suggested

by these reports are (1) prevention of environmental deprivation, (2) development of ability to adapt to out-of-school tasks now, and (3) establishment of a firm base for successful learning later. Insofar as early learnings contribute constructively, in general, to these outcomes—without risk to the child in other respects—early education must be considered effective. But the research findings above as well as others, provide little or no evidence suggesting that early education should be acquired in school instead of at home.

Hollos and Cowan (344) concluded that family ethics and values might well play a larger role than language stimulation and schooling in this respect. Goodnow and Bethon (282) also note that, in the normal course of events, children acquire the basic skills for logical thinking in conservation tasks without schooling. These conclusions were based on Goodnow's (280) work with unschooled Chinese boys in Hong Kong. And Price-Williams's work (549) among the illiterate Tiv of central Nigeria suggested that neurophysiological readiness led to comprehension of these logical concepts.

In the United States, Mermelstein and Shulman (464) found a similar occurrence among unschooled children in Virginia. Six- and nine-year-old black children from Prince Edward County, a community that had been without public schools for four years, were compared on conservation tasks with six- and nine-year-old black children who had had regular schooling in an adjoining county. The researchers expected to find no difference in performance between the two groups of six-year-olds, and no difference was found. But the fact that schooled nine-year-olds performed no better than unschooled children of the same age suggests that formal, structured learning may not help academic achievement in the early years of education as much as had been supposed, at least up to age nine.

The value of early schooling seems to come largely from its influence on general development rather than from its "success" in training children to perform certain academic-oriented tasks. Mermelstein and Meyer (463) question specific training for inducing conservation reasoning before the child has reasonable cognitive maturity. In fact, they suggest that for acquiring some abstract concepts, language and training may interfere with rather than facilitate learning.

Many tend to consider schooling effective, especially for the

190

disadvantaged, when children can do what they have been singularly trained to do, whether or not they understand it. For example, Deal (179) noted the improved performance of preschoolers with training and practice on specific mathematics items. But they had acquired no better general understanding of number concepts.

Indeed, many studies show learning and IQ gains in the preschool years. Yet disturbing questions remain: Does this early schooling provide the essential base for later school success? Does it increase competence to cope with present realities? Does it further complicate an already complex world? Are the IQ "gains" retained throughout school? While more research on these questions is needed, a few clues are appearing in preschool and kindergarten studies with both disadvantaged and middle-class children.

Preschool for the Disadvantaged

Effects of preschool programs on disadvantaged children and their families have been scrutinized carefully to determine justification for continued support by federal, state, and other public funds. After reviewing hundreds of studies, Stearns (653) summed up these effects: (1) preschools for the disadvantaged have made positive intellectual and social changes over the short run; (2) the effects on children's social and emotional development are uncertain, particularly over the long run; and (3) participation by parents in preschool programs leads to positive changes in the parents' attitudes toward the school, but not in their attitudes about themselves. Since the children showed growth and development, Stearns concluded that such programs might be justified as models for research and reform.

Several other studies have also noted positive effects of these early childhood programs. A report on the effects of different Head Start programs from 1966 to 1968 (506) indicated certain specific benefits for disadvantaged children: significant growth in the cognitive domain, adaptiveness to Stanford-Binet test conditions, more verbal activity and social interaction with children of other ethnic groups. (See chapter one on Head Start.)

Handler (314) found that preschool experience was important for the disadvantaged because family socialization patterns did not provide adequate training in school-related skills. And Lessler and Fox (424) noted sensitivity and receptiveness to the spoken word as the most significant effect of a Head Start program. This seems to compensate for a shortcoming in the family milieu.

Results of some early school programs show children's enjoyment and enthusiasm for school (315, 424). Researchers concluded that children progressed in learning how to feel, how to think for themselves, and how to make use of themselves in learning. They learned about themselves and about learning and felt good about their early school experience (648).

Better health and social behavior are other positive preschool outcomes for the economically disadvantaged (354). Hulan concludes, however, that there is no instant solution or panacea for the cumulative effects of malnutrition or for the lack of appropriate infant stimulation and rewarding experiences.

Effects of the Home Environment

Moon and Moore (486) analyzed test scores and teacher observations from the 1970 National Elementary School Survey (NESS)—covering about eighty thousand children in the second, fourth, and sixth grades from a national sample of about thirty-five hundred schools. They found: (1) There were marked differences between pupils identified as socioeconomically disadvantaged and those not so identified, both for achievement test scores and for pupil characteristics. (2) If kindergarten or preschool experience made any difference in later school achievement, it had greater benefit for pupils not identified as socioeconomically disadvantaged. (3) Such differences were minimal compared to those attributed to SES; the positive benefits of early school programs did not overcome the masking effect of other factors with disadvantaged children. (4) Older pupils in each grade achieved significantly better than younger pupils, but the differences became smaller as pupils progressed in school.

They concluded that the most meaningful differences related to family SES rather than to specific school programs. Many educators appear overconcerned that all children learn certain tasks at an early age, whereas greater emphasis should go toward coordinating programs for children with programs that will benefit and strengthen their families.

Blatt and Garfunkel (90) studied the effects of preschool intervention in the lives of lower-SES children, hoping to learn what might reduce later intellectual and academic deficits. They expected that good early schooling programs would effectively compensate disadvantaged youngsters. Their data revealed, however, that an enriched educational opportunity—as offered by preschools—is not enough. Instead, the home setting, has far greater potential for disadvantaged children than external manipulation of the school environment.

Home environments may also have negative effects. In one home-based preschool program of cognitive intervention for children of low-income families, Levenstein (425) found a wide range in gains made. All but one of the seven children who made low gains also demonstrated a common pattern of behavior, characterized by social and cognitive immaturity and an indication of unhappiness in family relationships. The home influence was positive, however, for thirty-three children in this particular program.

Parental involvement has been recognized as a vital factor in the present and future academic motivation of children in Head Start programs (731). The federal Home Start program, growing out of Head Start, was in part designed and initiated to develop such family-child interaction (608, 609). (See also chapter five.)

These findings and programs do not imply the homes and families of disadvantaged children are all they might be, even though they do exert tremendous influence. Indeed, intellectual inferiority has been traced to the lack of opportunity and stimulation so often found in these homes, and compensatory education has been expected to alleviate this lack (518). But the overriding evidence indicates that "compensatory education" as commonly conceived does not really or fully compensate. It is second best, a substitute for the primary family force in a child's life.

Highly Structured Preschool Programs

The Head Start program was the first modern, nationwide, federal attempt to promote the intellectual growth of disadvantaged preschoolers. Early evaluations of Head Start indicated that factors contributing to effective programs *for disadvantaged children* were a warm, supportive, and stimulating teacher in a task-oriented, academically structured situation, with emphasis on verbal development (518, 88).

These structured programs were necessary for disadvantaged

or educationally underprivileged children to achieve intellectual gains. An investigation of lower- and middle-class preschoolers showed that disadvantaged children *expect* external control. Less structured programs demand development of internal control, and internal control (or self-discipline) is a factor in self-confidence for later success in learning. Without a sound self-concept, the child is likely to be learning handicapped. Although children from sound home environments with little program structure have this quality, it is apparently best built (or rebuilt) in the disadvantaged child through a relatively highly structured, teacher-directed program (189, 188, 228).

Bissell (86) also found that, the greater a child's socioeconomic disadvantage, the more effective was a highly structured program in producing cognitive gains. The nondirective, less structured programs were more effective with the least disadvantaged. Bissell suggests that the disadvantaged have developed fewer resources to learn by themselves in unstructured programs than have the more advantaged students.

The necessity for structuring compensatory programs has also been reported by Clasen, Spear, and Tomaro (157) and by Larson and Olson (422), who assessed the effects of an all-day compensatory kindergarten. In this latter case, however, learning and intellectual growth rates diminished when focused saturation efforts stopped. A follow-through program was suggested as a step in remediation.

Children often lose the carefully nurtured gains of these structured preschool programs unless specific and knowledgeable attempts are made to maintain them (694, 388). In one study of first graders, researchers found few differences between disadvantaged children who had attended a Head Start program with no further intervention and those with no intervention at all. They concluded that learning habits of all children are well developed by age four, and intervention after that is not really effective without a planned follow-through (147). Activities designed to increase learning capacities through reading-readiness instruction and language training produce their most lasting effects when continued through kindergarten and into the primary grades (189).

A long-term plan, designed to keep culturally deprived children in a continuous, sequential program through preschool and the first grade, yielded significantly greater intellectual gains than traditional school programs. Children who remained in the program longest (two years preschool, one year first grade) achieved the most intellectual growth. Again, the structured nature of the activities and the continuous follow-through were credited for the positive results (685, 686).

Another tightly structured preschool program is the academically oriented model designed by Bereiter and Engelmann (76, 77). Reidford and Berzonsky (562) field-tested such a program for six months and found that children did achieve an IQ gain. Yet the total evaluation of their findings suggested that long-term programs extending through the early elementary school years should replace short-term programs for preschoolers.

The fast pace and intensive drill in the Bereiter-Engelmann program resulted in rapid attainment of basic academic concepts and an accompanying "gain" in IQ (75). But there is evidence that this academically oriented approach can cause later difficulties. Miller (476) compared the interaction of various Head Start curricula with subsequent schooling, discovering that children accustomed to the Bereiter-Engelmann structure appeared handicapped in kindergarten.

The many affective, cognitive, and sensory-motor variables discussed in other chapters of this book provide a wide spectrum of rationale convincing the objective ECE scholar that many factors suggest caution in urging academic structure or stimulation for most young children. Some of these factors—such as a sound self-concept, social stability, and untroubled neurological development—may have much greater relative value for the child's overall development than basic skills. Yet we risk these factors when we overstress structure and stimulation.

In fact, some years after his work with Engelmann, Bereiter (74) observed that the structured teaching of cognitive skills does not prepare a child for what lies beyond. He labeled the structured approach as *training* rather than *education*. Its influence on real development was minimal. The structured approach best services young children who are immature, reached better by a sensory approach than by conceptualizing. The former is more akin to training, the latter to education—utilizing the developing ability to reason abstractly.

Nimnicht (515), a chief psychologist for Head Start, also modified his theories on the need and desirability of early schooling. He suggested that "if mothers of young children would spend 20

195

minutes a day playing with their children in a way that would help them develop skills and concepts ... this time might be more productive than three hours a day in a Head Start classroom." In his experiments with such play (512, 513, 514), he was concerned both with helping children develop healthy self-concepts and with assisting parents to help their children develop intellectually, to strengthen parent-child attachments, and to become involved in the education decision-making process.

Many behaviorists appear to think of children almost as experimental animals. There is a danger here of neglecting the children's potential to develop feelings of freedom, independence, and self-discipline. As a consequence, tightly structured programs often deprive children of opportunities to develop in these crucial affective areas (708).

Along with structure and continuity, the most effective schools for young children have a larger proportion of available adults (644). Personal impact of the teacher is a decisive factor in effectiveness of programs for the disadvantaged. And the same adult(s) should be present daily, for to young children adult continuity is as important as program continuity. This fact constitutes one of the home's principal advantages.

A teacher-child ratio of 1 to 5 provides an opportunity to build motivating relationships and to reinforce learning (338). Many opinions exist on such ratios; depending on the age of the children and the warmth and ability of the care giver, they may range from 1 to 3 to 1 to 7. But probably they should be no larger than 1 to 7 for children under six years of age. Even in the elementary school, small group instruction of this kind promises greater academic success (249).

Actually, a teacher-child ratio of 1 to 1 is even more highly effective in early learning (527). Tutoring children at home and teaching mothers to work with their own children individually have both given positive learning results (388). Hamblin and Hamblin (307) experimented successfully with preschool peer tutoring in a beginning reading program; for both low- and medium-IQ children, performance increased with this personal help.

IQ and Other Measures of Progress

Although some programs for disadvantaged children have reportedly met with success in areas mentioned, others have failed to produce any particular gains, and some appear to incur losses. Asbury (29) found that a specialized training period for a short time did not result in a significant improvement in cognition related to verbal ability. The Westinghouse report on Head Start (716) likewise found short summer programs ineffective for lasting gains. Some Head Start enrichment programs resulted in no significant differences between Head Start and non–Head Start groups in achievement or in intellectual ability (89, 411, 158). In fact, Cartwright and Steglich (146) reported a non–Head Start control group superior to a Head Start group at the end of both the first and second years of school.

Some tests of disadvantaged preschoolers show improvement in certain areas although no special gain is apparent in intelligence. Sontag, Sella, and Thorndike (641) reported the significant progress of Head Start children in sensory and number concepts and word associations, but no difference in intelligence when compared with non–Head Start children. Saltz and Johnson (590) observed progress in both social and cognitive development from training in fantasy play and role enactment, but again there was no improvement in intelligence. Higher scores on school readiness tests have also followed early schooling (612, 680, 488), although there may have been no significant gain in IQ (371).

Initially low IQ scores of disadvantaged children do not necessarily represent a true measure of ability. Thus, the mental diversity between children of lower- and higher-socioeconomic levels may not be as great as it appears, even though dramatic but false IQ gains are likely to occur among the most disadvantaged. One evaluation of an inner-city preschool program (409) indicated that, the lower a child's initial IQ, the more likely he was to make large gains after sufficient experience with a preschool program. Children with a low initial IQ made their greatest gains in the second year of the program, while those with a higher IQ and higher socioeconomic status achieved the same gains during this first year.

The conclusions of Zigler and Butterfield (756) also raised questions about the authenticity of preschool IQ gains attributed to various programs. Their study found that standard testing procedures underestimated the culturally deprived child's intelligence. They suggested that what appeared to be increased intellectual ability in preschool children was really greater ability to use what was already there. (In a sense this reverts to the old controversy of heredity versus environment in the development of intelligence.)

For many disadvantaged children, Head Start programs have contributed to this greater ability to meet the intellectual challenges of kindergarten and first grade (66, 67, 1). But the dramatic gains of the preschool years were *not* repeated in early grade school, according to Deutsch, Taleporos, and Victor (184). This could also indicate the unrealistically low assessment of intelligence in preschool children who have not yet learned the academic "ropes" used in measuring cognitive ability.

Positive preschool effects on disadvantaged children have been marginally conducive to cognitive achievement during the first three grades of elementary school (716, 183, 700, 701, 702, 704), and they may last for four or even five years (389). Weikart and his associates (704) found that children who had participated in a preschool program demonstrated higher achievement in first and third grades than a control group, but their higher scores on IQ tests disappeared by the third grade. The children without preschool had begun to "catch up."

For preschool youngsters, a steady though gradual decline in measured IQ begins as early as kindergarten or first grade, even though groups with preschool appear to perform better academically than children with no preschool experience. These non-preschool children, on the other hand, show a gradual increase in IQ throughout kindergarten and first grade (477). These results suggest that most of the positive effects of a preschool program are insignificant after a year or two (337, 196).

Larson's findings (420, 421) are similar. Significant IQ gains in a Head Start group in rural Minnesota were stable through grade one. After kindergarten the learning rate of the Head Start children lagged behind those with no preschool, and after first grade those who had attended Head Start performed significantly below control groups on tests of word reading, paragraph meaning, vocabulary, and spelling.

Similarly, Van de Riet and Van de Riet (687) found that children from both an experimental Learning to Learn program and a traditional preschool were at first superior to those with no preschool in a number of developmental measures. At the end of the first grade, children from the experimental program were still superior in IQ, but the differences between the groups had begun to disappear because the nonpreschool group had improved.

Although carefully planned intervention may lead to IQ gains and better performance in early elementary school (294), differences not only in IQ but also in language and achievement begin to disappear in the first grade, losing any significance by the end of the fourth grade (295). Gray (293) concludes that even the best intervention programs do not make up for inadequate home or inappropriate school experience. The growing child must *continually* interact with his immediate environment if lasting changes are to occur.

A synthesis of these research findings suggests that the ability of the disadvantaged child to reach current educational standards depends upon (1) external control or structure representing limits consistent with the child's functional ability; (2) a continuous program extending into the elementary grades; and (3) continuity and accessibility of adults, whether teachers or parents.

When self-discipline (or internal control) is a goal of education during the preschool years, the external structure can be less rigid. According to the evidence reviewed here, cognitive gains are then smaller and develop more slowly. For the normal, undeprived child this is best. While highly regimented programs often result in greater immediate intellectual gains, these gains are relatively impermanent unless made after the first few years of elementary school. When parents and teachers insist that children formally learn basic academic skills before age seven or eight, learning situations must be laboriously structured. Such structure is unnecessary after children are slightly older; then they can accomplish in a few weeks or months what they might have taken years to do before—with less frustration and stress.

The effects of such regimented schooling *on both cognitive and affective development* indicate that the disadvantaged child's real deprivation may arise from a cultural discrepancy that leaves internal control undeveloped (86, 655). Without this basis for confidence and self-respect, motivation often lags. Schools may perpetuate this early deprivation by applying undue pressure for achievement that has little ultimate meaning for the child—because of cultural rather than pathological differences (46, 569).

In commenting on the common characteristics of preschool children from multiproblem families, Friedman (247) observes that the strong emphasis on cognitive development in their education may be inappropriate to the broader learning process. In his analysis of the early education needs of the disadvantaged, Friedman points out that only when developmental maturation is enhanced and supported can children be helped to acquire the personality and cognitive tools for realizing their full potential. The real effectiveness of early education lies more in released child potential than in quality of acquired information.

The Traditional Nursery School

The relaxed, loosely structured curriculum of the traditional nursery school is seldom reported in current research. Such a program—more promising for normal youngsters—has been of little value in helping disadvantaged children achieve cognitive gains (100). Even with parental involvement and later enriched classroom experience in the first and second grades, there were no real gains for children after three years in a nursery school program at Howard University (326). Nor has nursery school generally been a determinant of learning for more advantaged children (314). When children acquire a relatively high level of proficiency in school-related skills at home, notes Handler, nursery school experience has only a negligible effect on later school achievement.

"Traditional" Nursery Schools a Generation Ago

Before the sharply increased emphasis on early cognitive skills that came about in the late 1950s and 1960s, the programs of nursery schools were quite different from the structured curricula and academic objectives of current preschools. Older traditional nursery schools had little or no orientation to primary readiness. In effect, they were care centers seeking to provide optimum freedom in a creative, natural atmosphere without reference to academic knowledges and skills. Research efforts that focused on traditional nursery schools from the thirties to early sixties regularly revealed no significant intellectual effects on children (21, 279, 419, 502, 191, 529).

Even a generation ago, a year attending a superior nursery school appeared to produce almost no gains in intelligence scores. The superior program was, however, reported as encouraging independent thinking and intellectual curiosity through challenging experiences (85). Such unhurried experiences may

200

have contributed to intellectual development not immediately measurable, nurturing the children's affective development as well.

The usual outcomes of these nursery schools, then, especially prior to World War II, were personal and social in nature. Moustakas (502) summed up their greatest contribution as helping children develop social skills and emotional adjustment. Some researchers rated children with nursery school attendance as more sociable (321), more successful in social contacts (440), and more outgoing toward other children (351).

Their improved social behavior became more acceptable to teachers and other children (373), and solitary play merged into integrated group activities (530) that grew more spontaneous with increased social experience (632). The children tended to "grow up," to be more independent and to show more self-control and self-reliance as they progressed in nursery school (378, 683). But little has been done to determine the effects of even the better nursery school education on the older child and the adolescent.

With increasing nursery school attendance, children seemed to score higher on emotional maturity (378). Those schools judged as better sought to encourage attitudes that would help children handle their feelings (27), but conflicts, fighting, and quarreling seemed to increase with length of nursery school attendance (375)—raising questions as to the quality of socialization (see chapter thirteen on positive versus negative sociality). The children became less sensitive to suggestion or criticism, more active and resistant to authority (25), but better able to disguise or inhibit the outward expression of their fears (374).

In the late 1930s and during the 1940s intellectual development was a controversial question—caught in the greater nature-nurture debate. Wellman (712) and Rhinehart (564) believed that nursery school could influence IQ, but others were dubious (279, 536, 632, 525). The general attitude was that a significant IQ increase was not as important as the quality of effective intelligence—original ideas, creativity, productive enterprises, the questions asked, and the quality of explanations (502).

Nor were the effects of nursery school attendance clearly noticeable in kindergarten or elementary school. In the 1950s nursery school children were sometimes perceived by their later peers as more free and sure of themselves (13). They were more likely to be chosen as preferred playmates (26) and may have been more accepted by their peers (127). But kindergarten teachers' ratings for children with nursery school background were actually lower on personal adjustment and realtionships with other children. Brown and Hunt recognized that nursery school enrollments may have been influenced by the emotional needs or desires of parents, and poor personal adjustment could have begun before nursery school. Early nursery school attendance, in general, was not significant in social and emotional adjustments several years later (96, 191).

On tests of intelligence and educational performance, Douglas and Ross found that nursery school children made slightly higher scores at age eight than their nonnursery counterparts. Their scores were not significantly higher, however, and by age eleven they had lost their advantage. By age fifteen the nursery school children were slightly below the average of nonnursery school children. Palmer (529) reported similar findings in an evaluation of the effects of a junior kindergarten examined over a five-year period. Again there were early positive effects on achievement, but after four years they had disappeared.

There is a dearth of more recent research on traditional nursery schools. But we do know that this program generally produces negligible cognitive gains both for disadvantaged children (326) and for children of higher socioeconomic levels (314).

A Philosophical Question

In 1970 the Harvard Preschool Project and Ford Foundation jointly reported on research and educational practice as related to the first six years of life, calling attention of educational philosophers to moral and political overtones in the early schooling movement. They questioned the value of accelerating cognitive development in the preschool years, recognizing these years of a child's life as entities in themselves. Although pragmatic reasons for this unbalanced emphasis existed, undue pressures were pointed out as possibly dangerous and shortsighted (417).

The effects of increased time in school may have negative influences on young children—including poorer attitudes toward school the earlier they enrolled (574, 358). Witherspoon (733) found some evidence that both achievement and adjustment of

202

children through the third grade suffered when length of the school year was extended.

Robinson's (571) evaluations of early schooling effectiveness led her to conclude that intensive efforts to develop academic skills in early childhood correlate highly with frustration, anxiety, and apathy in later school years. The cognitive focus has fallen far short of producing significant, consistently sustained gains. And Rohwer (574) observed that, even when early schooling had apparently enhanced performance in school, performance in life was not adequately realized. Yet this must ever be the primary goal. (For related conclusions, see the section on early schooling effectiveness in chapter thirteen.)

12
A Positive Approach to
Early Learning

Synopsis. The present concern for early childhood education and for out-of-home care is not a new phenomenon. During the past two hundred years a number of ECE movements or cycles have attempted to improve social conditions by providing schools for children of the poor. As society became more complex in this century, more affluent parents sought nursery school experience for their children because of its presumed socialization and adjustment advantages. Some parents, however, may have been as much concerned for their own personal freedom—to work or to play—as for their children's welfare.

Many advocates claim that the current ECE drive is based on more concrete evidence than previous early childhood movements. But this is open to question.

It is likely true that the problems of disoriented families are more intense today. An increasingly complex technology has produced impersonal societies that often undermine feelings of self-worth and happy social intercourse.

We urgently need to find solutions to these problems. If children are to achieve self-worth and optimal development, it is even more important for them to enjoy the security of a stable family than to reach typical school expectations.

Most people still accept the family as the primary educational delivery system for young children. In fact, even while the trend moves toward earlier schooling, psychologists are more and more pointing to the home. Many early childhood specialists, and others interested in the child's welfare, suggest that educational programs for parents and future parents should receive society's and government's first consideration.

Family education generally produces desirable child development with much greater cost effectiveness than public care and other out-of-home programs for young children. A number of programs, such as Home Start, which bring child development services to children and families in their own homes, have successfully enhanced the quality of children's lives and built a base for learning upon existing family strengths. The home offers even greater possibilities as an effective learning environment and the parents as natural teachers than many people think—even for the years after the child starts to school.

Schools may be able to provide surrogate care and training for young children when homes are inadequate, when parents are otherwise unable to fulfill their responsibilities, or when other surrogate care (e.g., family day care) is not available. But schools are still institutionalized, and most of their programs tend to be structured. Research definitely questions the profitability of structured programs for most young children.

Even primary school age children usually do not perform well on abstract content until near the end of childhood or in early adolescence. Therefore, much that Western children now learn early can be more quickly and efficiently learned at a later age—with less repetition, apathy, and frustration. The earlier school years can then better emphasize physical health and affective, motor, and perceptual development, with the parents sharing home responsibility experiences, teaching their children to serve others as well as to be served.

A positive approach to early childhood education suggests a human ecological perspective for child development in relation to the family, the community, and the total culture. But priority should be given to development and informal education in the family.

ECE experimentation goes back well over two hundred years (448). Jean-Jacques Rousseau initiated ECE change in Europe with the publication of *Emile* in 1762, teaching that children should begin to develop the skills needed to understand the world and to shape their own futures.

Rousseau's idea that education should be appropriate to a child's development influenced Johann Basedow in Germany, who established a school in 1774 where he sought to stimulate children's reasoning faculties rather than to teach through memory only. From 1784 to 1808 Gotthilf Salzmann, also in Germany, advocated the influence of a natural environment in the country. About 1804 in Switzerland Phillipe de Fellenberg founded a similar program, adding agriculture and manual labor to his country program. Such educational opportunities also became available to poor children in the 1700s when Friedrich Von Rochow worked to bring schools, teachers, and textbooks to the peasants on his estate near Berlin (546).

Infant Schools, Kindergartens, and Nursery Schools

The Swiss educator Johann Pestalozzi (1746–1827) was especially interested in development of the infant mind and encouraged early learning of vocabulary through familiarity with materials and objects in the child's natural environment. According to Pestalozzi, the home was the only appropriate place for such early learning, and the mother was the best teacher (533)—except, of course, when circumstances make the home impossible.

The infant school was similar in its day to the nursery schools of our times. The history of the infant school movement in America, reviewed by May and Vinovskis (448), somewhat parallels the movement in Europe. To a considerable degree, we can trace American interest in early education of poor children to the English infant school movement that started in 1816 with the school founded by Robert Owen in New Lanark. A decade or so later, America followed the English example and organized infant school societies in a number of areas, including New York City and Philadelphia. By 1828 a number of infant schools were founded in and around Boston, which became the center of the infant school movement in America.

The primary focus was on the disadvantaged—to give religious and educational instruction to children from "unfavorable situations" (98), although some private infant schools were established for children of the better classes. This early education of the poor was to be the primary tool for permanently eliminating poverty.

In 1833, just as the ECE bandwagon was beginning to roll, Amariah Brigham startled the infant school advocates and the public as well by publishing *Remarks on the Influence of Mental Cultivation and Mental Excitement upon Health.* This book advocated more attention to health and physical development in early life, with less emphasis on cultivation of the mind. The Infant

School Society tried to explain its position as more a neighborhood nursery than a school, but enthusiasm rapidly declined and the schools soon ceased to function.

ECE proponents, however, again came alive with the kindergarten movement of the 1860s and 1870s. It was largely influenced by the Froebelian curriculum (248) of games, songs, and nature study, flourishing with greater public support than had the earlier infant schools. (Froebel, 1782–1852, was a contemporary of Pestalozzi.) As with Von Rochow, the English Infant School, and the eastern American schools of the early 1800s, the major objective was to alleviate problems of the underprivileged population by relating education to child development needs.

But now, in addition to problems of poverty, urbanization, and industrialization, a new need was evident in the U.S.—the acculturation of the children of immigrants into American society. In 1874 the National Education Association (NEA) formally recognized the work of kindergartens by establishing a special department for them. Soon the NEA recommended that kindergarten programs be part of the public school system.

Working for the disadvantaged and low-SES children generally continued to be a central ECE rationale. In 1907 Maria Montessori began her work with slum children in Rome, using the idea of a prepared environment to capitalize on the potential of children in their early years (560). In 1911 Margaret and Rachel McMillan, two sisters often credited as originators of the "nursery school" idea, sought to provide in their London school the qualities of a child-rearing environment available in more affluent homes (460).

After World War I interest in child development, as well as programs operated in child-study centers in many U.S. universities, tended to popularize nursery schools (20). For the first time in America, early childhood programs were established for a purpose other than to alleviate social ills. While the immediate health and happiness of children ostensibly received due consideration, longitudinal efforts to learn more about children and their development were an integral part of these research-oriented nursery schools (see chapter one).

It remained for federal legislation, under the U.S. Works Progress Administration (WPA) program of the depression years in the 1930s, to generate widespread government subsidies for nursery schools that mostly had unstructured programs. The American government continued through World War II to make ECE programs available to poor children (244). But after the late 1950s—the Sputnik era—the programs tended to be more structured, in the belief that children deserved more stimulation and socialization activities. But aside from these emergency periods, nursery school in the United States was limited largely to children in the middle and upper socioeconomic levels of society until the mid-1960s.

Parents concerned with their children's socialization and adjustment in an increasingly complex society sought the advantages they and others assumed good nursery schools would provide. There is little doubt, however, that some parents, conditioned by "freedom" from home duties due to women working during World War II, were as much concerned for their own freedom as for their children's welfare. Kanter (386) examined the standard routine of the nursery school experience and concluded that, although it may have helped socialize, it was oriented to bureaucratic reality rather than to the individual needs of the child.

Kanter observed that generally nursery school children learn little personal responsibility, participate in highly routinized play without internal motivation, and accept impersonal principles for relating to others. The school creates in effect a child's world resembling a large-scale formal organization (bureaucracy), and the child becomes an "organization child" with adaptive techniques to maintain status but with little initiative for individual achievement. He is, in fact, institutionalized. There are, of course, outstanding exceptions to this general rule, but the likelihood of maintaining such high-quality personnel and of financing low adult-child ratios for most children is virtually nil. European schools have proven this (487).

Rationale for Early Childhood Schools

The betterment of society has been the declared rationale running through most ECE movements (448, 647, 546). Experimenters and social reformers have provided schools for children when homes were deemed inadequate, but philosophers like Pestalozzi and Rousseau have maintained that homes are generally advantageous for early child rearing and training.

209

While obviously not advocating something altogether new, scholars and social reformers of the 1960s ostensibly based their ECE proposals on more concrete evidence than previous early childhood movements. Yet the quality of this supposedly research-related reasoning—as exemplified by Bloom (93, 94), Bruner (128), and others—must be scrutinized (see chapter seven for fuller discussion).

On the basis of his findings, Bloom proposed large-scale nursery school and kindergarten programs as the best solution to underachievement. Although early stimulation is certainly important, the kind and quality of such stimulation assumed by Bloom (and many whom he has influenced) have been sharply questioned. Critical analyses of Bloom's position by Bayley (53), Elkind (215), and Jensen (369) questioned the adequacy and correctness of this interpretation.

Bloom (94) suggested that early childhood programs be available first for disadvantaged children and eventually for all children. In spite of serious questions about the analytical quality of Bloom's work, some research basis exists to support ECE programs for the disadvantaged—as suggested in the previous chapter. However, his effort to generalize these ECE stimulation efforts for all children is clearly speculation—which has little, if any, systematic research base. It is much like ordering all children into hospitals because a few are sick.

Bloom concluded it was very unlikely that parents, particularly of culturally deprived children, could provide adequately for children's developmental needs, and so an important task of the schools was to help parents and supplement their efforts. As a result of such apparently scholarly thinking, many teachers have assumed they can outparent even relatively effective mothers and fathers. Such attitudes, conscious or unconscious, must be viewed with caution even when parents do not fully understand their children's developmental needs—and with alarm when they do. One of the overwhelming truths emerging from a study of more than seven thousand ECE research reports confirmed what many leading psychiatrists long have said: If we would spend more effort on working toward sound homes, educating for responsible parenthood, and providing the child a warm, responsive, and relatively free and consistent environment, we would develop much more creative and responsible children, save many damaged children, and save billions in tax dollars (497, 233).

Current Goals for Early Childhood Education

The problems of disoriented families in the wake of industrialization and urbanization are probably more intense today than in the days of infant schools and early kindergartens. Complex technologies generally produce impersonal societies that in turn undermine feelings of self-worth and happy social intercourse. Yet a careful study of the research relating to early childhood in today's society shows that, above all, a child's early education should contribute to self-fulfillment in the broadest sense (135), with an ultimate goal of teaching wholesome self-worth and altruistic regard for others (285).

We urgently need to humanize preschool education, with more attention to day-to-day quality of life and less to program outcomes or results (393). The core of this quality of life is the self-concept. Katz assigns high priority to the goal of helping children achieve such positive self-understanding through feeling respected and loved. She points out that the basic criteria children use to judge themselves are acquired very early within the family.

Aside from those families totally incapable of establishing reasonably sound value systems or those situations in which the family is broken beyond repair, it is more important for a child's total growth to measure up to his family's criteria than his school's expectations. When families are badly broken, a surrogate family is often the best remedy. Whatever the situation, adults must accept children's differences and treat their feelings and their freedom with respect—freedom to develop naturally, in the context of firm and kind parental shepherding.

Gordon's (285) emphasis of the self-concept as primary in early childhood education is similar to Katz's. He identifies the child's search for coherence, for meaning in his world, as central to his total development. When a child can achieve harmony with himself, with others, and with nature, he lives in an optimum situation for learning. Gesell concurs (263). When early education involves school as well as home, parents and teachers must work closely together, supplementing and complementing one another. Gordon concludes that children gain most from such experiences when school and home values are in harmony.

As support for children's positive self-concepts, Gordon (286) identified specific goals for early childhood education to develop: (1) questioning, open attitude; (2) respect for self and others; (3) sense of competence; (4) sense of responsibility; and (5) sense of commitment. Once more, Gordon emphasizes that family factors—especially parental openness, support, respect, and sharing—help children attain these goals. He adds that parents and families should be educated to believe in their own worth.

These goals for personal development in early childhood—fulfilling needs for attention, affection, and feelings of warmth and acceptance—are basic for early learning and for motivation in future learning. In fact, Zigler (754) concludes that over-emphasis on the intellectual aspect of child development is harmful when these crucial areas of personal development are ignored. Zigler points out that learning is an inherent feature of being human, and when appropriate conditions are established for general development, children *will* learn. Conversely, learning can be inhibited by inappropriate conditions that create an artificial environment (143), confuse a child's values (see chapter three), or detract from a child's sense of personal worth (550).

The caring function—providing love, attention, and appropriate activities and services—is far more important in early childhood education than acquiring information or cognitive stimulation (74). Schools reflect intellectual abilities; they do not create nor even necessarily develop them. Bereiter, along with Elkind (215, 216), Robinson (571), and Rohwer (574, 576), recommends that schools for young children drop their efforts to direct or shape intellectual development, even into the primary grades.

Priorities in Early Childhood Education

It is time to reassess our educational priorities. We must insure that programs for parents and future parents receive first consideration, concentrating on joint needs of children and family (596, 597, 598, 718, 719). Strengthening the family for its role in rearing and educating children—monitoring their development through medical, psychological, and educational resource centers and home-visiting programs—has been proposed by Barbrack and Horton (46), Gray (292), and B. White (719). Such an effort, they feel, would be far less costly—both in terms of money and child potential—and far more productive early childhood education than most out-of-home programs.

Cost Effectiveness

According to Burton White (719), in the early 1970s developmental day care cost an average of two to three thousand dollars per year *per child.* Some suggested much higher costs. Heber's Wisconsin program (324), which provided ideal adult-child ratios, cost about five thousand dollars per child. And inflation has now carried these costs to formidable levels for most families.

Parenthood education and parenting assistance for home education of children could, during the same era, be accomplished for three to five hundred dollars per year *per family.* And there were several children in many families. In 1970 Barbrack and Horton estimated that the average cost per child for a home visitor program over a five-year period would be less than $325 per year. The actual cost of such home-style education would thus be less than one-tenth that of first-rate day care, with much greater promise for most children.

On the other hand, if the state tries to provide care for all young children, as urged by many ECE entrepreneurs, financial limits will eventually ensure higher and higher ratios of children per adult caregiver. In central Europe this is often 1 to 25 or 1 to 40. And in France it reached 1 to 60, even 1 to 64, before authorities became desperate enough to try to reverse the trend (487).

As better-prepared families become more capable of providing for their own children, they might need less assistance (288). Furthermore, careful home education programs not only reach parents and present preschool children, but also (as Schaefer (594) and Gray (292) point out) tend to positively, if indirectly, affect preschool children yet to come and older siblings as well. Rothman (585) has suggested establishing a generous family assistance program, funded by federal or state funds, so that the poor need not be coerced into using day care centers.

Primitive societies educate their children almost entirely at home, although they often have some formal education when childhood is almost over—puberty rites and so on. But in technological cultures even early education tends to become totalitarian—something imposed from the top downward, with parents having progressively less control over their children's education. Parents, as well as society, must reorder their priorities; with guidance, parents must plan for time with their children to give them the confidence and security they need (666). Suviranta sums up the situation by urging recognition of parental duties and responsibilities as equivalent to any profession or job, as well as appreciation of the psychological and emotional impact of the well-ordered home on society.

Parent or Parenthood Education.*

A large body of research confirms the necessity of continuous early education for young children, but the *kind* of education is the question. Research also confirms the fact that parents are the most influential educators of their own children (593, 599). What parents do in a child's early years in managing the environment, being models for the child, and giving information influences both directly and indirectly a child's intellectual performance during these years and later on in school (286). And the value of a strong attachment, undiluted by out-of-home care, is far more urgent for efficient and effective learning—including later school—than commonly understood (see chapters two and three for an extended discussion).

This power of well-informed parental influence, if well motivated and directed, holds great promise for the child's general psychological development (134). Both parents have great influence, but educators are discovering in programs for young children that the mother generally has more influence on a child than anyone else (377).

From findings such as these, Schaefer (599) concluded that the education profession can best serve children by training and educating parents to care for and educate their own children. This supports Burton White's thesis (718, 719) that parent education should receive top priority in education planning, together with Gordon's (283) suggestion that parenthood education is an effective means for bringing about social change.

Parents need not be highly educated themselves in order to be good homemakers and child educators. Successful parent education programs have been conducted even by paraprofessionals (283,

---

*Some ECE people limit these terms, with *parent* applying only to parents and *parenthood* involving only those preparing to be parents. We generally use *parenthood education* in a generic sense—applying it to all.

289). It is the quality of family interaction that makes home education effective (593), and many parents are already doing the right thing (285). From a study of parenthood education using disadvantaged women to instruct indigent mothers in caring for and working with their children, Gordon (283) concluded that *how* a child is taught may be more important than *what* he is taught. He observed that, as the mothers' competence and sense of personal control increased, development of their infants and children improved.

In addition to giving parents confidence and personal competence, B. White (719) stressed the importance of educating parents to understand how children develop physically and socially and how they can provide safety and security within the home environment, leaving children free to explore and satisfy their developing curiosity about the world.

White (719) suggested required courses for parenthood education in high schools, high-quality public television programs, video-cassette or filmed minicourses in hospitals, adult education courses, and neighborhood resource centers for low-cost early detection of (with referral services for identification of) children's educational handicaps. The resource centers and home-visiting programs would also provide medical and educational assistance to parents as their children develop.

Experimentation with programs of this nature are encouraging. Already the home visitor–parent education approach, using nonprofessionals as educators, has proved unusually successful in producing long-term effects upon children's intellectual performance (287). And there undoubtedly are many other answers—such as well-conceived TV spots, interorganizational cooperation by parents' groups, etc.—that can go far toward educating parents' minds in behalf of their children.

Learning at Home

When parents become aware of their worth and responsibilities as teachers of their own children, even a very simple home with meager resources can be a secure and stimulating place for learning—the kind of natural stimulation appropriate for early childhood. Ordinary household items offer many kinds of sensory experiences, and participation in simple household tasks not only provides opportunities to improve motor skills but

215

also helps to develop a child's sense of responsibility and personal worth (56, 64, 492).

Programs to bring child development services to children and families in their own homes are based on this recognition of the home as a primary learning center (755, 521). Through paraprofessionals trained as home visitors, Home Start* has successfully served children from a wide variety of cultural and ethnic backgrounds—white, black, Eskimo, Navajo, migrant, Spanish-speaking, Chinese, and others. It has sought to assess nutrition and health needs, to provide information on nutrition, sanitation, safety, and early childhood development, and to provide direct health and social services or referrals when necessary. It has taught parents to use ordinary materials in the home or items from toy-lending libraries to expand the learning resources available to their children.

The Home Start program has confirmed that families definitely want to be part of a program supporting their own relationship to their children (521). It enhances the quality of children's lives and builds a base for learning upon existing family strengths (346). The program was centered in the home to produce better quality and more comprehensiveness for children's development and learning than was possible with Head Start (387).

Independent smaller experiments with home-centered learning have also been successful in helping parents to recognize themselves and their homes as important educational resources for their children (302, 461). Guernsey (302) reported some difficulty for working mothers who wished to participate in the program. This is often a matter of priorities, not only for the mothers who find it necessary to work, but also for the society that expects them to assume additional roles.

Young children who remain at home usually have an emotional advantage over those who receive early schooling. Weininger (706) reported the results of different learning experiences on five groups of young children matched for age, socioeconomic status, and intelligence. Four groups were in some kind of classroom situation, and one group remained at home. After six months all of the children had made about equal intellectual

*Home Start is an American ECE movement that emerged from Operation Head Start. It uses the home as the primary learning center.

progress, but the "at home" group showed significantly greater emotional growth.

Simpson (630) sees possibilities in the home as a learning environment throughout a child's education. She points out the opportunities for developing the child's concept of work and leisure and for learning occupational competencies. The learning of ethics, morals, management of resources, and preparation for responsible parenthood may all be home based. According to Simpson, this could greatly supplement the role of the school and increase its effectiveness.

In light of research evidence quoted above, the first and second recommendations of the Education Commission of the States (204) concerning statewide, publicly funded early childhood education are interesting: (1) Developing ways to reach the families of young children and to strengthen the ability for being good parents and (2) Involving parents in the formal education of their children.

Delayed Academic Skills

A positive approach to early learning should make possible the optimum all-round development of children. The weight of evidence from both research and practice reviewed thus far places the home and family well ahead of the school for assuring such development in most young children. What, then, is the role of the school in the child's total development?

Schools can provide surrogate care and training for young children when homes are totally inadequate or when parents are personally unable to fulfill their responsibilities for any of several reasons—financial, physical, psychological, maturational, and so forth. But a study of ninety European preschools, along with analyses of American preschools, found that the best preschools and kindergartens were those most closely simulating a good home (487). (See also the next chapter for details.)

And research has raised a serious question: Is intellectual competence in early childhood, or even in elementary school, necessary or desirable for eventual competence in later education and in life (574)? As noted earlier, experiments with paired-associate learning led Rohwer to the conclusion that learning skills are more easily developed through training during adolescence than during early childhood. Although children acquire the base for developing learning skills from their environment,

217

experiences, and relationships in early childhood, Rohwer found that they do not achieve the ability to make use of formal instruction and to retain abstract content until almost the end of childhood or early adolescence.

Rohwer (575) envisioned an elementary school where academic failure would not exist because children would work on projects or topics using nonacademic resources. Then, in the junior high school years, "all the learning necessary for success in meeting high school demands (could) be accomplished." He also expressed the belief that delaying formal instruction until the early adolescent years would increase ultimate academic success and decrease the negative attitudes toward school that appeared to develop in proportion to the years spent in school (574, 358, 197).

Research in the areas of neuropsychology and neurophysiology strongly and generally support Rohwer's thesis (see chapters eight and nine). His proposal could have further merit in that it would avoid the "intellectual burn" of children who struggle to keep up with academic activities before they are ready for total intellectual involvement (215).

Reasoning from the conclusions (1) that compensatory school programs focused on primary grades have not produced significant or sustained cognitive gains and (2) that intensive efforts to develop academic skills in early childhood correlate with apathy and reduced academic accomplishment in later school years, Robinson (571) also proposed early adolescence as the best time for academic learning. (See also chapter seven.) This could be especially advantageous for deprived children whose cognitive skills develop slowly.

Proposals like this are neither new nor revolutionary. Nor does this mean that no attention would be given to children's learning prior to their adolescent years. They would probably receive more satisfying attention than in traditional school programs. The emphasis likely should be on physical health and effective, motor, and perceptual development. With such a foundation, cognitive skills can be acquired easily and rapidly, even by children who normally find school achievement difficult. Those children who start school a year or two late, in the second or third grade, usually catch up with their peers and often pass them. And usually they come out better behaved and better socialized as well as higher achieving. In order to accommodate such late entrants, administrators should provide flexibility—ensuring that the usual lock-step progress through elementary school is not required. In fact, a teacher can use such flexibility to his advantage, especially by using the older students to help the younger and the stronger to assist the weaker (494, 492).

An Ecological Commitment

Schaefer (595, 600) points out the need for support of family care in children's education in order to maintain a life-space or ecological perspective for child development. The current focus upon professional and institutional resource for developing the individual apart from his family and cultural heritage has sometimes produced personal isolation.

Families, however, are often not adequate for the job without some assistance. Society has, in fact, trained them this way by diminishing and sometimes decreasing the parental role and accentuating its own institutions—preschools, care centers, kindergartens, and primary schools. This trend must be reversed if the child's freedom is to be ensured. Focusing on child development within a family and community network or system would provide more supportive relationships (600).

Crowded urban areas and family disintegration have particularly contributed to personal isolation for the child. Cities have become places where people learn to live without natural resources, where the rights of children are minimized, where a deteriorating environment influences human development and behavior (48). The major influences on learning in early childhood grow out of a child's total ecology—the immediate home and school setting as well as the large geographic setting and social system that affect the immediate setting (120). Positive progress in learning and development for all children depends to a great extent on a positive integration of these factors.

13

The Issues and Likely Solutions

Many outstanding examples of child care, preschool, kindergarten, and special programs for the disadvantaged exist in the U.S. and abroad (487). They are meeting needs more real than imagined. Yet often even they provide sanctuary for children who would be much better off in their homes and whose homes could readily provide such care. Regardless of funds available and approaches used, most early childhood education programs today are neither meeting the needs of children nor correcting the results and failures of child-rearing practices in the children's early years (597, 719).

The appropriate order of priorities has been skewed or ignored. We have assumed that children become best educated through contact with a professional in a classroom or other care center. But after nearly two decades of full-time research with children under six years old, Burton White has concluded from his experiments and observations that the *family* is the primary educational delivery system (719). He, along with many key ECE specialists, now believes that the highest educational priority in the nation should go to the family, not to developmental day-care centers nor to the preschool programs that abound. Similarly Sheldon White, after making a comprehensive study of federal ECE programs (723), expressed concern that the early schooling movement "might wipe out the gains special education has made and possibly ruin the future of early childhood education" (494).

The centrality of the home versus the school for the young child's education is a primary ECE issue today. This does not mean parent involvement in school activities, but full-time child and parent involvement in the home and its related activities *wherever possible*. For the child's first seven years or so, the school is at best a substitute and the teacher a surrogate. We should be concentrating *wherever possible* on educating for parenthood and improving the home, rather than on providing alternatives. And we should extend the meaning of "possible" if we want to save our society. The only exceptions should be those cases where the home cannot be made viable as the primary environment for the child. Many times it will be necessary to resort to substitutes and surrogates; yet to build sound children, we must make every effort to minimize early institutional life and maximize home influences.

Some ECE issues are more clearly defined than others, but most of them are interrelated. For the most part, the studies tell their own stories, and comments have been reserved for summaries and areas needing clarification. It is both necessary and urgent that we evaluate conventional wisdom, traditional practices, and current trends according to the questions and evidence arising from a systematic canvass of early childhood research. While some critics have insisted that much evidence supports the idea of early schooling for all (140), they have not yet made it available. There is little likelihood that any systematic body of such evidence exists.

In recent years, a number of thoughtful early childhood education leaders who had once strongly supported early schooling have reversed or sharply modified their positions. As noted in the previous chapter, many of them agree that certain ECE issues deserve careful and objective study and reassessment. We will summarize here some of the issues most frequently discussed and most needing reevaluation, with a goal of clearly translating theory and research-based facts into policy and practice.

Relative Effectiveness of Early Schooling

How effective is early schooling for children? This question challenges educational planners, legislators, trustees, administrators, teachers, parents, and those concerned about the welfare of society, culture, and country. Perhaps most of us equate learning with schools, but the home, during the child's earliest years, appears from the preponderance of research evidence to be his most likely learning laboratory. Formal education or even academic readiness should be kept on the back burner until the child has had time to reach a point of reasonable readiness for academic stimulation and for dilution of parental attachments. We also often equate low-SES homes with disadvantaged children and try to compensate for the assumed "disadvantage" by removing the children from an environment that may actually be best for them, thus in fact disadvantaging them, all the more.

Of course, many truly handicapped and otherwise disadvantaged youngsters at all SES levels do require the structured programs of good preschools, kindergartens, or primary schools. Yet this is no logical reason for generalizing this therapy to children who are not disadvantaged—any more than we hospitalize all children when a few have the "flu" or place all in casts when one breaks an arm. In fact, more germs may exist in the hospital than outside.

Nor do we have any reasonable assurance that preschools in general are as well run as those model schools so often used by researchers. Even the best school or care center is seldom, if ever, as effective as a relatively ordinary home. In fact, even in the inner cities there is reason to question whether the local school's basic environment is generally any better than the home's. Research has much yet to teach on this subject.

An analysis of eighty thousand young children from the National Elementary School Survey (HEW) indicates that, other than providing a publicly supported babysitting service, preschools in general are not serving our children well (486). If indeed we are simply providing out-of-home care, let us call it that, do it only where really needed, and do it very well, encouraging and carefully educating parents to care for their own when they can. No research exists in this chapter, in this book, or elsewhere on record that effectively and systematically leads to any other conclusion if we are primarily and objectively concerned with the freedom and welfare of little children—vis-à-vis parental "freedom," teacher unions, women's "lib" groups, commercial care givers, and other vested interests.

Family Restoration or Personal Accommodation

We must determine, then, whether we shall use the established facts of human ecology to restore family life or to accommodate those who place personal expedience and conventional

223

practices ahead of family welfare. For example, many parents send children to preschool because it is in style, convenient, or dictated by intuition or social pressures. And those forces are often more powerful than legal mandates. If a society flouts truth in dealing with its children, the freedom of all is at risk.

Home or School as the Basic ECE Delivery System

The school and other out-of-home care for young children must, of course, be evaluated against parent and home education. We have to provide out-of-home care for children whose parents cannot care for them, whether for physical, emotional, or financial reasons. Yet, wherever practical, as pointed out by Nimnicht (515), B. White (719), Schaefer (597), and others, the home should be the primary ECE delivery system.

Such a philosophy and practice need not deprive present preschool personnel of employment—as teacher unions so often fear. Some teachers can change their focus from the schoolroom to the home or to parent groups. They can educate parents in children's developmental needs and how best to meet these needs. In any event, the child's welfare must transcend employment concerns of teacher groups and must be carefully weighed in making decisions about parental employment (666). Nor does such policy demean womanhood. It ideally brings fathers together with mothers in support of women's highest calling—motherhood.

If the school has to provide the care, let it be as much as possible like a warm, responsive, consistent home. Following are some of the qualities and/or practices that Moore, Kordenbrock, and Moore (487) have found characteristic of outstanding preschools and care centers:

1. Warm, responsive, consistent teacher-caretakers
2. Small adult-child ratios
3. Residential houses, where possible, instead of school buildings
4. Children grouped in house rooms instead of classrooms, with children placed in family-type play groups of varying ages
5. Alertness to the frequent need to compensate for language and cultural differences
6. Daily homemaking experiences—including gardening,

224

cooking, cleaning, etc.—in lieu of more conventional kindergarten play

7. Programs free from formal teaching, academic orientation, or even stress on readiness for the primary grades
8. Adequate nap and other rest periods for all grades
9. Continuity of teacher or care giver personnel
10. A sense of parenthood more than pedagogy in care givers.

Family Authority and Responsibility

Who is primarily responsible for children? Assuming that authority and responsibility are commensurate, we conclude that, if parents are to have authority over their children, they must also accept responsibility for them. To the extent that parents delegate this *responsibility* to others, they also give up their *authority*. Suviranta (666) has noted that this shift of responsibility has already gone so far that education is in danger of becoming totalitarian, with parents having few rights even when the best interests of the child are at stake. In recent months and years a number of American mothers have been arrested, one recently jailed, for conscientiously keeping their children at home at ages six or seven. This violates constitutional freedom, as well as the rights and responsibilities of motherhood.

Parenthood Education

From the child's earliest years, he should be considered a future parent. This is a primary obligation of parenthood and of our schools at all levels. Yet the immediate needs of parents and expecting parents should be met with programs of all kinds, utilizing the wisest and most effective means of communication: television and radio spots and shows, printed media, community agencies, and so forth. The prime objectives of such programs should be to alert parents to children's developmental needs, to restore their confidence as parents, and to inspire warm, consistent responsiveness to their children—without the urge to be pedagogues.

Freedom for Parents or Children

Mothers sometimes desire freedom from home duties, including child care, in order to work or otherwise be "free." This is particularly true in those societies where life is essentially prepackaged, often taking much of the challenge out of homemaking and motherhood. For some mothers it is financially necessary to work, but for many it is not so cost effective as they would like to believe, as Suviranta has pointed out (666). (In some cases, of course, the father's employment may be in doubt.) The question, however, remains: Assuming that the child's best interests require a warm, responsive parent, are we fair to him when we unnecessarily abrogate parental responsibilities? Is the violation of the child's liberties a necessary concomitant of parental freedom? Or, is "freedom" really license?

The child's freedom to develop into a productive person depends substantially, as research clearly suggests, on the quality of his parental attachment. Therefore, isn't it reasonable to assume in most cases that a lack of attachment unnecessarily limits the child's freedom? The issue is a poignant one. When policy permits or encourages parental self-interest in the face of children's helplessness, reassessment of such policy—and practice—is urgently in order.

Care of Privileged or Underprivileged

As we have often pointed out, children of the poor or underprivileged more often need carefully planned out-of-home care than do children of more affluent families. But some people insist that, if public funding provides special services for the poor, it must also be available for all children (140). This reasoning, if logically extended to all areas of welfare, would ultimately lead to a total—and fiscally improbable—welfare state. In 1975 the *Wall Street Journal* reported that "there are already more Americans (80.6 million) being supported by tax dollars than there are workers in the private sector (71.6 million) to support them." And France has already demonstrated the disastrous results of uncontrolled ECE policies, with adult-child ratios running over 1 to 30 on an average and as high as 1 to 40, 1 to 50, and even more than 1 to 60 (487).

Early Screening

Early screening systems employing physicians, psychologists, and/or alert and well-prepared teachers should be established and made available for every child. Such screening programs would also, when necessary, help in determining the *nature* of the child's problem. Physicians should be alert to symptoms at birth, but the child should ideally have a yearly check up, par-

226

ticularly at or before school entry. This will help eliminate school failures and incorrect assessments of student problems.

Home or School Socialization of the Child

One commonly advanced rationale for early schooling is that it socializes young children. This depends upon the kind of sociability you prefer—positive and altruistic or negative and self-centered. Many parents confuse peer orientation and dependence with sociability when instead true sociality thrives on secure, independent thought.

Although the evidence may surprise parents and educators, it clearly points to the home as the primary socializing agency, no matter what approach is taken. For example: (1) Comparative entrance age studies find that children who start early to school are generally less socially mature in their later childhood and their high school years. (2) Teachers have subjectively found that early school entrants are more likely to have social maladjustment problems as they progress through school. (3) Children who have a secure home life until they are able to reason consistently and to establish their value systems—particularly if they carry responsibility *with the parents* in the home—will feel needed, wanted, and depended on. They will thus have a strong sense of self-worth—the basic dynamic of *positive* sociality and independent thought—and will not easily lock in to peer values, as early entrants usually do. They are less likely to become self-centered and peer dependent—in effect negatively socialized (see chapter eleven and references 25, 374, and 375).

Little if any research evidence supports the belief that young children need more social opportunities than normally come from a combination of parents, relatives, and neighborhood friends. In fact, in urban, suburban, rural, and even remote areas, most children develop better socially at home than in school. (Exceptions, of course, may be those homes that cannot provide reasonably sound parenting because of severe physical, cultural, emotional, or financial difficulties or parental ignorance or apathy.) In planning social opportunities, we often overlook the child's equally important need for solitude to work out his own fantasies—a basic activity for true sociality.

The Child's Need for Cognitive Stimulation

Another of the most frequently heard reasons for early schooling is mental stimulation. Except for some children who are deprived or handicapped, this theory simply is not consistent with research findings related to early learning. Nor for the most part is it successful in practice.

If, as neurophysiologists suggest, brain structure and function move along together, requiring a child to undertake tasks for which he is not fully prepared is risking damage to the central nervous system. It may also risk potential difficulties in the affective and motivational aspects of learning due to frustration, because the learning "tools" simply are not yet ready. Recent findings in the areas of neurophysiology, cognition, vision, hearing, and so on confirm this. They have raised serious questions about expecting children to pursue basic skills of reading, writing, and arithmetic on a deliberate academic basis before they are eight or ten years old. Only then have their neurological, cognitive, sensory, motor, and affective development *jointly* reached reasonable levels of maturity—what Moore calls the integrated maturity level (IML) (492). This appears to be the earliest safe time for school, even for gifted children.

If we expect reading and arithmetic based on understanding rather than on rote learning, delay of *formal* training in these areas appears wise—although informal education through warm parental responses is desirable. Some scholars and clinicians conclude that formal education should wait until ages ten to fourteen, or early adolescence (215, 236, 571, 574). Freedom within limits that permit the child to explore and test his own ideas and to develop practical skills—primarily with his parents—appears the best kind of "stimulation" for most children. Strong clinical and research evidence indicates that early exposure to the so-called stimulation of school often destroys childhood motivation for learning. By grade three or four many children become stranded on a motivational plateau, never recovering their early excitement for learning. Most primary teachers agree.

Children's Attitudes Toward School

Many parents think their young children are excited about school but do not stop to ask, "Why?" Is it because "all the kids are doing it"? Do they really enjoy school more than home? If they do, why? What of the quality—warmth, consistency, responsiveness—of the home compared with the school? Are homes really lacking in things that can interest young children? Is it only the social and psychological pressure of "everyone's doing it" that encourages early schooling? Or are parents simply unwilling to make the necessary sacrifices ensuring early childhood freedom, so urgently required for optimum development? Parents are frequently quite ready to submit to social pressures or conventional wisdom that meshes nicely with their own selfish inclinations.

Studies also clearly indicate that, the earlier children go to school, the worse their attitudes eventually are toward school, particularly as they enter their teens (358, 359, 433). Much more specific experimentation with parents and homes is now underway to provide sounder bases for parent education.

Structure or Freedom in the Young Child's Learning

While some preschools have excellent unstructured programs, most are readiness oriented—for reading, writing, arithmetic, language arts, etc. Such structure and regimentation seem helpful if we are determined to teach academic skills to the normal child before he is ready. Yet this is much like holding a young child up by his hands in the hope that we can hurry up his ability to walk—before he is ready. The question here is, why make him walk? If we are not worried about rushing a child into the basic skills, a virtually unstructured program with warmth, consistency, and concern for sound value development will—except for certain handicapped or disadvantaged children— provide the best readiness for learning. And the brighter the child, of course, the greater the risk of violating this readiness principle. The sharper the child, the more easily he is dulled, and he has more to lose.

Parents as Teachers

An alarming number of parents appear to have little confidence in their ability to "teach" their children. Research suggests that their ability to *care,* rather than to *teach,* is the criterion of parenthood during the early years, regardless of educational background. Sound care automatically provides sound teaching at this time. We should help parents understand the overriding importance of incidental teaching in the context of warm, consistent companionship. Such caring is usually the greatest teaching, especially if caring means sharing in the activities of the home—which for the young child represents his fore-taste of mature living, security, and independence. We have found no evidence for the common assumption that teachers can generally outparent parents.

Natural and Enriched Environments

Parents should also question much of the contemporary emphasis on special materials and equipment for learning in a child's environment. A clutter of toys can be more confusing than satisfying to a child. On the other hand, natural situations, with opportunities to explore, seldom overstimulate or trouble a small child. Furthermore, most children will find greater satisfaction and demonstrate greater learning from things they make and do *with* their parents or other people than from elaborate toys or learning materials. And there is no substitute for solitude—in the sandpile, mud puddle, or play area—for a young child to work out his own fantasies. Yet this privilege is often denied in our anxiety to institutionalize children.

Cost of Effective Child Care

An appropriate adult-child ratio is vital for children's development and learning (462). But the cost of providing the number of adults necessary for optimal care is high. Excellent parent and home education programs have been implemented, however, at much lower costs than possible for well-planned preschool or day-care programs. And these programs reach not just one child, but tend to flow throughout the whole family and community.

Costs in child services sometimes lead to confusion between educators and social work personnel and between the relative responsibilities of family physicians and publicly provided medical care. If our care system is to survive, costs of child care and child services must be evaluated from professional perspectives rather than political. B. White warns that otherwise the entire early childhood program may well be sacrificed (717).

School Entrance Age

The evidence overwhelmingly favors later entrance for most children. In fact—except for handicapped or seriously deprived children, who sometimes can profit from early structured learning—there is no systematic body of research evidence to the contrary. A nongraded primary room as a screening, adjusting, facility for children of varying physical and cognitive maturity would normally be the most efficient means of handling eight-year-old school beginners. Many will already know how to read, to write, or to do formal arithmetic, but few will be able to do all of these well, especially the latter two. And some, of course, will have virtually no background in these skills.

Returns from over three hundred correspondents who have entered schools at age eight or later indicate, however, that even in conventional school programs average youngsters can quickly progress and catch up. They often surpass—in motivation, achievement, behavior, sociality, and leadership—those who started school several years earlier. When they enter school these older children should normally be placed with their chronological and/or maturational peers.

There are many variations in state school laws, mandating enrollment anywhere from 8 years down to 5 ¾ years or younger. Seldom do they provide for the later maturation of boys, but dropout and delinquency statistics suggest that many boys suffer serious disadvantage from these laws, which are patently inconsiderate and unfair in our society. Such laws should either (1) be rewritten to provide the needed flexibility; (2) be tested at highest juridical levels; or, only after that failing, (3) be superseded by a federal law setting *general* enrollment age parameters consistent with systematic research evidence. Test cases presently in court may indeed bring state and/or federal court decisions that will have the effect of appropriate national mandate.

Differentiating Treatment
of Various Socioeconomic Levels

As pointed out earlier, it is impractical to demand the same tax-supported early childhood institutional care for those in middle- and higher-SES groups as for those in poverty. Such an attempt, carried to its ultimate logical conclusion, would result in a totalitarian welfare state. Some special services, such as medical and psychological screening for all children, may be better handled by public health or other agencies. But general early childhood assistance should be reserved for those incapable—for whatever reason—of caring for their children themselves.

Successful parenting, however, is *not* limited to middle- or

231

upper-income groups. Some of the best parents are found among the economically disadvantaged. And there are indifferent parents at all levels of society. So any plan for parent education, while first perhaps considering the poor, must not overlook the others.

School and Community Parent Education

Close cooperation between schools and other community agencies must exist for good parent or parenthood education programs. (Some proponents differentiate between *parent* and *parenthood* education, applying the latter term to education at school levels and to other premarriage groups.) Whether the primary responsibility is assumed by the school, community, church, or other agency, the *development* and *needs* of children must be the central focus of such education—not the "freedom" of parents, the job-arranging propensities of teacher unions, the zeal of women liberationists, or the advertising expertise of educational media people.

Research Analysis and Application

There is serious need for long-range ECE studies testing the recommendations of this book. Longitudinal research should, if possible, extend ten or fifteen years or more, comparing early entrants of five or six with later entrants of eight or nine. With only occasional exceptions (e.g., Davie, Butler & Goldstein (178), Mawhinney (447), and Forester (239)), ECE studies have covered relatively short time spans. Appraisals of Head Start and other programs have often been inconclusive for this reason. Meanwhile, the synergic effect of analyzing and interrelating studies from several ECE areas, as presented for example in this book, can provide much valuable information.

To gain as much understanding as possible of the real issues involved, we must interrelate research from all areas pertaining to the problem. At the same time, an effort should be made to (1) simplify explanations, (2) clarify findings, and (3) avoid use of complex or peculiarly professional terminology that so often obscures the message—even among ECE specialists and certainly among most educators and laymen. Data from carefully controlled studies can thus be available to educational planners and policy makers.

And we should not neglect or demean sound *clinical* data.

When carefully evaluated, it can provide excellent clues for further study and action.

Finally, it has long been assumed that researchers should not be advocates: that advocacy dilutes objectivity. We have come recently and somewhat reluctantly to believe, with excellent support, that this is not necessarily true. This long-held assumption seems to be one of the reasons that ECE facts from the various disciplines have been so scantily interrelated and poorly communicated. Truth is often threatening to those who find security in conventional practices, not daring to step out on new ground—or on old ground, rediscovered.

Subjecting expedient ways and conventional wisdom to honest scrutiny reveals their basic qualities. Such scrutiny is necessary for ECE research to benefit children fully. It is crucial that we reevaluate the trends of the times that do not clearly serve the needs of children. Where necessary, policies and practices—and legislation—must be altered if children are to realize their maximum potential. Attention to the *total* development of our children, however difficult to sell, is one of the most inexpensive and imperative kinds of insurance for the healthy survival of our society and civilization.

References

[1]Abelson, W. D. 1974. Head Start graduates in school: Studies in New Haven, Connecticut. In *Longitudinal evaluations of preschool programs,* ed. S. Ryan, pp. 1–14. Washington, D.C.: Office of Child Development. [134, 198]

[2]Abramson, P. R. 1973. Familial variables related to the expression of violent aggression in preschool-age children. *Journal of Genetic Psychology* 122:345–46. [45, 68, 134]

[3]Aguilar, M. J., and Williamson, M. L. 1968. Observations on growth and development of the brain. In *Human growth,* ed. D. B. Cheek. Philadelphia: Lea and Febiger. [134, 164, 176]

[4]Ahr, E. A. 1967*a*. The development of a group preschool screening test of early school entrance potentiality. *Psychology in the Schools* 4:59–63. [86]

[5]_____. 1967*b*. Early school admission: One district's experience. *Elementary School Journal* 67:231–36. [95, 97, 99]

[6]Ainsworth, M. D. S. 1963. The development of infant-mother interaction among the Ganda. In *Determinants of infant behaviour II,* ed. B. M. Foss, pp. 67–112. London: Methuen; New York: Wiley. [29]

[7]_____. 1969. Object relations, dependency, and attachment: A theoretical review of the infant-mother relationship. *Child Development* 40:969–1025. [29]

[8]_____. 1972. Attachment and dependency: A comparison. In *Attachment and dependency,* ed. J. L. Gewirtz, pp. 97–137. Washington, D.C.: V. H. Winston & Sons, Inc. [30, 31, 35]

[9]_____. 1973. The development of infant-mother attachment. In *Review of child development research,* eds. B. M. Caldwell and H. N. Ricciuti, vol. 3. Chicago: University of Chicago Press. [29, 30, 31, 33, 35]

[10]Ainsworth, M. D. S., and Bell, S. M. (no date) *Mother-infant interaction and the development of competence.* ED 065 180. [45]

[11]Alexander, F., and Staub, H. 1931. *The criminal, the judge, and the public.* New York: Macmillan. [57]

[12]Allen, F. H. 1958. The dilemmas of growth—for parents and children. *Child Study Journal* 35:4–7. [53]

[13]Allen, G. B., and Masling, J. M. 1957. An evaluation of the effects of nursery school training on children in the kindergarten, first and second grades. *Journal of Educational Research* 51:285–96. [202]

[14]Almy, Millie, et al. 1969. *Logical thinking in second grade.* ED 033 747. [136]

[15]Ames, L. B. 1963. Usefulness of the Lowenfeld mosaic test in predicting school readiness in kindergarten and primary school pupils. *Journal of Genetic Psychology* 103:75–91. [86]

[16]_____. 1969. Children with perceptual problems may also lag developmentally. *Journal of Learning Disabilities* 2:205–8. [150, 156]

[17]Ames, L. B., and August, J. 1966. Comparison of mosaic response of Negro and white primary-school children. [86, 93]

[18]Ames, L. B., and Chase, J. A. 1974. *Don't push your preschooler.* New York: Harper & Row. [72]

[19]Anastasi, A. 1958. Heredity, environment, and the question "how?" *Psychological Review* 65:197–208. [28]

[20]Anderson, J. E. 1956. Child development: An historical perspective. *Child Development* 27:181–96. [15, 208]

[21]Anderson, L. D. 1940. A longitudinal study of the effects of nursery-school training on successive intelligence test ratings. In *Yearbook of the National Society for the Study of Education,* vol. 39, part 2, pp. 3–10. [200]

[22]Anderson, R. C. 1965. Can first graders learn an advanced problem-solving skill? *Journal of Educational Psychology* 56:283–94. [134]

[23]Anderson, S. B. 1968. *The making of a pupil: Changing children into school children.* ED 037 235. [100, 101]

[24]Andreas, V. J. 1972. School entrance ages and subsequent progress. Master's thesis, University of Northern Colorado, Greeley, Colorado. [98, 110]

[25]Andrus, R., and Horowitz, E. L. 1938. The effect of nursery school training: Insecurity feelings. *Child Development* 9:169–74. [201, 227]

[26]Angell, D. B. 1954. Differences in social behavior between elementary school children who have attended nursery school and those who have not attended nursery school. Master's thesis, North Texas State College, Denton, Texas. [202]

[27]Appel, M. H. 1942. Aggressive behavior of nursery school children and adult procedures in dealing with such behavior. *Journal of Experimental Education* 11:185–99. [201]

[28]Arena, T. 1970. Social maturity in the prediction of academic achievement. *Journal of Educational Research* 64:21–22. [141]

[29]Asbury, C. A. 1970. Some effects of training on verbal mental functioning in Negro preschool children: A research note. *Journal of Negro Education* 39:100–103. [197]

[30]Asher, S. R., and Markell, R. A. 1973. Influence of interest on sex differences in reading comprehension. Paper presented at the annual meeting of the American Educational Research Association, 1973, at the University of Illinois–Urbana, Champaign, Illinois. [114]

[31]Atkinson, R. C. 1968. Computerized instruction and the learning process. *American Psychologist* 23:225–39. [176]

[32]Atkinson, R. C., and Fletcher, J. D. 1972. Teaching children to read with a computer. *The Reading Teacher* 25:319–27. [176]

[33]Austin, G. R. 1972. International comparative study of school-related achievement as it reflects effects of early childhood education. Working document. Paris: Centre for Educational Research and Innovation. [140]

[34]Ausubel, D. P. 1962. Can children learn anything that adults can and more effectively? *Elementary School Journal* 62:270–72. [136]

[35]Ausubel, D. P., and Ausubel, P. 1963. Ego development among segregated Negro children. In *Education in depressed areas,* ed. A. H. Passow, pp. 109–41. New York: Columbia University Teachers College Press. [59]

[36]Ayres, J. A. 1968. Reading—a product of sensory integrative processes. In *Perception and reading,* ed. H. K. Smith, pp. 77–82. Newark, Del.: International Reading Association. [106, 112]

[37]Baer, C. J. 1958. The school progress and adjustment of underage and overage students. *Journal of Educational Psychology* 49:17–19. [141]

[38]Baldwin, A. L.; Kalhounr, J.; and Breese, F. H. 1945. *Patterns of parent behavior.* Psychological Monographs, vol. 58, no. 3 (serial no. 268). Westport, Conn.: Greenwood Press. [41]

236

[39]Ball, R. S. 1970. *The relation of certain home environment factors to the thinking abilities of three-year-old children.* ED 039 041. [66]

[40]Balow, I. H. 1963. Sex differences in first grade reading. *Elementary English* 40:303–6, 320. [109]

[41]Balow, I. H., and Balow, B. 1964. Lateral dominance and reading achievement in the second grade. *American Educational Research Journal* 1:139–43. [111, 149]

[42]Bandura, A., and Huston, A. 1961. Identification as a process of incidental learning. *Journal of Abnormal and Social Psychology* 63:311–18. [55]

[43]Bandura, A.; Ross, D.; and Ross, S. A. 1961. Transmission of aggression through imitation of aggressive models. *Journal of Abnormal and Social Psychology* 52:575–82. [55]

[44]Bandura, A., and Walters, R. H. 1963. *Social learning and personality development.* New York: Holt, Rinehart & Winston. [55]

[45]Baratz, S. S., and Baratz, J. C. 1970. Early childhood intervention: The social science base of institutional racism. *Harvard Educational Review* 40:29–50. [79]

[46]Barbrack, C. R., and Horton, D. M. 1970. Educational intervention in the home and paraprofessional career development: A second generation mother study with an emphasis on costs and benefits. DARCEE papers and reports, vol. 4, no. 4. Nashville, Tenn.: George Peabody College for Teachers. [199, 212]

[47]Barry, H.; Bacon, M. K.; and Child, E. L. 1957. A cross-cultural survey of some sex differences in socialization. *Journal of Abnormal Social Psychology* 55:327–32. [178]

[48]Bauch, J. P. 1971. Cities: An alien environment for young children. *Peabody Journal of Education* 48:122–24. [219]

[49]Baumrind, D. 1967. *Child care practices anteceding three patterns of preschool behavior.* Genetic Psychology Monographs 75:43–88. Provincetown, Mass.: Journal Press. [42, 45]

[50]Baumrind, D., and Black, A. E. 1967. Socialization practices associated with dimensions of competence in preschool boys and girls. *Child Development* 38:291–327. [45]

[51]Bayley, N. 1958. Individual patterns of development. *Child Development* 27:45–74. [128, 129, 130]

[52]———. 1966. The two-year-old. Paper read at Education Improvement Program, May 5, 1966, at Duke University, Durham, North Carolina. [133]

[53]———. 1970. Development of mental abilities. In *Carmichael's manual of child psychology,* ed. J. Mussen, 1:1163–1209. New York: Wiley & Sons. [128, 181, 182, 183, 184, 185, 210]

[54]Bayley, N., and Schaefer, E. S. 1964. *Correlations of maternal and child behaviors with the development of mental abilities.* Monographs of the Society for Research in Child Development, vol. 29, no. 6 (serial no. 97). Chicago: University of Chicago Press. [181, 182, 185]

[55]Beasley, D. S., and Beasley, D. C. 1973. Auditory reassembly abilities of black and white first- and third-grade children. *Journal of Speech and Hearing Research* 16:213–21. [92, 93]

[56]Beck, H. L. 1973. *Don't push me, I'm no computer.* New York: McGraw-Hill. [216]

237

⁵⁷Beery, J. W. 1967. Matching of auditory and visual stimuli by average and retarded readers. *Child Development* 38:827–33. [157]

⁵⁸Beilin, H., and Franklin, I. C. 1962. Logical operations in area and length measurement: Age and training effects. *Child Development* 33:607–18. [134, 136]

⁵⁹Bell, R., and Costello, N. 1964. Three tests for sex differences in tactile sensitivity in the newborn. *Biologia Neonatorum* 7:335–47. [177]

⁶⁰Bell, R., and Darling, J. F. 1965. The prone head reaction to the human neonate: Relation with sex and tactile sensitivity. *Child Development* 36:943–49. [177]

⁶¹Bell, S. M. 1970. The development of the concept of object as related to infant-mother attachment. *Child Development* 41:291–311. [30, 32]

⁶²_____. 1971. Early cognitive development and its relationship to infant-mother attachment: A study of disadvantaged Negro infants. Final report, Project No. 508, Johns Hopkins University. Washington, D.C.: OE, U.S. Department of Health, Education, and Welfare. [30, 31, 45]

⁶³_____. 1975. Letter to R. S. Moore, 10 September 1975. [31]

⁶⁴Bell, T. H. 1973. *Your child's intellect.* Salt Lake City, Ut.: Olympus Publishing Company. [216]

⁶⁵Beller, E. K. 1962. A study of dependency and aggression in early childhood. Progress report, project M-849, Child Development Center, New York. [186]

⁶⁶_____. 1967. *A study of cognitive and social functioning, Project II; A study of the attitudes of parents of deprived children, Project III.* ED 025 310. [198]

⁶⁷_____. 1974. Impact of early education on disadvantaged children. In *Longitudinal evaluations of preschool programs*, ed. S. Ryan, pp. 15–48. Washington, D.C.: Department of Health, Education, and Welfare. [198]

⁶⁸Beller, E. K. and Neubauer, P. B. 1963. Sex differences and symptom patterns in early childhood. *Journal of Child Psychiatry* 2:414–33. [182]

⁶⁹Bennett, E. L., et al. 1964. Chemical and anatomical plasticity of brain. *Science* 146:610–19. [146]

⁷⁰Bennett, E. L.; Rosenzweig, M. R.; and Diamond, M. C. 1970. Time courses of effects of differential experiences on brain measures and behavior of rats. In *Molecular approaches to learning and memory,* ed. W. L. Byrne, pp. 55–89. New York: Academic Press. [171]

⁷¹Bentzen, F. 1963. Sex ratios in learning and behavior. *American Journal of Orthopsychiatry* 33:92–98. [185]

⁷²Bercovici, A., and Feshbach, N. 1973. *Teaching styles of mothers of "successful" readers and "problem" readers in the first grade.* ED 076 962. [41]

⁷³Bereiter, C. 1967. *Acceleration of intellectual development in early childhood.* ED 014 332. [109, 133, 134]

⁷⁴_____. 1972. Schools without education. *Harvard Educational Review* 42:390–413. [195, 212]

⁷⁵Bereiter, C., and Engelmann, S. 1966a. *Effectiveness of direct verbal instruction on IQ performance and achievement in reading and arithmetic.* ED 030 496. [195]

⁷⁶_____. 1966b. Observations on the use of direct instruction with young disadvantaged children. *Journal of School Psychology* 4:55–62. [195]

⁷⁷_____. 1966c. *Teaching the disadvantaged child in the preschool.* Englewood Cliffs, N.J.: Prentice-Hall. [195]

⁷⁸Berger, H. 1932. Ueber das Elektorenzephalogramm des Menschen. IV

238

Mitteilung. *Archiv fuer Psychiatrie* 97:6–26. [168]

[79]Berk, L. E.; Rose, M. H.; and Stewart, D. 1970. Attitudes of English and American children toward their school experience. *Journal of Educational Psychology* 61:33–40. [78]

[80]Bigelow, G. S. 1971. Field dependence—field independence in 5- to 10-year-old children. *Journal of Educational Research* 64:397–400. [129, 131]

[81]Bing, E. 1963. Effect of child-rearing practices on development of differential cognitive abilities. *Child Development* 34:631–48. [182]

[82]Birch, H. G., and Belmont, L. 1965. Lateral dominance, lateral awareness, and reading disability. *Child Development* 36:57–71. [149]

[83]Birch, H. G., and Bortner, M. 1966. Stimulus competition and category usage in normal children. *Journal of Genetic Psychology* 109:195–204. [138]

[84]Birch, H. G., and Lefford, A. 1963. *Intersensory development in children.* Monographs of the Society for Research in Child Development, vol. 28, no. 5 (serial no. 89). Chicago: University of Chicago Press. [133, 154]

[85]Bird, G. E. 1940. Effect of nursery school attendance upon mental growth of children. In *Yearbook of the National Society for the Study of Education,* vol. 39, part 2, pp. 81–84. [200]

[86]Bissell, J. S. 1970. The cognitive effects of preschool programs for disadvantaged children. Doctoral thesis, Harvard University, Cambridge, Massachusetts. [93, 194, 199]

[87]_____. 1973. Planned variation in Head Start and Follow Through. In *Compensatory education for children ages 2 to 8,* ed. J. C. Stanley, pp. 63–107. Baltimore, Md.: The Johns Hopkins University Press. [20, 21]

[88]Blank, M. H., and Solomon, F. 1969. How shall the disadvantaged child be taught? *Child Development* 40:47–61. [76, 77, 193]

[89]Blatt, B., and Garfunkel, F. 1965. *A field demonstration of the effects of nonautomated responsive environments on the intellectual and social competence of educable mentally retarded children.* ED 010 289. [197]

[90]_____. 1969. *The educability of intelligence.* Washington, D.C.: Council for Exceptional Children. [192]

[91]Bledsoe, J. C. 1967. Self-concepts of children and their intelligence achievement, interests, and anxiety. *Childhood Education* 43:436–38. [52, 179]

[92]Blehar, M. 1974. Anxious attachment and defensive reactions associated with day care. *Child Development* 45:683–92. [34]

[93]Bloom, B. S. 1964. *Stability and change in human characteristics.* New York: Wiley. [128, 210]

[94]_____. 1965. *Early learning in the home.* ED 019 127. [210]

[95]Blum, D. M., and Chagnon, J. G. 1967. The effect of age, sex, and language on rotation in a visual-motor task. *Journal of Social Psychology* 71:125–32. [41]

[96]Bonney, M. E., and Nicholson, E. L. 1958. Comparative social adjustments of elementary school pupils with and without preschool training. *Child Development* 29:125–33. [202]

[97]Bookbinder, G. E. 1967. The preponderance of summer-born children in E.S.N. classes: Which is responsible: Age or length of infant schooling? *Educational Research* 9:213–18. [98]

[98]*Boston Recorder and Religious Telegraph* (newspaper), July 9, 1829, p. 4 (Infants teaching adults). [207]

239

[99]Bottrill, J. H. 1967. Effects of preschool experience on the school readiness level of privileged and underprivileged children. *Exceptional Children* 34:275. [92]

[100]Bouchard, R. A., and Mackler, B. 1967. *A prekindergarten program for four-year-olds with a review of the literature on preschool education.* ED 026 124. [200]

[101]Bowerman, C. E., and Kinch, J. W. 1959. Changes in family and peer orientation of children between the 4th and 10th grades. *Social Forces* 37:206–11. [55]

[102]Bowlby, J. 1952. *Maternal care and mental health.* Geneva: World Health Organization. [36, 54]

[103]————. 1953. Some pathological processes set in train by early mother-child separation. *Journal of Mental Science* 99:265–72. [34]

[104]————. 1965. *Child care and the growth of love.* Baltimore: Penguin. [29, 31, 34]

[105]————. 1967. *Maternal care and mental health.* New York: Schocken Books. [34]

[106]————. 1969. *Attachment and loss,* vol. 1. New York: Basic Books. [29, 34, 35]

[107]————. 1973. *Attachment and loss, II: Separation, anxiety, and anger.* New York: Basic Books. [34]

[108]Brackbill, Y. 1973. Continuous stimulation reduces arousal level: Stability of the effect over time. *Child Development* 44:43–46. [71, 72]

[109]Braga, J. L. 1969. Analysis and evaluation of early admission to school for mentally advanced children. *Journal of Educational Research* 63:103–6. [95]

[110]————. 1971. Early admission: Opinion versus evidence. *Elementary School Journal* 72:35–46. [95]

[111]Brandis, W., and Bernstein, B. 1974. *Selection and control: Teachers' ratings of children in the infant school.* London: Routledge and Kegan Paul. [37, 39, 124]

[112]Brazelton, T. B. 1974. *Toddlers and parents: A declaration of independence.* New York: Delacorte Press. [50]

[113]Brazziel, W. 1967. Two years of Head Start. *Phi Delta Kappan* 48:344–48. [19]

[114]Brekke, V. W.; Williams, J. D.; and Harlow, S. D. 1973. Conservation and reading readiness. *Journal of Genetic Psychology* 123:133–38. [114]

[115]Brenner, A., and Stott, L. H. 1973. *School readiness factor analyzed.* Detroit: Merrill-Palmer Institute. [86, 87, 88, 180, 183, 185, 186]

[116]Briggs, P. F., and Tellegen, A. 1970. Further normative data on a Frostig subtest, eye-hand coordination. *Perceptual and Motor Skills* 30:640–42. [149]

[117]Brison, D. W. 1966. Acceleration of conservation of substance. *Journal of Genetic Psychology* 109:311–22. [134]

[118]Bronfenbrenner, U. 1970. *Two worlds of childhood: U.S. and U.S.S.R.* New York: Simon and Schuster. [24, 55, 61, 68]

[119]————. 1973. The social ecology of human development. In *Brain and intelligence: The ecology of child development,* ed. Frederick Richardson, pp. 113–129. Hyattsville, Md.: National Educational Press. [24, 46]

[120]————. 1974. The origins of alienation. *Scientific American* 231:53–61. [219]

[121]Brook, J. S. 1970. A test of Piaget's theory of "nominal realism." *Journal of Genetic Psychology* 116:165–75. [137]

[122]Brookover, W. B. 1969. Self-concept and achievement. Paper presented at

the annual meeting of the American Educational Research Association, February 1969, Los Angeles. [50]

[123]Brookover, W. B.; Patterson, A.; and Thomas, S. 1962. Self-concept of ability and school achievement. USOE Project No. 845. East Lansing: Michigan State University. [50]

[124]_____. 1964. Self-concept of ability and school achievement. *Sociology of Education* 37:271-78. [50]

[125]Brophy, J. E. 1970. Mothers as teachers of their own preschool children: The influence of socioeconomic status and task structure on teaching specificity. *Child Development* 41:79-94. [37]

[126]Brown, A. L. 1973. Conservation of numbers and continuous quantity in normal, bright, and retarded children. *Child Development* 44:376-79. [95, 99]

[127]Brown, A. W., and Hunt, R. 1961. Relations between nursery school attendance and teachers' ratings of some aspects of children's adjustment in kindergarten. *Child Development* 32:585-96. [202]

[128]Bruner, J. S. 1960. *The process of education.* Cambridge, Mass.: Harvard University Press. [127, 210]

[129]Bryant, P. E., and Trabasso, T. 1971. Transitive inferences and memory in young children. *Nature* 232:456-58. [134]

[130]Bryden, M. P. 1972. Auditory-visual and sequential-spatial matching in relation to reading ability. *Child Development* 43:824-32. [112]

[131]Budoff, M., and Quinlan, D. 1964. Auditory and visual learning in primary grade children. *Child Development* 35:583-86. [90, 112]

[132]Buktenica, N. A. 1968. *Visual learning: Dimensions in early learning series.* ED 027 089. [152]

[133]Busse, T. V., et al. 1972. Environmentally enriched classrooms and the cognitive and perceptual development of Negro preschool children. *Journal of Educational Psychology* 63:15-21. [73, 77]

[134]Butler, A. L. 1970. *Current research in early childhood education.* Washington, D.C.: American Association of Elementary-Kindergarten-Nursery Educators. [214]

[135]_____. 1971. *Recent research in early childhood education.* ED 058 970. [211]

[136]Cairns, R. B. 1972. Attachment and dependency: A psychobiological and social-learning synthesis. In *Attachment and dependency,* ed. J. L. Gewirtz, pp. 29-80. Washington, D.C.: V. H. Winston & Sons.

[137]Caldwell, B. M. 1972. What does research teach us about day care: For children under three. *Children Today* 1:6-11. [67]

[138]Caldwell, B. M., and Ricciuti, H. N., eds. 1973. *Review of child development research,* vol. 3. Chicago: University of Chicago Press. [9]

[139]California (People of the State of) vs. Larry and Nell Williams. 1973. Office of the District Attorney (for the St. Helena School District), Napa County, California. [86]

[140]California State Department of Education. 1972. *Early childhood education: Report of the task force on early childhood education.* Sacramento: California State Department of Education. [23, 222, 226]

[141]Caplin, M. D. 1966. The relationship between self-concept and academic achievement and between level of aspiration and academic achievement. Doctoral dissertation, Columbia University, New York, New York. [50]

[142]Carlsmith, L. 1964. Effect of early father absence on scholastic aptitude.

241

Harvard Educational Review 34:3-21. [182]

[143]Carpenter, E., and Shipley, E. 1962. *Freedom to move.* ED 020 778. [70, 71, 72, 77, 212]

[144]Carroll, M. L. 1963. Academic achievement and adjustment of underage and overage third graders. *Journal of Educational Research* 56:415-19. [184]

[145]Carter, L. B. 1956. The effect of early school entrance on the scholastic achievement of elementary school children in the Austin public schools. *Journal of Educational Research* 50:91-103. [185]

[146]Cartwright, W. J., and Steglich, W. G. 1965. *Report of the effectiveness of project Head Start, Lubbock, Texas.* ED 019 131. [197]

[147]Cawley, J. F.; Burrow, W. H.; and Goodstein, H. A. 1970. Performance of Head Start and non-Head Start participants at first grade. *Journal of Negro Education* 39:124-31. [194]

[148]Chalfant, J. C., and Scheffelin, M. A. 1969. *Central processing dysfunctions in children: A review of research.* Washington, D.C.: Department of Health, Education, and Welfare. [145]

[149]Chansky, N. M. 1963. Age, IQ, and improvement of reading. *Journal of Educational Research* 56:439. [109]

[150]Chissom, B. S. 1971. A factor-analytic study of the relationship of motor factors to academic criteria for first- and third-grade boys. *Child Development* 42:1133-43. [90, 132]

[151]Chomsky, C. 1972. Language development after age six. In *Readings in child behavior and development,* ed. C. S. Lavatelli and F. Stendler, pp. 271-82. New York: Harcourt Brace Jovanovich. [137]

[152]Choppin, B. H. 1969. The relationship between achievement and age. *Educational Research* 12:22-29. [96]

[153]Cicirelli, V. G.; Evans, J. W.; and Schiller, J. S. 1970. The impact of Head Start: A reply. *Harvard Educational Review* 40:105-29. [19]

[154]Clarizio, H. F. 1968. Maternal attitude change associated with involvement in project Head Start. *Journal of Negro Education* 37:106-13. [47]

[155]Clarke, A. D. B. 1968. Learning and human development. *British Journal of Psychiatry* 114:1061-77. [134, 135]

[156]Clarke, H. H., and Drowatzky, J. N. 1972. Mental, social, and physical characteristics of boys underaged and modal-aged in elementary school. *Elementary School Journal* 73:26-35. [95]

[157]Clasen, R. E.; Spear, J. E.; and Tomaro, M. P. 1969. A comparison of the relative effectiveness of two types of preschool compensatory programming. *Journal of Educational Research* 62:401-5. [194, 197]

[158]Cline, M., and Dickey, M. 1968. *An evaluation and follow-up study of summer 1966 Head Start children in Washington, D.C.* ED 020 794.

[159]Coffman, A. O., and Dunlap, J. 1967. *Effects of assessment and personalized programming for subsequent intellectual development of prekindergarten and kindergarten children.* ED 013 663. [141, 185]

[160]Cole, M., and Bruner, J. S. 1972. Preliminaries to a theory of cultural differences. In *Early childhood education,* ed. I. J. Gordon, pp. 161-79. Chicago: University of Chicago Press. [66, 67, 72, 78, 79]

[161]Coleman, H. M. 1968. Visual perception and reading dysfunction. *Journal of Learning Disabilities* 1:116-23. [152, 184]

[162]Collard, R. R. 1971. Exploratory and play behaviors of infants reared in

an institution and in lower- and middle-class homes. *Child Development* 42:1003–15. [69, 75]

[163]Colton, F. V. 1972. Cognitive and affective reactions of kindergartners to video displays. *Child Study Journal* 2:63–66. [71, 72]

[164]Condrey, J. C.; Siman, M. L.; and Bronfenbrenner, U. 1968. Characteristics of peer- and adult-oriented children. Unpublished manuscript, Department of Child Development, Cornell University. [55]

[165]Conners, C. K.; Schuette, C.; and Goldman, A. 1967. Informational analysis of intersensory communication in children of different social class. *Child Development* 38:251–66. [68, 132, 157]

[166]Coopersmith, S. 1967. *The antecedents of self-esteem.* San Francisco: W. H. Freeman & Co. [50, 51, 52, 53, 55]

[167]Corbin, P. H. 1961. The electroencephalogram in normal children from one to ten years of age: A study with observations on the use of frequency analysis. Master's thesis, University of Minnesota, Minneapolis. [169]

[168]Cox, F. N., and Campbell, D. 1968. Young children in a new situation with and without their mothers. *Child Development* 39:123–31. [34]

[169]Crandall, V., and Rabson, A. 1960. Children's repetition choices in an intellectual achievement situation following success and failure. *Journal of Genetic Psychology* 97:161–68. [182]

[170]Crandall, V., et al. 1964. Parents' attitudes and behaviors and grade school children's academic achievements. *Journal of Genetic Psychology* 104:53–66. [181]

[171]Cravioto, J.; DeLicardie, E. R.; and Birch, H. G. 1966. Nutrition, growth, and neurointegrative development: An experimental and ecologic study. *Pediatrics* 38:319–72. [150]

[172]Crosby, R. M. N., and Liston, R. A. 1968. *The waysiders.* New York: Delacorte. [106, 108]

[173]Crovetto, A. M.; Fischer, L. L.; and Boudreaux, J. L. 1967. *The preschool child and his self-image.* Division of Instruction and Division of Pupil Personnel, New Orleans Public Schools. [59, 60]

[174]Cutts, N., and Moseley, N. 1957. *Teaching the disorderly pupil in elementary and secondary school.* New York: Longmans. [185]

[175]D'Andrade, R. G. 1966. Sex differences and cultural institutions. In *The development of sex differences,* ed. E. E. Maccoby, pp. 56–81. Stanford, Calif.: Stanford University Press. [178]

[176]Daugherty, L. G. 1963. Working with disadvantaged parents. *NEA Journal* 52:18–20. [52]

[177]Davidson, H. H., and Lang, G. 1960. Children's perceptions of their teachers' feelings toward them related to self-perception, school achievement, and behavior. *Journal of Experimental Education* 29:107–18. [52]

[178]Davie, R.; Butler, N.; and Goldstein, H. 1972. *From birth to seven.* New York: Longmans, Green. [232]

[179]Deal, Therry N. 1966. *Effects of a structured program of preschool mathematics on cognitive behavior.* ED 015 791. [134, 191]

[180]deHirsch, K.; Jansky, J. J.; and Langford, W. S. 1966. *Predicting reading failure.* New York: Harper & Row. [110]

[181]Denenberg, V. H. 1969. Animal studies of early experience: Some principles which have implications for human development. In *Minnesota symposia*

on child psychology, ed. J. P. Hill, 3:31-45. Minneapolis: University of Minnesota Press. [67]

[182]Dennis, W. 1942. The performance of Hopi children on the Goodenough Draw-A-Man test. *Journal of Comparative Psychology* 34:341-48. [72, 78]

[183]Deutsch, M., et al. 1971. *Regional research and resource center in early childhood.* ED 055 649. [198]

[184]Deutsch, M.; Taleporos, E.; and Victor, J. 1974. A brief synopsis of an initial enrichment program in early childhood. In *Longitudinal evaluations of preschool programs,* ed. S. Ryan, pp. 49-60. Washington, D.C.: Office of Child Development.

[185]Devereau, E. C. 1970. The role of peer-group experience in moral development. In *Minnesota symposia on child psychology,* ed. J. P. Hill, 4:94-140. Minneapolis: University of Minnesota Press. [59, 182]

[186]DeWitt, B. F. 1961. An analysis of the effect of chronological age as a factor in achievement in the elementary school. Doctoral dissertation, State University of Iowa, Iowa City, Iowa. [141, 185]

[187]Dickinson, D. J., and Larson, J. D. 1963. The effects of chronological age in months on school achievement. *Journal of Educational Research* 56:492-93. [95, 99]

[188]DiLorenzo, L. T. 1971. Which way for Pre-K: Wishes or reality? *American Education* 7:28-32. [194]

[189]DiLorenzo, L. T., and Salter, R. 1968. An evaluative study of pre-kindergarten programs for educationally disadvantaged children: Follow-up and replication. *Exceptional Children* 35:111-19. [194]

[190]Donaldson, R. S., and Kohl, S. G. 1965. Perinatal mortality in twins by sex. *American Journal of Public Health* 55:1411-18. [180]

[191]Douglas, J. W. B., and Ross, J. M. 1964. The later educational progress and emotional adjustment of children who went to nursery schools or classes. *Educational Research* 7:73-80. [200, 202]

[192]Douglass, M. P. 1968. Innovation and the credibility gap. Paper presented to the California Elementary School Administrators Association and the California Association for Supervision and Curriculum Development, January 1968, Palo Alto, California. [192]

[193]Downing, J. 1970. Children's concepts of language in learning to read. *Educational Research* 12:106-12. [113]

[194]Drews, E. M., and Teahen, J. E. 1967. Parental attitudes and academic achievement. *Journal of Clinical Psychology* 13:328-32. [45]

[195]Dublin, L. I. 1965. *Factbook on man.* New York: Macmillan. [180]

[196]Dunlap, J. M., and Coffman, A. L. 1970. *The effects of assessment and personalized programming on subsequent intellectual development of prekindergarten and kindergarten children.* ED 045 198. [198]

[197]Dunn, J. A. 1968. The approach-avoidance paradigm as a model for the analysis of school anxiety. *Journal of Educational Psychology* 59:388-94. [218]

[198]du Preez, I. F., and Moore, R. S. 1976. Compulsory school entrance age and attendance laws and their implications for the education of young children. Unpublished manuscript, Hewitt Research Foundation, Berrien Springs, Michigan. [86]

[199]Durkin, D. 1961. Children who learned to read at home. *Elementary School Journal* 62:14-18. [37, 76, 94, 107]

244

[200]_____. 1962. An earlier start in reading. *Elementary School Journal* 63:146–51. [109]

[201]_____. 1963. Children who read before grade 1: A second study. *Elementary School Journal* 64:143–48. [107, 108, 109]

[202]_____. 1970. What does research say about the time to begin reading instruction? *Journal of Educational Research* 64:52–56. [40 114]

[203]Dyer, D. W., and Harcum, E. R. 1961. Visual perception of binary pattern by preschool children and by school children. *Journal of Educational Psychology* 52:161–65. [151]

[204]*Early Childhood Development.* 1971. Alternatives for program implementation in the states: A report of the Education Commission of the States. Report No. 22. Early Childhood Report No. 1. [217]

[205]Eccles, J. C. 1968. Chairman's opening remarks. In *Growth of the nervous system*, ed. G. E. W. Wolstenholme and M. O'Connor, pp. 1–2. Boston: Little, Brown and Co. [170]

[206]_____. 1970. *Facing reality.* New York: Springer-Verlag. [171]

[207]_____. 1974. Neurosciences: Our brains and our future. In *The greatest adventure*, ed. E. H. Kone and H. J. Jordan, p. xxxiii. New York: The Rockefeller University Press. [161]

[208]Edwards, J. B. 1974. A developmental study of the acquisition of some moral concepts in children aged 7 to 15. *Educational Research* 16:83–93. [54, 182]

[209]Ekholm, J. 1967. Postnatal changes in cutaneous reflexes and in the discharge pattern of cutaneous and articular sense organs. *Acta Physiologica Scandinavica*, supplement 297. [166]

[210]Eklund, S. J. 1970. Competitiveness in boys as related to academic achievement and mothers' achievement orientation. DARCEE papers and reports, vol. 2, no. 7. Nashville, Tenn.: George Peabody College for Teachers. [181]

[211]Elkind, D. 1961*a*. The development of quantitative thinking: A systematic replication of Piaget's studies. *Journal of Genetic Psychology* 98:37–46. [129, 130]

[212]_____. 1961*b*. Children's discovery of the conservation of mass, weight, and volume: Piaget replication study II. *Journal of Genetic Psychology* 98:218–27. [129]

[213]_____. 1961*c*. The development of the additive composition of classes in the child: Piaget replication study III. *Journal of Genetic Psychology* 99:51–57. [129]

[214]_____. 1961*d*. Children's conceptions of right and left: Piaget replication study IV. *Journal of Genetic Psychology* 99:269–76. [138]

[215]_____. 1969. Piagetian and psychometric conceptions of intelligence. *Harvard Educational Review* 39:319–37. [129, 189, 210, 212, 218, 228]

[216]_____. 1970*a*. The case for the academic preschool: Fact or fiction? *Young Children* 25:132–40. [24, 71, 102, 129, 189, 212]

[217]_____. 1970*b*. *Children and adolescents.* New York: Oxford Press. [24, 125]

[218]Ellingson, R. J. 1972. Development of wakefulness-sleep cycles and associated EEG patterns in mammals. In *Sleep and the maturing nervous system*, ed. C. D. Clemente, D. P. Purpura, and F. E. Mayer, pp. 166–73. New York: Academic Press. [168]

[219]Ellingson, R. J., and Wilcott, R. C. 1960. Development of evoked respon-

ses in visual and auditory cortices of kittens. *Journal of Neurophysiology* 23:363–75. [145, 151]

[220]Emde, R. N., and Metcalf, D. R. 1970. An electroencephalographic study of behavioral rapid eye movement states in the newborn. *Journal of Nervous and Mental Disease* 150:370–76. [168]

[221]Engel, M. n.d. Rapunzel, Rapunzel, let down your golden hair: Some thoughts on early childhood education. Unpublished manuscript, National Demonstration Center in Early Childhood Education, U.S. Office of Education, Washington, D.C. [43]

[222]Engelmann, S. 1967. *Teaching formal operations to preschool advantaged and disadvantaged children.* ED 019 990. [133]

[223]Erikson, E. 1950. *Childhood and society.* New York: Norton. [51]

[224]Escalona, S. 1974. The present state of knowledge and available techniques in the area of cognition. In *Methodological approaches to the study of brain maturation and its abnormalities,* ed. D. P. Purpura and G. P. Reaser, pp. 135–40. Baltimore: University Park Press. [173]

[225]Fanaroff, A.; Kennell, J. H.; and Klaus, M. H. 1972. Follow-up of low birth weight infants—the predictive value of maternal visiting patterns. *Pediatrics* 49:287–90. [31]

[226]Farber, A. E. 1970. A comparison of the effect of verbal and material reward on the learning of lower class preschool children. DARCEE papers and reports, vol. 4, no. 8. Nashville, Tenn.: George Peabody College for Teachers. [67]

[227]Farber, B. 1962. Marital integration as a factor in parent-child relations. *Child Development* 33:1–14. [43, 50, 52]

[228]Featherstone, H. J. 1973. *Cognitive effects of preschool programs on different types of children.* ED 082 838. [194]

[229]Feigenbaum, K. D.; Geiger, D.; and Crevoshay, S. 1970. An exploratory study of the 3-, 5-, and 7-year-old female's comprehension of cooperative and uncooperative social interaction. *Journal of Genetic Psychology* 116:141–48. [130]

[230]Felker, D. 1974. *Building positive self-concepts.* Minneapolis: Burgess Publishing Company. [50, 58]

[231]Feshbach, N. 1969. Student teacher preferences for elementary school pupils varying in personality characteristics. *Journal of Educational Psychology* 60:126–32. [183]

[232]Feyberg, P. S. 1966. Concept development in Piagetian terms in relation to school attainment. *Journal of Educational Psychology* 57:164–68. [141]

[233]Fisher, J. T., and Hawley, L. S. 1951. *A few buttons missing.* Philadelphia: J. B. Lippincott Co. [96, 100, 101, 211]

[234]Flammer, D. P. 1971. Self-esteem, parent identification and sex role development in preschool age boys and girls. *Child Study Journal* 2:39–45. [179]

[235]Fletcher, J. D., and Atkinson, R. C. 1972. Evaluation of the Stanford CAI program in initial reading. *Journal of Educational Psychology* 63:597–602. [176]

[236]Flory, C. D. 1936. *Osseous development in the hand as an index of skeletal development.* Monographs of the Society for Research in Child Development, vol. 1, no. 3. Chicago: University of Chicago Press. [179, 180, 228[

[237]Flower, R. M. 1968. The evaluation of auditory abilities in the appraisal of children with reading problems. In *Perception and reading,* ed. H. K. Smith, pp. 21–24. Newark, Del.: International Reading Association. [112]

246

[238]Forbes, G. B., and Dykstra, A. 1971. Children's attribution of negative traits to authority figures as a function of family size and sex. *Psychological Reports* 28:363–66. [26, 186]

[239]Forester, J. J. 1955. At what age should a child start school? *School Executive* 74:80–81. [56, 95, 99, 141, 232]

[240]Forgione, P. D., and Moore, R. S. 1975. The rationales for early childhood education policy making. Prepared for the U.S. Office of Economic Opportunity under Research Grant No. 50079-G-73/01 to the Hewitt Research Foundation, Berrien Springs, Michigan. ED 114 208. [42, 86]

[241]Formaneck, R., and Woog, P. 1971. Attitudes of preschool and elementary school children to authority figures. *Child Study Journal* 1:100–110. [58, 183]

[242]Fortenberry, W. D. 1969. *An investigation of the effectiveness of a special program upon the development of visual perception for word recognition of culturally disadvantaged first grade students.* ED 036 411. [112]

[243]Fowler, W. 1962. Cognitive learning in infancy and early childhood. *Psychological Bulletin* 59:116–52. [128]

[244]Frank, L. 1962. The beginnings of child development and family life education in the 20th century. *Merrill-Palmer Quarterly* 8:207–27. [209]

[245]Frerichs, A. H. 1971. Relationship of self-esteem of the disadvantaged to school success. *Journal of Negro Education* 40:117–120. [59]

[246]Freyman, R. 1965. Further evidence of the effect of date of birth on subsequent school performance. *Educational Research* 8:58–64. [110]

[247]Friedman, R. 1974. Characteristics of early education needs of disadvantaged children. *Child Welfare* 53:93–97. [199]

[248]Froebel, F. 1896. *The education of man.* New York: D. Appleton and Company. [208]

[249]Frost, J. L. 1967. *A study of the effects of an elementary school enrichment program on the school achievement of welfare recipient children.* ED 016 734. [196]

[250]Frostig, M. 1968. Visual modality, research, and practice. In *Perception and reading*, ed. H. K. Smith, pp. 25–33. Newark, Del.: International Reading Association. [110, 112]

[251]Frostig, M.; Lefever, W.; and Whittlesey, J. 1963. Disturbances in visual perception. *Journal of Educational Research* 57:160–62. [91, 150, 152, 156]

[252]Furth, H. G. 1963. Conceptual discovery and control on a pictorial part-whole task as a function of age, intelligence, and language. *Journal of Educational Psychology* 54:191–96. [138, 183]

[253]_____. 1966 *Thinking without language.* New York: Free Press. [90]

[254]Galambos, R. 1967. Brain correlates of learning. In *The neurosciences: A study program*, ed. G. C. Quarton, T. Melnechuk, and F. O. Schmitt, pp. 637–43. New York: The Rockefeller University Press. [172]

[255]Garai, J. E., and Scheinfeld, A. 1968. *Sex differences in mental and behavioral traits.* Genetic Psychology Monographs 77:169–299. Provincetown, Mass.: Journal Press. [180]

[256]Gardner, R. W., and Moriarty, A. 1968. *Personality development at preadolescence.* Seattle: University of Washington Press. [185]

[257]Gaskill, A. R., and Fox, W. C. 1964. How useful are psychological tests for screening underage school beginners? *Journal of Educational Research* 57:333–36. [95]

[258]Geber, M. 1958. The psycho-motor development of African children in

247

the first year, and the influence of maternal behavior. *Journal of Social Psychology* 47:185–95. [30, 32, 45]

259Gelles, H. M., and Coulson, M. C. 1959. At what age is a child ready for school? *School Executive* 78:29–31. [88]

260Gershaw, N. J., and Schwarz, J. C. 1971. The effects of a familiar toy and mother's presence on exploratory and attachment behaviors in young children. *Child Development* 42:1662–66. [34]

261Geschwind, N. 1964. The development of the brain and the evolution of language. *Monograph Series on Language and Linguistics, no. 17*, ed. C. I. J. M. Stuart, pp. 155–69. Washington, D.C.: Georgetown University Press. [157]

262_____. 1965. Disconnexion, syndromes in animals and man. *Journal of Experimental Psychology* 88:237–94, 585–644. [163]

263Gesell, A. 1940. *The first five years of life.* New York: Harper & Row. [121, 211]

264Gesell, A., and Ilg, F. L. 1943. *Infant and child in the culture of today.* New York: Harper & Row. [71]

265Gewirtz, H. B., and Gewirtz, J. L. 1969. Caretaking settings, background events, and behavior differences in four Israeli child-rearing environments: Some preliminary trends. In *Determinants of infant behavior IV,* ed. B. M. Foss, pp. 229–52. London: Methuen. [29]

266Gewirtz, J. L. 1965. The course of infant smiling in four child-rearing environments in Israel. In *Determinants of infant behavior III,* ed. B. M. Foss, pp. 205–60. London: Methuen; New York: Wiley. [29]

267_____. 1972a. *Attachment and dependency.* Washington, D.C.: V. H. Winston & Sons. [29]

268_____. 1972b. Attachment, dependence, and a distinction in terms of stimulus control. In *Attachment and dependency,* ed. J. L. Gewirtz, pp. 139–77. Washington, D.C.: V. H. Winston & Sons. [30, 31, 32, 76]

269_____. 1972c. On the selection and use of attachment and dependence indices. In *Attachment and dependency,* ed. J. L. Gewirtz, pp. 179–215. Washington, D.C.: V. H. Winston & Sons; New York: Wiley. [30, 31]

270Gewirtz, J. L., and Gewirtz, H. B. 1965. Stimulus conditions, infant behaviors, and social learning in four Israeli child-rearing environments: A preliminary report illustrating differences in environment and behavior between the "only" and the "youngest" child. In *Determinants of infant behavior III,* ed. B. M. Foss, pp. 161–84. London: Methuen; New York: Wiley. [31, 32]

271Gibbs, F. A., and Gibbs, E. L. 1951. *Atlas of electroencephalography.* Reading, Mass.: Addison-Wesley Publishing Co. [168, 169]

272Gill, M. P. 1969. Pattern of achievement as related to the perceived self. Paper read at the annual meeting of the American Educational Research Association, February 1969, Los Angeles, California. [50]

273Gill, N.; Herdtner, T. J.; and Lough, L. 1968. Selected perceptual and socio-economic variables, body-orientation instruction, and predicted academic success in young children. *Childhood Education* 45:52–54. [66]

274Girona, R. 1972. Changes operated in institutionalized children as a result of controlled interaction with a "significant adult." *Journal of Educational Research* 65:343–46. [53]

275Glueck, S., and Glueck, E. 1950. *Unraveling juvenile delinquency.* Cambridge, Mass.: Harvard University Press. [57]

[276] _____. 1968. *Delinquents and nondelinquents in perspective.* Cambridge, Mass.: Harvard University Press. [57]

[277] _____. 1974. *Of delinquency and crime: A panorama of years of search and research.* Springfield, Ill.: Charles C. Thomas. [57]

[278]Golden, M., et al. 1969. *Social class differentiation in cognitive development: A longitudinal study.* ED 033 754. [79]

[279]Goodenough, F. L., and Maurer, K. A. 1940. The mental development of nursery school children compared with that of non-nursery school children. In *Yearbook of the National Society for the Study of Education,* vol. 39, part 2, pp. 161–78. [29, 200, 201]

[280]Goodnow, J. J. 1962. *A test of milieu differences with some of Piaget's tasks.* Psychological Monographs, vol. 76, no. 36 (serial no. 555). Westport, Conn.: Greenwood Press. [74, 190]

[281] _____. 1968 (date of study). Cultural variations in cognitive skills. In *Cross-cultural studies,* ed. D. R. Price-Williams, pp. 246–64. Baltimore: Penguin, 1969. [139]

[282]Goodnow, J. J., and Bethon, G. 1966. Piaget's tasks: Effects of schooling and intelligence. *Child Development* 37:573–82. [74, 114, 190]

[283]Gordon, I. J. 1969. *Relationship between observed home behavior variables and infant performance at age one.* Gainesville, Fla.: Institute for Development of Human Resources, University of Florida. [214, 215]

[284] _____. 1971. Early stimulation through parent education. In *Readings in research in developmental psychology,* ed. I. J. Gordon, pp. 146–54. Glenview, Ill.: Scott, Foresman & Co. [47]

[285] _____. 1972a. Success and accountability. *Childhood Education* 48:338–47. [211, 215]

[286] _____. 1972b. *What do we know about parents-as-teachers?* ED 065 788. [212, 214]

[287] _____. 1973. *A home learning center approach to early stimulation.* Gainesville, Fla.: Institute for Development of Human Resources, University of Florida. [215]

[288]Gordon, I. J., and Guinagh, B. J. 1969. *A home learning center approach to early stimulation.* ED 056 750. [213]

[289]Gordon, I. J., et al. 1969. *Reaching the child through parent education: The Florida approach.* ED 057 880. [215]

[290]Gott, M. A. 1963. The effect of age difference at kindergarten entrance on achievement and adjustment in elementary school. Doctoral dissertation, University of Colorado, Boulder, Colorado. [95, 98, 141]

[291]Granger, R. L., et al. 1969. *The impact of Head Start: An evaluation of the effects of Head Start on children's cognitive and effective development,* vol. 1. Report to the U.S. Office of Economic Opportunity by Westinghouse Learning Corporation and Ohio University, Athens, Ohio. Washington, D.C.: U.S. Office of Economic Opportunity. [19]

[292]Gray, S. W. 1971. The child's first teacher. *Childhood Education* 48:127–29. [212, 213]

[293] _____. 1974. Children from three to ten: The early training project. In *Longitudinal evaluations of preschool programs,* ed. S. Ryan, pp. 61–67. Washington, D.C.: Office of Child Development. [199]

[294]Gray, S. W., and Klaus, R. 1965. An experimental preschool program for

culturally deprived children. *Child Development* 36:887–98. [199]

²⁹⁵_____. 1970. The early training project: A seventh year report. *Child Development* 41:909–24. [199]

²⁹⁶Greathouse, B. 1972. The effects of toy talk training and experience on low income black mothers and their pre-school children. Doctoral dissertation, University of Arizona, Tucson, Arizona. [75, 77]

²⁹⁷Green, D. R., and Simmons, S. V. 1962. Chronological age and school entrance. *Elementary School Journal* 63:41–47. [97, 98]

²⁹⁸Greenfield, P. M. 1966 (date of study). On culture and conservation. In *Cross-cultural studies,* ed. D. R. Price-Williams, pp. 211–45. Baltimore: Penguin, 1969. [139]

²⁹⁹Gross, M. 1967. *Learning readiness in two Jewish groups: A study in "cultural deprivation."* ED 026 126. [93]

³⁰⁰Grossman, B. D. 1969. Extracurricular parent-child contact and children's socially reinforced task behavior. *Journal of Genetic Psychology* 114:291–99. [181]

³⁰¹Grossman, M., and Philips, M. 1973. Ocular motility and reading skills. *Child Study Journal* 3:39–45. [112]

³⁰²Guernsey, J. 1972. South Umpqua's kitchen classrooms. *American Education* 8:24–27. [216]

³⁰³Hall, J. W. 1969. Errors in word recognition and discrimination by children of two age levels. *Journal of Educational Psychology* 60:144–47. [137]

³⁰⁴Hall, R. V. 1963. Does entrance age affect achievement? *Elementary School Journal* 63:391–96. [184, 185]

³⁰⁵Halliwell, J. W. 1966. Review the reviews on entrance age and school success. *Journal of Educational Research* 59:395–401. [95]

³⁰⁶Halliwell, J. W., and Stein, B. W. 1964. Achievement of early and late school starters. *Elementary English* 41:631–39. [100, 141]

³⁰⁷Hamblin, J. A., and Hamblin, R. L. 1972. On teaching disadvantaged preschoolers to read: A successful experiment. *American Educational Research Journal* 9:209–16. [196]

³⁰⁸Hamburg, D. A. 1966. Effects of progesterone on behavior. In *Endocrines and the nervous system,* ed. R. Levine. Baltimore: Williams and Wilkins. [177]

³⁰⁹Hamburg, D. A., and Lunde, D. T. 1966. Sex hormones in the development of sex differences in human behavior. In *The development of sex differences,* ed. E. E. Maccoby, pp. 1–24. Stanford, Calif.: Stanford University Press. [176, 177, 178]

³¹⁰Hammill, D. D., and Larsen, S. C. 1974. The relationship of selected auditory perceptual skills and reading ability. *Journal of Learning Disabilities* 7:429–35. [112]

³¹¹Hampleman, R. S. 1959. A study of the comparative reading achievements of early and late school starters. *Elementary English* 36:331–34. [110]

³¹²Hampson, J. G. 1955. Hermaphroditic appearance, rearing, and eroticism in hyperadrenocorticism. *Bulletin Johns Hopkins Hospital* 96:265–73. [178]

³¹³Hampson, J. L., and Hampson, J. G. 1961. The ontogenesis of sexual behavior in man. In *Sex and internal secretions,* vol. 2, ed. W. C. Young. Baltimore: Williams and Wilkins. [178]

³¹⁴Handler, E. 1972. Comparative effectiveness of four preschool programs: A sociological approach. *Child Welfare* 51:550–61. [191, 200, 202]

³¹⁵Harding, J. 1966. *A comparative study of various project Head Start programs.*

250

ED 019 987. [192]

[316]Harlen, W. 1968. The development of scientific concepts in young children. *Educational Research* 11:4-13. [130]

[317]Harlow, H. F., and Zimmerman, R. R. 1959. Affectioned responses in the infant monkey. *Science* 130:421-32. [29]

[318]Hartup, W. W., ed. 1972. *The young child: Reviews of research,* vol. 2. Washington, D.C.: National Association for the Education of Young Children. [9]

[319]Hartup, W. W., and Smothergill, N. L., eds. 1967. *The young child: Reviews of research.* Washington, D.C.: National Association for the Education of Young Children. [9]

[320]Harvey, O. J., et al. 1966. Teachers' belief systems and preschool atmospheres. *Journal of Educational Psychology* 57:373-81. [68, 79]

[321]Hattwick, L. W. 1946. The influence of nursery school attendance upon the behavior and personality of the preschool child. *Journal of Experimental Education* 5:180-90. [201]

[322]Havighurst, R. J.; Gunther, M.; and Pratt, I. 1946. Environment and the Draw-A-Man test: The performance of Indian children. *Journal of Abnormal and Social Psychology* 41:50-63. [72, 78]

[323]Hawk, T. L. 1967. Self-concepts of the socially disadvantaged. *Elementary School Journal* 67:196-206. [59]

[324]Heber, R., and Garber, H. 1970. *An experiment in the prevention of cultural-familial mental retardation.* Proceedings of the Second Congress of the International Association for the Scientific Study of Mental Deficiency, 25 August–2 September 1970, Warsaw, Poland. [67, 213]

[325]Heffernan, H. 1968. A vital curriculum for today's young child. In *Early childhood education rediscovered,* ed. J. L. Frost, pp. 492-97. New York: Holt, Rinehart and Winston. [114]

[326]Herzog, E.; Newcomb, C. H.; and Cisin, I. H. 1974. Double deprivation: The less they have, the less they learn. In *Longitudinal evaluations of preschool programs,* ed. S. Ryan, pp. 69-93. Washington, D.C.: Office of Child Development. [200, 202]

[327]Hess, R. D. 1969. Maternal behavior and the development of reading readiness in urban Negro children. Unpublished paper, University of Chicago. [46, 107]

[328]Hess, R. D., and Shipman, V. C. 1968. Maternal attitudes toward the school and the role of pupil: Some social class comparisons. In *Developing programs for the educationally disadvantaged,* ed. A. H. Passow, pp. 109-29. New York: Columbia University Teachers College Press. [40]

[329]Hess, R. D., et al. 1971. Parent involvement in early education. In *Day care: Resources for decision,* ed. E. H. Grotberg, pp. 265-312. Washington, D.C.: Office of Economic Opportunity. [47]

[330]Hilgartner, H. 1962. The frequency of myopia found in individuals under 21 years of age. Unpublished manuscript, Austin, Texas. (First reported by Mosdle Boland.) [152]

[331]_____. 1974. Letter to R. S. Moore, 18 November 1974. [152]

[332]Hillerich, R. L. 1964. Eye-hand dominance and reading achievement. *American Educational Research Journal* 1:121-26. [111, 149]

[333]Himwich, H. E. 1973. Early studies of the developing brain. In *Biochemistry of the developing brain,* ed. W. Himwich. New York: Marcel Dekker. [166]

[334]Himwich, W. A. 1962. Biochemical and neurophysiological development of the brain in the neonatal period. *International Review of Neurobiology* 4:117–58. [167]

[335]Hirst, W. E. 1970. *Prediction of reading success.* ED 040 825. [107, 109]

[336]Hobson, J. R. 1948. Mental age as a workable criterion for school admission. *Elementary School Journal* 48:312–21. [95, 97, 99]

[337]Hodges, W. L., and Spicker, H. H. 1967. The effects of preschool experiences on culturally deprived children. In *The young child: Reviews of research,* eds. W. W. Hartup and N. L. Smothergill, pp. 262–89. Washington, D.C.: National Association for the Education of Young Children. [92, 198]

[338]Hodgins, A., and Karnes, M. B. 1966. *The effects of a highly structured preschool program on the measured intelligence of culturally disadvantaged four-year-old children.* ED 019 116. [196]

[339]Hoffman, E. 1971. Pre-kindergarten experiences and their relationships to reading achievement. *Illinois School Research* 8:6–12. [108]

[340]Hoffman, L. W., and Hoffman, M. L., eds. 1966. *Review on child development research,* vol. 2. New York: Russell Sage Foundation. [9]

[341]Hoffman, M. L. 1963. Child-rearing practices and moral development: Generalizations from empirical research. *Child Development* 34:295–318. [51, 53]

[342]Hoffman, M. L., and Hoffman, L. W., eds. 1964. *Review of child development research,* vol. 1. New York: Russell Sage Foundation. [9]

[343]Holden, M. H., and MacGinitie, W. H. 1972. Children's conceptions of word boundaries in speech and print. *Journal of Educational Psychology* 63:551–57. [113]

[344]Hollos, M., and Cowan, P. A. 1973. Social isolation and cognitive development: Logical operations and role-taking abilities in three Norwegian social settings. *Child Development* 44:630–41. [73, 190]

[345]Holmes, D., and Holmes, M. B. 1966. *An evaluation of differences among different classes of Head Start participants.* ED 015 012. [66, 75, 76, 77, 79]

[346]*Home Start demonstration program: An overview. 1973.* ED 077 583. [216]

[347]Honig, A. S.; Caldwell, B. M.; and Tannenbaum, J. 1970. Patterns of information processing used by and with young children in a nursery school setting. *Child Development* 41:1045–65. [69]

[348]Honzik, M. P. 1957. Developmental studies of parent-child resemblance in intelligence. *Child Development* 28:215–27. [185]

[349]_____. 1967. Environmental correlates of mental growth: Prediction from the family setting at 21 months. *Child Development* 38:337–64. [67, 75]

[350]Hooper, F. H. 1969. The Appalachian child's intellectual capabilities: Deprivation or diversity. *Journal of Negro Education* 38:224–35. [72, 77, 78]

[351]Horowitz, E. L., and Smith, R. B. 1939. Social relations and personality patterning in preschool children. *Journal of Genetic Psychology* 54:337–52. [201]

[352]Horowitz, F. D., and Resenfeld, H. M. 1966. *Comparative studies of a group of Head Start and a group of non-Head Start preschool children.* ED 015 013. [77]

[353]Huberty, C. J., and Swan, W. W. 1974. Preschool classroom experience and first-grade achievement. *Journal of Educational Research* 67:311–16. [140]

[354]Hulan, J. R. 1972. Head Start program and early school achievement. *Elementary School Journal* 73:81–94. [192]

[355]Humphrey, T. 1953. The relation of oxygen deprivation to fetal reflex arcs and the development of fetal behavior. *Journal of Psychology* 35:3–43. [165]

252

[356]Hunt, J. McV. 1961. *Intelligence and experience.* New York: The Ronald Press Company. [18]

[357]Hurley, J. R. 1959. Maternal attitudes and children's intelligence. *Journal of Clinical Psychology* 15:291–92. [41]

[358]Husén, T., ed. 1967. *International study of achievement in mathematics: A comparison of twelve countries I, II.* New York: John Wiley & Sons. [8, 96, 140, 202, 218, 229]

[359]_____. 1972. Letter to R. S. Moore, 23 November 1972. [8, 229]

[360]Huttenlocher, P. R. 1966. Development of neuronal activity in neocortex of the kitten. *Nature* 211:91–92. [145]

[361]Hydén, H. 1972. Changes in brain protein during learning. In *Macromolecules and behavior,* ed. G. B. Answell and P. B. Bradley, pp. 3–26. Baltimore: University Park Press. [171]

[362]Hyvarinen, J. 1966. Analysis of spontaneous spike potential activity in developing rabbit diencephalon. *Acta Physiologica Scandinavica,* Supplement 68. [166]

[363]Ilg, F. L., and Ames, L. B. 1950. Developmental trends in reading behavior. *Journal of Genetic Psychology* 76:291–311. [91, 108, 109, 110]

[364]Ilika, J. 1969. *Age of entrance into the first grade as related to rate of scholastic achievement.* ED 028 843. [98]

[365]Impellizzeri, I. H. 1967. Auditory perceptual ability of normal children aged five through eight. *Journal of Genetic Psychology* 111:289–94. [153]

[366]James, W. 1890. *Principles of psychology,* 2 vols. Magnolia, Mass.: Peter Smith. [51]

[367]Jeffery, W. E. 1969. Early stimulation and cognitive development. In *Minnesota symposia on child psychology,* ed. J. P. Hill, 3:46–65. Minneapolis: University of Minnesota Press. [71]

[368]Jenkins, G. G. 1956. Responsibility of children: The contribution of the home. *Child Study* 33:3–6. [54]

[369]Jensen, A. R. 1969. *Understanding readiness: An occasional paper.* ED 032 117. [87, 100, 101, 128, 210]

[370]Jensen, A. R., and Rohwer, W. D. 1965. Syntactical mediation of serial and paired-associate learning as a function of age. *Child Development* 36:601–8. [137]

[371]Jensen, J., and Kohlberg, L. 1966. *Report of a research and demonstration project for culturally disadvantaged children in the Ancona montessori school.* ED 015 014. [197]

[372]Jersild, A. T. 1968. *Child psychology.* Englewood Cliffs, N.J.: Prentice-Hall. [180]

[373]Jersild, A. T., and Fite, M. D. 1939. *The influence of nursery school experience on children's social adjustments.* New York: Columbia University Teachers College Press. [201]

[374]Jersild, A. T., and Holmes, F. B. 1935. *Children's fears.* New York: Columbia University Teachers College Press. [201, 227]

[375]Jersild, A. T., and Markey, F. V. 1935. *Conflicts between preschool children.* New York: Columbia University Teachers College Press. [201, 227]

[376]Jessen, B. L., and Kaess, D. W. 1973. Effects of training on intersensory communication by three- and five-year-olds. *Journal of Genetic Psychology* 123:115–22. [157]

253

[377] Jester, R. E. 1969. *Focus on parent education as a means of altering the child's environment.* ED 033 758. [214]

[378] Joel, W. 1939. The influence of nursery school education upon behavior maturity. *Journal of Experimental Education* 8:164–65. [201]

[379] Joint Commission on Mental Health of Children. 1973. *Mental health: From infancy through adolescence.* New York: Harper & Row. [178, 186]

[380] Jones, P. A. 1972. Home environment and the development of verbal ability. *Child Development* 43:1081–86. [77]

[381] Jordan, T. E. 1971. Longitudinal study of preschool development. *Exceptional Children* 37:509–12. [66, 79]

[382] Kagan, J. 1970. On class differences and early development. In *Education of the infant and young child,* ed. V. H. Denenberg, pp. 10–15. New York: Academic Press. [93, 94]

[383] Kagan, J., and Moss, H. A. 1962. *Birth to maturity.* New York: Wiley. [186]

[384] Kagan, J., and Sigel, I. E. 1963. The psychological significance of styles of conceptualization. In *Basic cognitive processes in children,* ed. J. C. Wright and J. Kagan. Monographs of the Society for Research in Child Development, vol. 28, no. 2. Chicago: University of Chicago Press. [183, 186]

[385] Kagan, J.; Zelazo, P.; and Kearsley, R. 1976. Good daycare: Does it affect children? *Carnegie Quarterly* 24:3–5. [33]

[386] Kanter, R. M. 1972. The organization child: Experience management in a nursery school. *Sociology of Education* 45:186–212. [209]

[387] Kapfer, S. 1972. Report of first national Home Start conference, 3–7 April 1972, St. Louis, Missouri. Washington, D.C.: Office of Child Development. [216]

[388] Karnes, M. B. 1968. *A research program to determine the effects of various preschool intervention programs on the development of disadvantaged children and the strategic age for such intervention.* ED 017 319. [194, 196]

[389] Karnes, M. B.; Zehrbach, R. R.; and Teska, J. A. 1974. The Karnes preschool program: Rationale, curricula offerings, and follow-up data. In *Longitudinal evaluations of preschool programs,* ed. S. Ryan, pp. 95–108. Washington, D.C.: Office of Child Development. [198]

[390] Kastel, Janet. 1973. Taped interview with Raymond S. Moore, October 1973, Hewitt Research Center, Berrien Springs, Michigan. [32]

[391] Katkovsky, W.; Preston, A.; and Crandall, V. J. 1964a. Parents' attitudes toward their personal achievements and toward the achievement behaviors of their children. *Journal of Genetic Psychology* 104:67–82. [181]

[392] _____. 1964b. Parents' achievement attitudes and their behavior with their children in achievement situations. *Journal of Genetic Psychology* 104:105–21. [38, 181]

[393] Katz, L. G. 1973. Humaneness in preschool. *Illinois Teacher for Contemporary Roles* 16:179–82. [211]

[394] Kaufman, A. S., and Kaufman, N. L. 1972. Tests built from Piaget's and Gesell's tasks as predictors of first-grade achievement. *Child Development* 43:521–35. [86]

[395] Keasey, C. T., and Charles, D. C. 1967. Conservatism of substance in normal and mentally retarded children. *Journal of Genetic Psychology* 111:271–79. [114, 139]

[396] Keislar, E. R., and Stern, C. 1970. Differentiated instruction in problem

254

solving for children of different mental ability levels. *Journal of Educational Psychology* 61:445–50. [134, 135]

[397]Keister, B. V. 1941. Reading skills acquired by five-year-old children. *Elementary School Journal* 41:587–96. [110, 134]

[398]Kendler, T. S. 1972. An ontogeny of mediational deficiency. *Child Development* 43:1–17. [131, 132]

[399]King, I. B. 1955. Effect of age of entrance into grade I upon achievement in elementary school. *Elementary School Journal* 55:331–36. [95, 98, 141, 185]

[400]King, M. 1971. The development of some intention concepts in young children. *Child Development* 42:1145–52. [138]

[401]Klaus, M. H., et al. 1972. Maternal attachment: Importance of the first post-partum days. *New England Journal of Medicine* 286:460–63. [36]

[402]Klaus, R., and Gray, S. 1968. *The early training project for disadvantaged children: A report after five years.* Monographs of the Society for Research in Child Development vol. 33, no. 4. Chicago: University of Chicago Press. [68, 79]

[403]Klausmeier, H. J. 1963. Effects of accelerating bright older elementary pupils: A follow-up. *Journal of Educational Psychology* 54:165–71. [96]

[404]Klesius, S. E. 1971. *Perceptual-motor development and reading: A closer look.* ED 050 916. [112]

[405]Kohlberg, L. 1968. Early education: A cognitive-developmental view. *Child Development* 39:1013–62. [88, 89]

[406]Kohlberg, L., and Zigler, E. 1967. *The impact of cognitive maturity on the development of sex-role attitudes in the years 4 to 8.* Genetic Psychology Monographs 75:89–165. Provincetown, Mass.: Journal Press. [182]

[407]Kollros, J. J. 1968. Order and control in neurogenesis (As exemplified by the lateral motor column). In *Developmental biology*, Suppl. 2:274–305. New York: Academic Press. [170]

[408]Kounin, J. S., and Gump, P. V. 1961. The comparative influence of punitive and non-punitive teachers upon children's concepts of school misconduct. *Journal of Educational Psychology* 52:44–49. [59]

[409]Kraft, I., et al. 1968. *Prelude to school: An evaluation of an inner-city preschool program.* ED 033 750. [197]

[410]Krantz, M. 1972. Haptic recognition of objects in children. *Journal of Genetic Psychology* 120:121–33. [157]

[411]Krider, M. A., and Petsche, M. 1967. *An evaluation of Head Start preschool enrichment programs as they affect the intellectual ability, the social adjustment, and the achievement level of five-year-old children enrolled in Lincoln, Nebraska.* ED 015 011. [197]

[412]Krippner, S. 1971. On research in visual training and reading disability. *Journal of Learning Disabilities* 4:65–76. [107, 150]

[413]Krus, P., and Rubin, R. A. 1974. *Use of family history data to predict educational functioning from ages five through seven.* ED 090 274. [38]

[414]Kunz, J., and Moyer, J. E. 1969. A comparison of economically disadvantaged and economically advantaged kindergarten children. *Journal of Educational Research* 62:392–95. [70]

[415]L'Abate, L. 1962. Consensus of choice among children: A test of Piaget's theory of cognitive development. *Journal of Genetic Psychology* 100:143–49. [130, 131]

[416]Labov, W. 1970. The logical non-standard English. In *Language and Poverty*,

ed. F. Williams, pp. 153–89. Chicago: Markham Press. [90]

[417]LaCrosse, R. E., et al. 1970. *The first six years of life: A report on current research and educational practice.* Genetic Psychology Monographs 82:161–266. Provincetown, Mass.: Journal Press. [189, 202]

[418]Lamb, H. E., et al. 1965. *The development of self-other relationships during project Head Start.* ED 015 008. [60]

[419]Lamson, E. E. 1940. A follow-up study of a group of nursery school children. In *Yearbook for the National Society for the Study of Education,* vol. 39, part 2, pp. 231–36. [200]

[420]Larson, D. E. 1969. *The effect of a preschool experience upon intellectual functioning among four-year-old, white children in rural Minnesota.* ED 039 030. [198]

[421]_____. 1972. *Stability of gains in intellectual functioning among white children who attended a preschool program in rural Minnesota.* ED 066 227. [198]

[422]Larson, R. G., and Olson, J. L. 1968. Compensatory education: How much is enough? *Journal of Negro Education* 37:164–67. [194]

[423]Lee, P. C., and Wolinsky, A. L. 1973. Male teachers of young children: A preliminary study. *Young Children* 28:342–52. [179, 186]

[424]Lessler, K., and Fox, R. E. 1969. An evaluation of a Head Start program in a low population area. *Journal of Negro Education* 38:46–54. [191, 192]

[425]Levenstein, P. 1969. Individual variation among preschoolers in cognitive intervention program in low-income families. Paper presented at the Council for Exceptional Children, Conference on Early Childhood Education, 12 December 1969, New Orleans, Louisiana. [40, 45, 193]

[426]_____. 1971. Learning through (and from) mothers. *Childhood Education* 48:130–34. [38]

[427]Levenstein, P., and Levenstein, S. 1971. Fostering learning potential in preschoolers. *Social Casework* 52:74–78. [77]

[428]Levinson, B. M. 1961. Parental achievement drives for preschool children, and the Vineland social maturity scale, and the social deviation quotient. *Journal of Genetic Psychology* 99:113–28. [39]

[429]Levy, D. M., and Tulchin, S. H. 1925. The resistant behavior of infants and children. *Journal of Experimental Psychology* 8:209–24. [182]

[430]Lewis, H. 1954. *Deprived children.* London: Oxford University Press. [35]

[431]Lewis, M. 1966. Probability learning in young children: The binary choice paradigm. *Journal of Genetic Psychology* 108:43–48. [138]

[432]Liddle, G. P., and Rockwell, R. E. 1964. The role of parents and family life. *Journal of Negro Education* 33:311–17. [30, 46]

[433]Liljefors, R. 1974. Interview with R. S. Moore, April 1974. [8, 229]

[434]Litman, F. 1969. *Environment influences on the development of abilities.* ED 032 126. [77]

[435]Little, W. B.; Kenny, C. T.; and Middleton, M. H. 1973. Differences in intelligence among low socioeconomic class Negro children as a function of sex, age, educational level of parents, and home stability. *Journal of Genetic Psychology* 123:241–50. [44]

[436]Low, S., and Spindler, P. G. 1968. *Child care arrangements of working mothers in the United States.* Children's Bureau Publication no. 461. Washington, D.C.: U.S. Department of Health, Education, and Welfare. [42]

[437]Ludlam, W. 1974. Young readers may harm eyes. *South Bend* (Indiana) *Tribune,* 12 December 1974, p. 34. [151]

[438]Maccoby, E. E. 1966. Sex differences in intellectual functioning. In *The development of sex differences,* ed. E. E. Maccoby, pp. 25–55. Stanford, Calif.: Stanford University Press. [179, 184, 185, 186]

[439]Maccoby, E. E.; Dowley, E. M.; and Degerman, J. W. 1965. Activity level and intellectual functioning in normal preschool children. *Child Development* 36:761–70. [186]

[440]Mallay, H. 1935. Growth in social behavior and mental activity after six months in nursery school. *Child Development* 6:303–9. [201]

[441]Manis, M. 1958. Personal adjustment, assumed similarity to parents, and inferred parental evaluations of the self. *Journal of Consulting Psychology* 22:481–85. [52]

[442]Mannio, F. V. 1966. A cohort study of school withdrawals with implications for mental health. *Community Mental Health Journal* 2:146–51. [179, 185]

[443]Mariam, Sister. 1954. A comparative study of the reading disability in neurologically organized and neurologically disorganized fifth grade children. Doctoral dissertation, Loyola University, Chicago. [149]

[444]Marshall, H. H. 1969. Learning as a function of task interest, reinforcement, and social class variables. *Journal of Educational Psychology* 60:133–37. [70, 72]

[445]Marty, R., and Scherer, J. 1964. Critères de maturation des systèmes afférents corticaux. *Progressive Brain Research* 4:222–36. [153, 166]

[446]Mason, G. E., and Prater, N. J. 1966. Social behavioral aspects of teaching reading to kindergarteners. *Journal of Educational Research* 60:58–61. [183]

[447]Mawhinney, P. E. 1964. We gave up on early entrance. *Michigan Educational Journal* 41:25. [95, 97, 135, 232]

[448]May, D., and Vinovskis, M. 1972. A ray of millennial light: Early education and social reform in infant school movement in Massachusetts, 1826–1840. Paper presented at the Clark University Conference on Family and Social Structure, 22 April 1972, Clark University, Worcester, Massachusetts. [16, 206, 207, 209]

[449]Mayeske, G. W. 1972. Similarities and dissimilarities in the dependence of achievement on family background and school factors for students of different and ethnic group membership. Paper presented to the American Educational Research Association, April 1972, Chicago, Illinois. [37]

[450]McAulay, J. D. 1961. What understandings do second grade children have of time relationships? *Journal of Educational Research* 54:312–14. [138]

[451]McCandless, B. 1967. *Children: Behavior and development.* New York: Holt, Rinehart and Winston. [37, 38]

[452]McCarthy, D. J. 1955. Pre-entrance variables and school success of under-age children. *Harvard Educational Review* 25:266–69. [86, 88]

[453]McCracken, R. A. 1966. A two-year study of the reading achievement of children who were reading when they entered first grade. *Journal of Educational Research* 59:207–10. [113]

[454]McDill, E. L.; McDill, M. S.; and Sprehe, J. T. 1969. *Strategies for success in compensatory education: An appraisal of evaluation research.* Baltimore: The Johns Hopkins Press. [189]

[455]McGeoch, J. A., and Irion, A. L. 1952. *The psychology of human learning.* 2d ed. New York: Longmans, Green. [90]

[456]McGurk, H., and Lewis, M. 1972. *Birth order: A phenomenon in search of an*

257

explanation. ED 067 156. [31]

[457] McKay, C. L., and Ryan, A. P. 1974. Visual characteristics of submarine school candidates, submariners, and Navy divers. Naval Submarine Medical Research Laboratory, Report no. 767. Groton, Conn.: Bureau of Medicine and Surgery, Navy Department, Submarine Base. [152]

[458] McLean, D. 1954. Child development: A generation of research. *Child Development* 25:3–8. [15]

[459] McLeod, J.; Markowsky, M. D.; and Leong, C. K. 1972. A follow-up of early entrants to elementary schools. *Elementary School Journal* 73:10–19. [95]

[460] McMillan, M. 1919. *The nursery school.* London: J. M. Dent and Sons. [208]

[461] McNally, L. 1973. *Living room school project: Final evaluation report, 1972–73.* ED 082 850. [216]

[462] Meers, D. 1970. *International day care: A selective review and psychoanalytic critique.* Washington, D.C.: Office of Economic Opportunity. [230]

[463] Mermelstein, E., and Meyer, E. 1969. Conservation training techniques and their effects on different populations. *Child Development* 40:471–90. [190]

[464] Mermelstein, E., and Shulman, L. S. 1967. Lack of formal schooling and the acquisition of conservation. *Child Development* 38:39–52. [74, 114, 190]

[465] Metcalf, D. R. 1974. Letter to R. S. Moore, 22 March 1974. [111, 145, 148, 149]

[466] ———. 1975. *An investigation of cerebral lateral functioning and the EEG.* Report of a study made for the U.S. Office of Economic Opportunity under Research Grant No. 50079-G-73-02-1 to Hewitt Research Foundation, Berrien Springs, Michigan. ERIC No. pending. [139, 148]

[467] Metcalf, D. R., and Jordon, K. 1972. EEG ontogenesis in normal children. In *Drugs, development, and cerebral function,* ed. W. L. Smith, pp. 125–44. Springfield, Ill.: Charles C. Thomas. [147]

[468] Meyers, E. 1966. Self-concept, family structure, and school achievement: A study of disadvantaged Negro boys. Doctoral dissertation, University of Florida, Gainesville. [52]

[469] Michigan (People of the State of) vs. Larry W. and Judy B. O'Guin. 1973. District Court, 96th Judicial District, Marquette, Michigan. [86]

[470] Michigan (People of the State of) vs. Judy Waddell. 1975–76. District Court, 5th Judicial District, St. Joseph, Michigan. [86]

[471] Milgram, N. A., and Furth, H. G. 1967. Factors affecting conceptual control in normal and retarded children. *Child Development* 38:531–43. [129, 132]

[472] Milgram, N. A., and Ozer, M. N. *The effects of neurological and environmental factors on the language development of Head Start children—an evaluation of the Head Start program.* ED 017 317. [150]

[473] Miller, D. L. 1972. Preschoolers' perceptions of parental attributes and their effect on behavior in nursery school. *Child Study Journal* 2:197–203. [39, 45]

[474] Miller, G. W. 1970. Factors in school achievement and social class. *Journal of Educational Psychology* 61:260–69. [140]

[475] Miller, J. W. 1968. *Development of children's ability to coordinate perspectives.* ED 016 516. [130, 132]

[476] Miller, L. B. 1971. *Experimental variation of Head Start curricula: A comparison of current approaches.* Annual Progress Report, 1 March 1971 to 31 May 1971.

Louisville, Ky.: University of Louisville, Department of Psychology. [195]
477_____. 1972. *Four preschool programs: Their dimensions and effects.* Annual Progress Report, 1 June 1971 to 31 May 1972. Louisville, Ky.: University of Louisville, Department of Psychology. [198]
478Miller, W. H. 1969. When mothers teach their children. *Elementary School Journal* 70:38–42. [46]
479Milner, E. A. 1951. A study of the relationship between reading readiness in grade one school children and patterns of parent-child interactions. *Child Development* 22:95–112. [45, 107, 108, 109]
480Minton, C.; Kagan, J.; and Levine, J. A. 1971. Maternal control and obedience in the two-year-old. *Child Development* 42:1873–94. [40]
481Minuchin, S., et al. 1967. *Families of the slums: An exploration of their structure and treatment.* New York: Basic Books. [38]
482Mischel, W. 1966. A social-learning view of sex differences in behavior. In *The development of sex differences,* ed. E. E. Maccoby, pp. 56–81. Stanford, Calif.: Stanford University Press. [182]
483Money, J. 1967. Sex hormones and other variables in human eroticism. In *Sex and internal secretions,* vol. 2, ed. W. C. Young, pp. 1383–1400. Baltimore: Williams and Wilkins. [178]
484Money, J.; Hampson, J. G.; and Hampson, J. L. 1957. Imprinting and the establishment of gender roles. *A.M.A., Archives of Neurology and Psychiatry* 77:333–36. [178]
485Monod, N., and Ducas, D. 1968. The prognostic value of the electroencephalogram in the first two years of life. In *Clinical electroencephalography of children,* ed. P. Kellaway and I. Petersén, pp. 61–76. New York: Grune and Stratton. [169]
486Moon, R. D., and Moore, R. S. 1975. *The effect of early school entrance on the school achievement and attitudes of disadvantaged children.* Report of a study made for the U.S. Office of Economic Opportunity under Research Grant No. 50079-G-73/02 to the Hewitt Research Foundation, Berrien Springs, Michigan. ED 146 198. [185, 192, 223]
487Moore, D. R.; Kordenbrock, K.; and Moore, R. S. 1976. Lessons from Europe: A report on European preschools and child care. *Childhood Education* 53:66–70. [69, 85, 87, 209, 213, 217, 221, 224, 226]
488Moore, R. E., and Ogletree, E. J. 1973. A comparison of the readiness and intelligence of first grade children with and without a full year of Head Start training. *Education* 93:266–70. [197]
489Moore, R. S. 1973. Unpublished school entry-age reports. On file at Hewitt Research Foundation, Berrien Springs, Michigan. [96, 101]
490_____. 1976a. Socialization of young children. A paper commissioned by and presented to the International Academy for Preventive Medicine, Bad Nauheim, Germany, 11 June 1976. Hewitt Research Foundation, Berrien Springs, Michigan. [60]
491_____. 1976b. Motherhood on trial. *Liberty* 71:3–5. [86]
492Moore, R. S., and Moore, D. N. 1975. *Better late than early.* New York: Reader's Digest Press. [92, 101, 216, 219, 228]
493Moore, R. S., and Moore, D. R. 1972a. The dangers of early schooling. *Harper's Magazine* 245:58–62. [101, 102]
494_____. 1972b. Early schooling for all? *Congressional Record,* 16 October

259

1972, pp. E8726–40. [219, 221]

[495]_____. 1973. How early should they go to school? *Childhood Education* 50:14–20. [24]

[496]Moore, R. S.; Moon, R. D.; and Moore, D. R. 1972. The California report: Early schooling for all? *Phi Delta Kappan* 53:615–21. [24, 185]

[497]Moore, R. S., et al. 1975. *Influences on learning in early childhood*. Report of a study made for the U.S. Office of Economic Opportunity under Research Grant No. 50079-G-73/01 to the Hewitt Research Foundation, Berrien Springs, Michigan. ED 144 711. [211]

[498]Morency, A. 1968. Auditory modality, research, and practice. In *Perception and reading*, ed. H. K. Smith, pp. 17–21. Newark, Del.: International Reading Association. [110, 155, 156]

[499]Morency, A., and Wepman, J. M. 1973. Early perceptual ability and later school achievement. *Elementary School Journal* 73:323–27. [90, 156]

[500]Moss, H. A. 1967. Sex, age, and state as determinants of mother-infant interaction. *Merrill-Palmer Quarterly* 13:19–36. [180]

[501]Moss, H. A., and Kagan, J. 1958. Maternal influences on early IQ scores. *Psychological Reports* 4:655–61. [181, 185]

[502]Moustakas, C. E. 1952. Personality studies conducted in nursery schools. *Journal of Educational Research* 46:161–77. [200, 201]

[503]Mumpower, D. L. 1970. Sex ratios found in various types of referred exceptional children. *Exceptional Children* 36:621–22. [185]

[504]Nagera, H. 1966. *Early childhood disturbances, the infantile neurosis, and the adulthood disturbances*. New York: International Universities Press. [43]

[505]Nathanson, I. T.; Towne, L. E.; and Aub, J. C. 1941. Normal excretion of sex hormones in childhood. *Endocrines* 28:851–65. [177, 180]

[506]National evaluations. 1972. *Effects of different Head Start program approaches on children of different characteristics: Report on analysis of data from 1966–67 and 1967–68*. ED 072 859. [191]

[507]Neale, D. C., and Proshek, J. M. 1967. School-related attitudes of culturally disadvantaged elementary school children. *Journal of Educational Psychology* 58:238–44. [78]

[508]Nelson, K. E., and Earl, N. 1973. Information search by preschool children: Induced use of categories and category hierarchies. *Child Development* 44:682–85. [134, 135]

[509]Nelson, W. E., ed. 1967. *Textbook of pediatrics*, 8th ed. Philadelphia: W. B. Saunders Company. [147, 148, 169]

[510]Neubauer, P. B. 1956. The child's growth toward maturity. *Child Study* 33:31–34. [54]

[511]Newton, F. H. 1972. Letter to R. S. Moore, 24 October 1972. [152]

[512]Nimnicht, G. P. 1970a. *Overview of responsive model program*. ED 045 207. [196]

[513]_____. 1970b. *A progress report on the parent/child course and toy library*. ED 045 206. [196]

[514]Nimnicht, G. P., et al. 1971. *A report on the evaluation of the parent/child toy-lending library program*. ED 069 655. [196]

[515]Nimnicht, G. P. 1972. Letter to R. S. Moore, 29 September 1972. [23, 195, 224]

[516]Noback, C. R., and Purpura, D. P. 1961. Postnatal ontogenesis of neurons

in cat neocortex. *Journal of Comparative Neurology* 117:291-307. [165]
    [517]Northway, M. L. 1968. The stability of young children's social relations. *Educational Research* 11:54-57. [58]
    [518]O'Brien, R. A., and Lopate, P. 1968. *Preschool programs and the intellectual development of disadvantaged children.* ED 024 473. [193]
    [519]O'Brien, T., and Shapiro, B. J. 1968. The development of logical thinking in children. *American Educational Research Journal* 5:531-42. [138]
    [520]Odom, R. D. 1967. Problem-solving strategies as a function of age and socioeconomic level. *Child Development* 38:747-52. [138]
    [521]O'Keefe, R. A. 1973. Home Start: Partnership with parents. *Children Today* 2:12-16. [216]
    [522]Olmsted, P. P., and Jester, R. E. 1972. *How mothers teach.* ED 063 549. [40]
    [523]Olson, W. C. 1947. Experiences for growing. *NEA Journal* 36:502-3. [88, 186]
    [524]Osborne, R. T., and Lindsey, J. M. 1965. *A longitudinal investigation of change in the factorial composition of intelligence with age in young school children.* ED 026 149. [128]
    [525]Page, J. D. 1940. The effect of nursery school attendance upon subsequent IQ. *Journal of Psychology* 10:221-30. [201]
    [526]Palermo, D. S., and Molfese, D. L. 1972. Language acquisition from age five onward. *Psychological Bulletin* 78:409-28. [137]
    [527]Palmer, F. H. 1968. *Early intellective training and school performance: Summary of NIH grant no. HD-02253.* ED 025 324. [196]
    [528]Palmer, J. A. 1966a. *"Preschool" education, pros and cons: A survey of "preschool" education with emphasis on research past, present, and future.* ED 016 525. [129]
    [529]_____. 1966b. *The effects of junior kindergarten on achievement—the first five years.* ED 016 526. [200, 202]
    [530]Parten, M. D. 1932. Social participation among preschool children. *Journal of Abnormal and Social Psychology* 27:243-69. [201]
    [531]Payne, J. S., et al. 1973. *Head Start: A tragicomedy with epilogue.* New York: Behavioral Publications. [19]
    [532]Peisach, E., and Wein, N. 1970. Relationship of conservation explanations to item difficulty. *Journal of Genetic Psychology* 117:167-80. [139]
    [533]Pestalozzi, J. H. 1898. *Letters on early education.* Syracuse, N.Y.: C. W. Bardeen. [207]
    [534]Peters, A., and Muir, A. R. 1959. The relationship between axons and schwann cells during development of peripheral nerves in the rat. *Quarterly Journal of Experimental Psychology* 44:117-30. [166]
    [535]Petersén, I.; Eeg-Olofsson, O.; and Selldín, V. 1968. Paroxysmal activity in EEG of normal children. In *Clinical electroencephalography of children,* ed. P. Kellaway and I. Petersén. pp. 167-88. New York: Grune and Stratton. [169]
    [536]Peterson, T. J. 1937. A preliminary study of the effects of previous nursery school attendance upon five-year-old children entering kindergarten. In *Studies in preschool education.* University of Iowa Studies in Child Welfare, vol. 14. Iowa City: University of Iowa Press. [201]
    [537]Phillips, J. L. 1969. *The origins of intellect: Piaget's theory.* San Francisco: W. H. Freeman & Company. [61, 137]

261

[538]Piaget, J. 1952. *The origins of intelligence in children* (translated by M. Cook). New York: International Universities Press. [61, 89, 129, 130, 137]

[539]_____. 1961. The genetic approach to the psychology of thought. *Journal of Educational Psychology* 52:275-81. [130]

[540]_____. 1964. Development and learning. *Journal of Research in Science Teaching* 2:176-86. [130]

[541]_____. 1970. *Science of education and the psychology of the child.* New York: Viking Press. [125, 126]

[542]Piaget, J.; Inhelder, B.; and Szeminska, A. 1960. *The child's conception of geometry.* New York: Basic Books. [136]

[543]Pidgeon, D. A. 1965. Date of birth and scholastic performance. *Educational Research* 8:3-7. [98]

[544]Pishkin, V., and Willis, D. J. 1974. Age, sex, and socioeconomic factors in concept identification. *Psychology in the Schools* 2:85-90. [78]

[545]Polansky, N. A., et al. 1970. Two modes of maternal immaturity and their consequences. *Child Welfare* 49:312-23. [39]

[546]Pollard, H. M. 1974. *Pioneers of popular education.* Westport, Conn.: Greenwood Press. [207, 209]

[547]Pontius, A. A. 1972. Neurological aspects in some type of delinquency, especially among juveniles. *Adolescence* 7:289-308. [56]

[548]Prestige, M. C. 1970. Differentiation, degeneration, and the role of the periphery: Quantitative considerations. In *The neurosciences,* ed. F. O. Schmitt. New York: The Rockefeller University Press. [170]

[549]Price-Williams, D. R. 1961. A study concerning concepts of conservation of quantities among primitive children. *Acta Psychologica* 18:297-305. [190]

[550]Purkey, W. W. 1970. *Self-concept and school achievement.* Englewood Cliffs, N.J.: Prentice-Hall. [51, 212]

[551]Purpura, D. P., and Shade, J. P. 1964. Growth and maturation of the brain. *Progressive Brain Research* 4:110. [165]

[552]Purpura, D. P.; Shofer, R. J.; and Noback, C. R. 1964. Comparative ontogenesis of structure-function relations in cerebral and cerebellar cortex. *Progressive Brain Research* 4:187-221. [166]

[553]Quigley, H. 1973. The pre-reading vocabulary of children leaving nursery school. *Educational Research* 16:28-33. [106, 113]

[554]Rabinowicz, T. 1974. Some aspects of the maturation of the human cerebral cortex. In *Pre- and post-natal development of the human brain,* ed. S. R. Berenberg, M. Caniaris, and N. P. Masse, pp. 44-56. Basel: S. Karger. [164]

[555]Radin, N. 1967. *The role of socialization and social influence in a compensatory preschool program.* ED 017 337. [79]

[556]_____. 1971. Maternal warmth, achievement motivation, and cognitive functioning in lower-class preschool children. *Child Development* 42:1560-65. [40, 45]

[557]_____. 1973. Observed paternal behaviors as antecedents of intellectual functioning in young boys. *Developmental Psychology* 8:369-76. [40]

[558]Radin, N., and Kamii, C. K. 1965. The child-rearing attitudes of disadvantaged Negro mothers and some educated implications. *Journal of Negro Education* 34:138-46. [40]

[559]Radke, M.; Trager, H. G.; and Davis, H. 1949. *Social perceptions and attitudes of children.* Genetic Psychology Monographs 40:327-447. Provincetown,

Mass.: Jouranl Press. [60]

560Rambusch, N. M. 1962. *Learning how to learn.* Baltimore: Helicon Press. [208]

561Reid, J. F. 1966. Learning to think about reading. *Educational Research* 9:56–62. [113]

562Reidford, P., and Berzonsky, M. 1969. Field test of an academically oriented preschool. *Elementary School Journal* 69:271–76. [195]

563Reilly, D. H. 1971. Auditory-visual integration, sex, and reading achievement. *Journal of Educational Psychology* 62:482–86. [183, 184]

564Rhinehart, J. B. 1942. Some effects of a nursery school parent education program on a group of three-year-olds. *Journal of Genetic Psychology* 61:153–61. [201]

565Richmond, B. O., and Norton, W. A. 1973. Creative production and developmental age in disadvantaged children. *Elementary School Journal* 73:279–84. [80]

566Riles, W. 1972. *The early childhood education program proposal.* Sacramento: California State Department of Education. [101]

567Riley, D. A.; McKee, J. P.; and Hadley, R. W. 1964. Prediction of auditory discrimination learning and transposition from children's auditory ordering ability. *Journal of Experimental Psychology* 67:324–29. [153]

568Riley, D. A., et al. 1967. Auditory discrimination in children: The effect of relative and absolute instructions on retention and transfer. *Journal of Experimental Psychology* 73:581–88. [153]

569Rist, R. C. 1970. Student social class and teacher expectations: The self-fulfilling prophecy in ghetto education. *Harvard Educational Review* 40:411–51. [79, 199]

570Robinson, H. B., and Robinson, N. M. 1971. Longitudinal development of very young children in a comprehensive day care program: The first two years. *Child Development* 42:1673–83. [79]

571Robinson, M. L. 1973. *Compensatory education and early adolescence.* Menlo Park, Calif.: Stanford Research Center. [24, 71, 101, 102, 203, 212, 218, 228]

572Robinson, R. J., and Tizard, J. P. M. 1966. The central nervous system in the newborn. *British Medical Journal* 22:49–55. [146, 147, 148, 150]

573Roff, M. 1971. *Childhood antecedents in the mental health development of three groups of adult males: Neurotics—severe bad conduct cases, and controls.* Minneapolis: Institute of Child Development, University of Minnesota. [45]

574Rohwer, W. D. 1971. Prime time for education: Early childhood or adolescence? *Harvard Educational Review* 41:316–41. [8, 24, 71, 100, 101, 102, 140, 188, 189, 202, 203, 212, 217, 218, 228]

575_____. 1973. Improving instruction in the 1970's—what could make a significant difference? Paper presented at the American Educational Research Association meeting, 1973, New Orleans, Louisiana. [24, 71, 189, 218]

576_____. 1975. Inequality in school success: The neglect of individuals. Address at National Education Association Conference on Educational Neglect, February 1975, Washington, D.C. [71, 100, 102, 212]

577Rohwer, W. D., et al. 1971. Population differences and learning proficiency. *Journal of Educational Psychology* 62:1–14. [72, 77, 78]

578Rosen, B. M.; Bahn, A. K.; and Kramer, M. 1964. Demographic and diagnostic characteristics of psychiatric clinic out-patients in the U.S.A., 1961.

American Journal of Orthopsychiatry 34:455–68. [179]

[579]Rosen, C. L., and Ohnmacht, F. 1968. Perception, readiness, and reading achievement in first grade. In *Perception and reading,* ed. H. K. Smith, pp. 33–39. Newark, Del.: International Reading Association. [184]

[580]Rosenthal, M. 1969. *A comparison of reading readiness achievement of kindergarten children of disparate entrance ages.* ED 033 745. [87]

[581]Rosenzweig, M. R.; Bennett, E. L.; and Diamond, M. C. 1972. Brain changes in response to experience. *Scientific American* 226:22–29. [67, 69, 71, 146]

[582]Rosner, J. 1972. *The development and validation of an individualized perceptual skills curriculum.* Pittsburgh: Learning Research and Development Center, University of Pittsburgh. [112, 156]

[583]_____. 1973. Language arts and arithmetic achievement, and specifically related perceptual skills. *American Educational Research Journal* 10:59–68. [90, 157]

[584]Ross, D., and Ross, S. 1969. Leniency toward cheating in preschool children. *Journal of Educational Psychology* 60:483–87. [61]

[585]Rothman, S. M. 1973. Liberating day care: A modest proposal. *Phi Delta Kappan* 55:132–35. [213]

[586]Rubin, R. 1972. Sex differences in effects of kindergarten attendance on development of school readiness and language skills. *Elementary School Journal* 72:265–74. [184, 185]

[587]Rudel, R. G., and Denckla, M. B. 1976. Relationship of IQ and reading score to visual, spatial, and temporal matching tasks. *Journal of Learning Disabilities* 9:169–78. [110, 162]

[588]Rudnick, M.; Sterritt, G. M.; and Flax, M. 1967. Auditory and visual rhythm perception and reading ability. *Child Development* 38:581–87. [109, 110, 112, 157]

[589]Ruebush, B. E. 1963. Child psychology. In *Yearbook of the National Society for the Study of Education,* vol. 62, part 1, pp. 460–515. [35]

[590]Saltz, E., and Johnson, J. 1973. *Training for thematic-fantasy play in culturally disadvantaged children: Preliminary results.* ED 086 334. [30, 44, 197]

[591]Satz, P., and Friel, J. 1974. Some predictive antecedents of specific reading disability: A preliminary two-year follow-up. *Journal of Learning Disabilities* 7:437–44. [111]

[592]Scarfe, N. V. 1972. The importance of security in the education of young children. *International Journal of Early Childhood* 4:27–30. [68]

[593]Schaefer, E. S. 1969. *Need for early and continuing education.* ED 040 750. [214, 215]

[594]_____. 1970. Need for early and continuing education. In *Education of the infant and young child,* ed. V. H. Denenberg, pp. 61–82. New York: Academic Press. [213]

[595]_____. 1971. Toward a revolution in education: A perspective from child development research. *National Elementary School Principal* 51:18–25. [24, 219]

[596]_____. 1972a. Does early education pay off? *PTA Magazine* 67:8–10, 30. [24, 212]

[597]_____. 1972b. Parents as educators: Evidence from cross-sectional, longitudinal, and intervention research. *Young Children* 27:227–39. [46, 212, 221, 224]

[598]_____. 1972c. Letter to R. S. Moore, 18 July 1972. [212]

[599]_____. 1973. *Child development research and the educational revolution: The child, the family and the education profession.* ED 078 972. [24, 214]

[600]_____. 1974. The ecology of child development: Implications for research and the professions. Paper presented at the Symposium on the Role of Psychology in Studying and Helping Families with Problems, American Psychological Association, August 1974, New Orleans, Louisiana. [219]

[601]Scheibel, A. B. 1962. Neural correlates of psychophysiological developments in the young organism. *Recent Advances in Biological Psychiatry* 4:313–27. [166]

[602]Scherer, J. 1968. Electrophysiological aspects of cortical development. *Progressive Brain Research* 22:480–90. [145, 166, 167]

[603]Schulz, D. 1972. *The changing family: its functions and future.* Englewood Cliffs, N.J.: Prentice-Hall. [40]

[604]Schwartz, I. R.; Pappas, G. O.; and Purpura, D. P. 1968. Fine structure of neurons and synapses in the feline hippocampus during postnatal ontogenesis. *Experimental Neurology* 22:394–407. [165]

[605]Scott, J. P. 1960. Comparative social psychology. In *Principles of comparative psychology*, eds. R. H. Waters, D. A. Rethingshafer, and W. E. Caldwell, pp. 250–88. New York: McGraw-Hill. [29]

[606]_____. 1963. *The process of primary socialization in canine and human infants.* Monographs of the Society for Research in Child Development, vol. 28, no. 1 (serial no. 85). Chicago: University of Chicago Press. [11, 29]

[607]Scott, P. M. 1972. About research. In *The young child: Reviews of research,* vol. 2, ed. W. W. Hartup, pp. 1–23. Washington, D.C.: National Association for the Education of Young Children.

[608]Scott, R. 1973. Home Start: Family-centered preschool enrichment for black and white children. *Psychology in the Schools* 10:140–46. [193]

[609]_____. 1974. Research and early childhood: The Home Start project. *Child Welfare* 53:112–19. [193]

[610]Sears, R. R. 1972. Attachment, dependency, and frustration. In *Attachment and dependency*, ed. J. L. Gewirtz, pp. 1–27. Washington, D.C.: V. H. Winston & Sons. [31]

[611]Secord, P. 1967. *A social psychological analysis of the transition from home to school.* ED 015 017. [77]

[612]Seidel, H. E.; Barkley, M. J.; and Stith, D. 1967. Evaluation of a program for project Head Start. *Journal of Genetic Psychology* 110:185–97. [197]

[613]Shapiro, B. J., and O'Brien, T. C. 1970. Logical thinking in children ages six through thirteen. *Child Development* 41:823–29. [134]

[614]Shapiro, E., and Biber, B. 1972. The education of young children: A developmental-interaction approach. *Teachers College Record* 74:55–79. [67, 68]

[615]Shaw, M. C., and Dutton, B. E. 1965. The use of the parent-attitude research inventory with the parents of bright academic underachievers. In *The self in growth, teaching, and learning: Selected readings*, ed. D. E. Hamachek, pp. 493–500. Englewood Cliffs, N.J.: Prentice-Hall. [52]

[616]Shearer, E. 1967. The effect of date of birth on teachers' assessments of children. *Educational Research* 10:51–56. [99]

[617]Sheldon, W. D. 1970. *Teaching reading to the disadvantaged: Progress and promise.* ED 045 311. [108, 109]

[618]Shepherd, C. W. 1969. Childhood chronic illness and visual motor perceptual development. *Exceptional Children* 36:39–42. [150]

[619]Shields, M. M., and Steiner, E. 1973. The language of three-to-five-year-olds in preschool education. *Educational Research* 15:97–105. [98]

[620]Shriner, T., and Daniloff, R. 1970. Reassembly of segmented CVC syllables by children. *Journal of Speech and Hearing Research* 13:537–47. [92]

[621]Sigel, I. E., and Hooper, F. 1968. *Logical thinking in children.* New York: Holt, Rinehart and Winston. [89]

[622]Sigel, I. E.; Jarman, P.; and Hanesian, H. 1963. Styles of categorization and their perceptual, intellectual, and personality correlates in young children. Unpublished paper, Merrill-Palmer Institute. [186[

[623]Sigel, I. E., and Mermelstein, E. 1965. Effects of nonschooling on Piagetian tasks of conservation. Paper presented at American Psychological Association meeting, September 1965, Chicago, Illinois. [74]

[624]Sigel, I. E., et al. 1972. *Psycho-educational intervention beginning at age two: Reflections and outcomes.* ED 069 161. [183]

[625]Silberberg, N. E., and Silberberg, M. C. 1969. Myths in remedial education. *Journal of Learning Disabilities* 2:209–17. [111]

[626]Silberberg, N. E., and Iversen, I. A. 1972. The effects of kindergarten instruction in alphabet and numbers on first grade reading. *Journal of Learning Disabilities* 5:254–61. [109]

[627]Simmons, S. V. 1958. A study of the chronological age of children in relation to their achievement in school. Unpublished paper, Emory University, Atlanta, Georgia. [97]

[628]Simon, M. D. 1959. Body configuration and school readiness. *Child Development* 30:493–512. [90]

[629]Simonsen, K. M. 1947. *Examination of children from children's homes and day nurseries.* Copenhagen: NYT Nordisk Forlag Arnold Busck. [36]

[630]Simpson, E. J. 1973. The home as a career education center. *Exceptional Children* 39:626–30. [217]

[631]Skeels, H. M. 1966. *Adult status of children with contrasting early life experiences.* Monographs of the Society for Research in Child Development, vol. 31, no. 3 (serial no. 105). Chicago: University of Chicago Press. [34]

[632]Skeels, H. M., et al. 1938. *A study of environmental stimulation: An orphanage preschool project.* University of Iowa Studies in Child Welfare, vol. 15, no. 4. Iowa City: University of Iowa Press. [39, 44, 201]

[633]Skoglund, S. 1960. The activity of muscle receptors in the kitten. *Acta Physiologica Scandinavica* 50:203–21. [166]

[634]_____. 1969. Growth and differentiation. *Annual Review of Physiology* 31:19–42. [146, 166]

[635]Smith, J. R. 1937. The origin and genesis of rhythm in the electroencephalogram. *Psychological Bulletin* 34:534–35. [168]

[636]Smith, Mildred B. 1968. School and home: Focus on achievement. In *Developing programs for the educationally disadvantaged,* ed. A. H. Passow, pp. 89–107. New York: Columbia University Teachers College Press. [52, 76]

[637]Smith, Marshall P. 1968. Intellectual differences in five-year-old underprivileged girls and boys with and without prekindergarten school experiences. *Journal of Educational Research* 61:348–50. [185]

[638]Smith, N. B. 1965. Early reading: Viewpoints. *Childhood Education*

42:229–41. [108]

⁶³⁹Soares, A. T., and Soares, L. M. 1969. Self-perceptions of culturally disadvantaged children. *American Educational Research Journal* 6:31–45. [60]

⁶⁴⁰Soares, L. M., and Soares, A. T. 1970–71. Self-concepts of disadvantaged and advantaged students. *Child Study Journal* 1:69–73. [60]

⁶⁴¹Sontag, M.; Sella, A. P.; and Thorndike, R. L. 1969. The effect of Head Start training on the cognitive growth of disadvantaged children. *Journal of Educational Research* 62:387–89. [197]

⁶⁴²Spaulding, R. L., and Katzenmeyer, W. G. 1969. *Effects of age of entry and duration of participation in a compensatory education program.* ED 043 380. [95]

⁶⁴³Spelke, E., et al. 1973. Father interaction and separation protest. *Developmental Psychology* 9:83–90. [33]

⁶⁴⁴Spicker, H. H. 1971. Intellectual development through early childhood education. *Exceptional Children* 37:629–40. [196]

⁶⁴⁵Spitalny, T. 1957. Battles and "best friends" in the nursery school. *Child Study* 34:8–12. [61]

⁶⁴⁶Spitz, R. A. 1949. The role of ecological factors in emotional development in infancy. *Child Development* 20:145–55. [41, 42]

⁶⁴⁷Spodek, B. 1973. *Early childhood education.* Englewood Cliffs, N.J.: Prentice-Hall. [209]

⁶⁴⁸Sprigle, H. 1974. Learning to learn program. In *Longitudinal evaluations of preschool programs,* ed. S. Ryan, pp. 109–24. Washington, D.C.: Office of Child Development. [192]

⁶⁴⁹Stanley, J. C., ed. 1972. *Preschool programs for the disadvantaged: Five experimental approaches to early education.* Proceedings of the first annual Hyman Blumberg Symposium on Research in Early Childhood Education. Baltimore: The Johns Hopkins University Press. [22]

⁶⁵⁰_____. 1973. *Compensatory education for children, ages two to eight: Recent studies of educational intervention.* Proceedings of the second annual Hyman Blumberg Symposium on Research in Early Childhood Education. Baltimore: The Johns Hopkins University Press. [22]

⁶⁵¹Stanners, R. F., and Soto, D. H. 1967. Developmental changes in the recognition of beginning segments of English words. *Journal of Educational Psychology* 58:273–77. [110]

⁶⁵²Stanwyck, D. J.; Felker, D. W.; and VanMondfrans, A. P. 1971. An examination of the learning consequences of one kind of civil disobedience. *Educational Theory* 21:146–94. [50]

⁶⁵³Stearns, M. S. 1971. *Report on preschool programs: The effects of preschool programs on disadvantaged children and their families. Final report.* ED 062 025. [191]

⁶⁵⁴Steinhilber, A. W., and Sokolowski, C. J. 1966. *State law on compulsory attendance.* Washington, D.C.: Office of Education. [86]

⁶⁵⁵Stephens, M. W., and Delys, P. 1973. External control expectancies among disadvantaged children at preschool age. *Child Development* 44:670–74. [199]

⁶⁵⁶Stern, C. 1967. Acquisition of problem-solving strategies in young children and its relation to verbalization. *Journal of Educational Psychology* 58:245–52. [134]

⁶⁵⁷Stevenson, H. W., and Siegel, A. 1969. Effects of instructions and age on retention of filmed content. *Journal of Educational Psychology* 60:71–74. [112, 151, 153]

267

[658]Stevenson, H. W.; Williams, A. M.; and Coleman, E. 1971. Interrelations among learning and performance tasks in disadvantaged children. *Journal of Educational Psychology* 62:179-84. [66, 77, 78]

[659]Stone, J. L., and Church, J. 1973. *Childhood and adolescence.* New York: Random House. [41]

[660]Strag, G. A., and Richmond, B. O. 1973. Auditory discrimination techniques for young children. *Elementary School Journal* 73:447-54. [153]

[661]Strauss, S., and Langer, J. 1970. Operational thought inducement. *Child Development* 41:163-75. [139]

[662]Streff, J. W. 1974. Preliminary report on visual changes of children in Cheshire public schools. Unpublished manuscript, Vision Research, Gesell Institute, New Haven, Connecticut. [151]

[663]Strom, R. D. 1965. What is the school speed-up doing to children? *Elementary School Journal* 65:206-7. [142]

[664]Sullivan, H. S. 1953. *The interpersonal theory of psychiatry.* New York: W. W. Norton and Company. [51, 53]

[665]Sutton, M. J. 1969. Children who learned to read in kindergarten: A longitudinal study. *Reading Teacher* 22:595-602. [108]

[666]Suviranta, A. 1973. Home economics answer to the problems raised in industrialized countries. In *XIIth Congress of the International Federation for Home Economics, Final Report,* pp. 92-99. Boulogne, France: Fédération internationale pour l'économie familiale. [214, 224, 225, 226]

[667]Sweet, J. R., and Thornburg, K. R. 1971. Preschoolers' self and social identity within the family structure. *Journal of Negro Education* 40:22-27. [56]

[668]Tanner, J. M. 1961. *Education and physical growth.* New York: International Universities Press. [146, 147, 148, 149, 179, 185]

[669]_____. 1962. *Growth at adolescence.* 2d ed. Oxford: Blackwell Scientific Publications. [180]

[670]Taylor, B. J., and Howell, R. J. 1973. The ability of three-, four-, and five-year-old children to distinguish fantasy from reality. *Journal of Genetic Psychology* 122:315-18. [130]

[671]Theis, S. V. 1924. *How foster children turn out.* New York: State Charities Aid Association. Publication no. 165. [34, 36]

[672]Tocco, T. S., and Bridges, C. M. 1973. The relationship between the self-concepts of mothers and their children. *Child Study Journal* 3:161-79. [52]

[673]Tolor, A.; Scarpetti, W.; and Lane, P. A. 1967. Teachers' attitudes toward children's behavior revisited. *Journal of Educational Psychology* 58:175-80. [67, 79]

[674]Towler, J. O. 1968. *Training effects and concept development—A study of the conservation of continuous quantity in children.* ED 016 533. [134]

[675]Trowbridge, N. T. 1969. *Project IMPACT research report 1968-1969.* Washington, D.C.: U.S. Office of Education Cooperative Research Report. [60]

[676]_____. 1970. Effects of socioeconomic class on self-concept of children. *Psychology in the Schools* 7:304-6. [60]

[677]_____. 1972. Self-concept and socioeconomic status in elementary school children. *American Educational Research Journal* 9:525-37. [60]

[678]Tuddenham, R. D. 1952. *Studies in reputation: I. Sex and grade differences in school children's evaluation of their peers. II. The diagnoses of social adjustment.* Psychological Monographs, vol. 66, no. 333. Westport, Conn.: Greenwood Press. [186]

[679]Tulkin, S. R., and Kagan, J. 1972. Mother-child interaction in the first year of life. *Child Development* 43:31–41. [38, 45, 68, 79]

[680]Turner, R. V., and DeFord, E. F. 1970. *Follow-up study of pupils with differing preschool experiences.* ED 042 810. [197]

[681]Tyler, F. B.; Rafferty, J. E.; and Tyler, B. B. 1962. Relationships among motivations of parents and their children. *Journal of Genetic Psychology* 101:69–81. [179, 182]

[682]Tyler, S. 1970. *Cognitive anthropology.* New York: Holt, Rinehart and Winston. [66]

[683]Van Alstyne, D., and Hattwick, L. A. 1939. A follow-up study of the behavior of nursery school children. *Child Development* 10:43–72. [201]

[684]Vance, B. J. 1967. *The effect of preschool group experience on various language and social skills in disadvantaged children.* ED 019 989. [75]

[685]Van de Riet, V., and Resnick, M. B. 1972a. *A sequential approach to early childhood and elementary education, phase III.* ED 067 150. [195]

[686]_____. 1972b. *A longitudinal study of the intellectual growth of culturally disadvantaged children in a sequential learning to learn program.* ED 070 791. [195]

[687]Van de Riet, V., and Van de Riet, H. 1967. *An evaluation of the effects of a unique sequential learning program on culturally deprived preschool children.* ED 019 994. [55, 198]

[688]Van der Veen, F., et al. 1964. Relationships between the parents' concept of the family and family adjustment. *American Journal of Orthopsychiatry* 34:45–55. [55]

[689]Vande Voort, L.; Serf, G. M.; and Benton, A. L. 1972. Development of audio-visual integration in normal and retarded readers. *Child Development* 43:1260–72. [157]

[690]Vaughan, H. 1974. Studies in neuropsychology. In *Methodological approaches to the study of brain maturation and its abnormalities,* ed. D. P. Purpura and G. P. Reaser, pp. 107–12. Baltimore: University Park Press. [169]

[691]Vernon, P. E. 1965. Ability factors and environmental influences. *American Psychologist* 20:723–33. [72, 73, 74]

[692]_____. 1967 (date of study). Abilities and educational attainments in an East African environment. In *Cross-cultural studies,* ed. D. R. Price-Williams, pp. 76–91. Baltimore: Penguin, 1969. [78]

[693]Wachs, T. D., et al. 1967. *Cognitive development in infants of different age levels and from different environmental backgrounds.* ED 015 786. [71]

[694]Waller, D. A., and Conners, C. K. 1966. *A follow-up study of intelligence changes in children who participated in project Head Start.* ED 020 786. [194]

[695]Washburn, T. C.; Medearis, D. N.; and Childs, B. 1965. Sex differences in susceptibility to infections. *Pediatrics* 35:57–69. [180]

[696]Wattenberg, W. W., and Clifford, C. 1964. Relation of self-concepts to beginning achievement in reading. *Child Development* 35:461–67. [108]

[697]Weber, G. 1971. *Inner-city children can be taught to read: Four successful schools.* Washington, D.C.: Council for Basic Education. [78, 109]

[698]Webster, S. W. 1965. Some correlates of reported academically supportive behaviors of Negro mothers toward their children. *Journal of Negro Education* 34:114–20. [56]

[699]Wei, T. T. D.; Lavatelli, C. B.; and Jones, R. S. 1971. Piaget's concept of classification: A comparative study of socially disadvantaged and middle-class

269

young children. *Child Development* 42:919–27. [93, 133]

[700]Weikart, D. P. 1970a. *The cognitively oriented curriculum: A framework for preschool teachers.* ED 044 535. [198]

[701]_____. 1970b. *Longitudinal results of Ypsilanti Perry preschool project.* ED 044 536. [124, 198]

[702]_____. 1972. Relationship of curriculum, teaching, and learning in preschool education. In *Preschool programs for the disadvantaged,* ed. J. C. Stanley. Baltimore: The Johns Hopkins University Press. [198]

[703]Weikart, D. P., and Lambie, D. Z. 1969. *Ypsilanti-Carnegie infant education project progress report.* Department of Research and Development, Ypsilanti Public Schools, Ypsilanti, Michigan. [38]

[704]Weikart, D. P.; Deloria, D. J.; and Lawsor, S. 1974. Results of a preschool intervention project. In *Longitudinal evaluations of preschool programs,* ed. S. Ryan, pp. 125–33. Washington, D.C.: Office of Child Development. [198]

[705]Weininger, O. 1956. The effects of early experience on behavior and growth characteristics. *The Journal of Comparative and Physiological Psychology* 49:1–9. [67]

[706]_____. 1974. *Early school entry: A study of some difference in children remaining at home and those attending school.* ED 096 003. [216]

[707]_____. 1975a. Yesterday I talked to my child: An approach to developmental linguistics. Unpublished manuscript, Ontario Institute for Studies in Education, Toronto, Ontario. [39]

[708]_____. 1975b. Personal communication with Raymond S. Moore. [50, 74, 196]

[709]_____. 1975c. Misery or magic: Reading as a process. *Educational Courier* 45(May 1975):8–11. [113, 114]

[710]Weiss, P. 1958. Summary and evaluation. In *The chemical basis of development,* ed. W. D. McElroy and B. Glass. Baltimore: Hopkins Press. [172]

[711]Weller, G. M., and Bell, R. Q. 1965. Basal skin conductance and neonatal state. *Child Development* 36:647–57. [177]

[712]Wellman, B. L. 1934. Growth in intelligence under differing school environments. *Journal of Experimental Education* 3:59–83. [201]

[713]Wells, M. E. 1970. Preschool play activities and reading achievement. *Journal of Learning Disabilities* 3:214–19. [108]

[714]Wepman, J. M. 1960. Auditory discrimination, speech, and reading. *Elementary School Journal* 60:325–33. [153]

[715]_____. 1968. The modality concept. In *Perception and reading,* ed. H. K. Smith, pp. 1–6. Newark, Del.: International Reading Association. [111, 154, 156]

[716]Westinghouse Learning Corporation/Ohio University. 1970. The impact of Head Start: An evaluation of the effects of Head Start on children's cognitive and affective development. In *The disadvantaged child,* ed. J. L. Frost and G. R. Hawkes. 2d ed., pp. 197–201. Boston: Houghton Mifflin. [197, 198]

[717]White, B. L. 1972. *Setting priorities in early education.* Paper presented at Education Commission of States Conference, December 1972, Denver, Colorado. [24, 230]

[718]_____. 1973. *Making sense out of our education priorities.* ED 085 087. [24, 212, 214]

[719]_____. 1974. Reassessing our educational priorities. In *Implementing child*

development programs: Report of an August, 1974, national symposium, pp. 8–18. Denver, Col.: Education Commission of the States. [212, 213, 214, 215, 221, 224]

[720]White, R. W. 1959. Motivation reconsidered: The concept of competence. *Psychological Review* 68:297–333. [50]

[721]White, S. H. 1968. Some educated guesses about cognitive development in the preschool years. In *Early education: Current theory, research, and practice,* ed. R. Hess and R. M. Bear, pp. 203–14. Chicago: Aldine. [24]

[722]_____. 1969. Statement in hearings before the select subcommittee on education. In *Comprehensive preschool education and child day-care act of 1969,* pp. 46–62. Washington, D.C.: U.S. Congress, House, 20 November 1969. [24]

[723]_____. 1973. Federal programs for young children. Unpublished manuscript. Cambridge, Mass.: Huron Institute. [24, 221]

[724]Whiteman, M. 1967. Children's conceptions of psychological causality. *Child Development* 38:143–55. [129, 131]

[725]Whiting, B., and Edwards, C. P. 1973. A cross-cultural analysis of sex differences in the behavior of children aged three through eleven. *Journal of Social Psychology* 91:171–88. [178, 181]

[726]Whiting, J., and Whiting, B. 1962 (date of study). Reference from annotated bibliography compiled by R. M. Oetzel. In *The development of sex differences,* ed. E. E. Maccoby. Stanford, Calif.: Stanford University Press, 1966. [186]

[727]Wiener, G. G.; Rider, R. V.; and Oppel, W. 1963. Some correlates of IQ changes in children. *Child Development* 34:61–67. [42]

[728]Williams, H. L. 1970. Aspects of human intelligence. In *The neurosciences,* ed. F. O. Schmitt. New York: The Rockefeller University Press. [173]

[729]Williams, J. P.; Blumberg, E. L.; and Williams, D. V. 1970. Cues used in visual word recognition. *Journal of Educational Psychology* 61:310–15. [112]

[730]Williams, R. 1971. Testing for number readiness: Application of the Piagetian theory of the child's development of the concept of number. *Journal of Educational Research* 64:394–96. [138]

[731]Willmon, B. 1969. Parent participation as a factor in the effectiveness of Head Start programs. *Journal of Educational Research* 62:406–10. [193]

[732]Willoughby, R. H. 1973. Age and training effects in children's conditional matching to sample. *Child Development* 44:143–48. [134, 135]

[733]Witherspoon, R. L. 1968. *Effect of trimester school operation on the achievement and adjustment of kindergarten and first through third grade children.* ED 020 003. [202]

[734]Witkin, H. A., et al. 1954. *Personality through perception.* New York: Harper. [183, 186]

[735]Wolf, R. M. 1964. Identification and measurement of environmental process variables related to intelligence. Doctoral dissertation. University of Chicago. [29, 75]

[736]Wolff, P. 1965. Unpublished paper presented at the Tavistock Conference on determinants of infant behavior, September 1965, London, England. [177]

[737]Wolff, P.; Levin, J. R.; and Llongobardi, E. T. 1974. Activity and children's learning. *Child Development* 45:221–23. [29, 70]

[738]Worcester, D. A. 1956. *The education of children of above-average mentality.* Lincoln: University of Nebraska Press. [96]

[739]Wylie, R. C. 1961. *The self-concept: A critical survey of pertinent research liter-*

271

ature. Lincoln: University of Nebraska Press. [51]

[740]Yakovlev, P. I. 1972. Letter to R. S. Moore, 25 July 1972. [145, 146, 162]

[741]Yakovlev, P. I., and Lecours, A. R. 1967. The myelogenetic cycles of regional maturation of the brain. In *Regional development of the brain in early life,* ed. A. Minkowski, pp. 34–44. Oxford: Blackwell Scientific Publications. [147]

[742]Yarrow, L. J. 1956. The development of object relationships during infancy and the effects of a disruption of early mother-child relationships (abstract). *American Psychologist* 11:423. [29]

[743]_____. 1961. Maternal deprivation: Toward an empirical and conceptual reevaluation. *Psychological Bulletin* 58:459–90. [35]

[744]_____. 1964. Separation from parents during early childhood. In *Child development research I,* ed. M. L. Hoffman and L. W. Hoffman, pp. 89–130. New York: Russell Sage Foundation. [29, 35, 36]

[745]_____. 1967. The development of focused relationships during infancy. In *Exceptional infant,* vol. 1, ed. J. Hellmuth, pp. 429–42. Seattle, Wash.: Special Child Publications. [29]

[746]_____. 1972. Attachment and dependency: A developmental perspective. In *Attachment and dependency,* ed. J. L. Gewirtz, pp. 81–95. Washington, D.C.: V. H. Winston & Sons. [30, 31, 76]

[747]Yarrow, L. J., and Pedersen, F. A. 1972. Attachment: Its origins and course. In *The young child: Reviews of research,* ed. W. W. Hartup, pp. 54–66. Washington, D.C.: National Association for the Education of Young Children. [29]

[748]Yarrow, M. R. 1973. Research on child rearing as a basis for practice. *Child Welfare* 52:209–19. [28]

[749]Young, B. W. 1969. *Inducing conservation of number, weight, volume, area, and mass in preschool children.* ED 028 822. [134]

[750]Young, F. A. 1962. The effect of nearwork illumination level on monkey refraction. *American Journal of Optometry and Archives of American Academy of Optometry* 39:60–67. [151]

[751]_____. 1963. The effect of restricted visual space on the refractive error of the young monkey eye. *Investigative Ophthalmology* 2:571–77. [151]

[752]_____. 1970. Development of optical characteristics for seeing. In *Early experience and visual information processing in perceptual and reading disorders,* ed. F. A. Young and D. B. Lindsley, pp. 35–61. Washington, D.C.: National Academy of Sciences. [150, 151]

[753]Young, F. A., et al. 1969. The transmission of refractive errors within Eskimo families. *American Journal of Optometry and Archives of American Academy of Optometry* 46:676–85. [151]

[754]Zigler, E. 1968. *Training the intellect versus development of the child.* ED 034 573. [24, 212]

[755]_____. 1971. Opening address at Home Start Planning Conference, 21–22 October 1971, Office of Child Development, Washington, D.C. [24, 216]

[756]Zigler, E., and Butterfield, E. C. 1968. Motivational aspects of changes in IQ test performance of culturally deprived nursery school children. *Child Development* 39:1–14. [197]

Index

Motor and sensorimotor skills, 115, 122, 127, 132, 155, 157, 164–65, 173, 185, 195, 215, 218
Multidisciplinary, *see* research interdisciplinary
Myelination, 165
  see also brain
Myopia (nearsightedness), *see* eyes, vision

Napa County, Calif., 24
National Education Association, 208
Nearsightedness, *see* eyes, vision
Needs, *see* child-rearing
Netherlands, 140
Neuropsychology, 144–51
Neurophysiology, 5, 159–73, 228
New England, 178
New Lanark, 207
New York City, 207
Nigeria, 190
Nimnicht, Glen, 21, 22
Nongraded schools, 231
Norway, 73

Obedience, *see* discipline
Office of Economic Opportunity, *see* United States
O'Guin, Larry, 25
Okinawa, 178
Orchard Town, 178
Out-of-family care, 2, 36, 41, 42
  see also home and family
Owen, Robert, 207

Parent-child relationship, 43–46, 52, 93–95
  attachment and dependency, *see* attachment
  communication and directions, 38–39, 56
  see also home and family, teaching, rejection, separation
Parent education, 38, 214
Parenthood education, 222–23, 225
Parent involvement, 193
  see also Head Start, Home Start
Parental approval, 52

Parental authority and responsibility, *see* authority
Parental consistency, 52, 54
Parental example, 53
Parental frustration, 39
Parental maturity, 41
Parents
  and parent surrogates, 35
  as teachers, 229–30
  positive influence of, 39, 40, 77
  see also practical suggestions
Peers, culture and influence, 55–56
Pennsylvania, 86
Perception and skills and discrimination, 90–94, 112, 153–57, 185, 195, 218
  auditory, 3, 90, 91, 115, 145, 150, 153, 157, 184, 185
  intersensory, 4, 90, 154–57
  visual, 3, 4, 90, 112, 115, 145, 150–57, 184, 185
  see also senses
Person-permanence, 32
Pestalozzi, Johann, 207, 208, 209
Phi Delta Kappan, 5
Philadelphia, 207
Philippines, 178
Piaget, Jean, 122, 128
  operational periods or stages of growth, 3, 122–26
  see also REFERENCES
Plasticity
  of the brain, 169–73
  of the eye, 150
Play and playthings, 37, 114
  see also learning, toys
Point Barrow, Alaska, 151
Policy, public, 1, 2, 29, 86–87, 95–102
  see also laws
Poverty, 93
Practical suggestions for various age levels:
  for building academic readiness, 102–4
  for building value systems, self-worth and positive sociality, 61–64
  for facilitating good reading

277

279

Virginia, 190
Vision, development of, 115,
   150–53, 163–64
   maturity, 150–53, 184
   myopia, 151–52
   see also perception, visual
Von Rochow, Friedrich, 207, 208

Waddell, Judy, 25
Wall Street Journal, 226
Warmth, *see* love
Weikart, David, 21, 22
Wepman, Joseph, 4

Western societies, 30
Westinghouse Report, 19, 197
Williams, Larry, 24
Wolfe, Dan, 21
Women's liberation groups, *see*
   vested interests
World War I, 17, 208
World War II, 17, 182, 201, 209
Woodworth, Robert S., 16
Work, 37
Working mothers, 14, 42
Writing, 231

Zigler, Edward, 19

About the Authors

RAYMOND S. MOORE is a widely quoted authority on the relative effectiveness of home care and schooling of young children. A developmental psychologist, he has been public elementary teacher, principal and city school superintendent, college dean and president, graduate programs officer for the U.S. Office of Education, advisor to the White House, the U.S. Congress, for HEW, for many states, for Canada, and for a number of overseas governments. He is now president of the Hewitt Research Center, a national foundation for efficiency in education with particular emphasis on the relationship of the young child, the family, and the school. He teaches or lectures at Andrews, Indiana, and Nova universities and the International Graduate School of Education. A writer for many professional journals, Dr. Moore is author or contributor to more than 40 books.

DOROTHY N. MOORE is a reading specialist and author in early childhood education. Her extensive background in teaching and consulting in public and private primary schools and universities recommends her as the coauthor of this book, as does her experience as head of a cerebral palsy clinic in a major California medical school and her training as a homemaker. She and her husband have two children of their own and have adopted or provided foster care for many others.

T. JOSEPH WILLEY is a Loma Linda, California, medical school professor and also a research colleague of Sir John Eccles, Nobel laureate in neurophysiology at the State University of New York. Dr. Willey is primarily responsible for chapter nine on brain development and learning.

DENNIS R. MOORE, a Hewitt Research Associate, is a former primary school teacher who is teaching developmental psychology in a Nevada community college. He worked particularly with Dr. Willey and others in developing the pioneering chapters on neuropsychology and neurophysiology.

KATHLEEN KORDENBROCK, also a Hewitt Research Associate, and former elementary school teacher, is an early childhood specialist with the Sacramento, California, City Schools. Also a linguist, she was a lead investigator in the Hewitt study of European preschools.